MUST KNOW

MIDDLE SCHOOL ELA

Find out the important stuff in a flash

Master English Language Arts skills in no time!

Bonus Flashcard App

Kelly Scardina

Mc Graw Hill

New York   Chicago   San Francisco   Athens   London   Madrid
Mexico City   Milan   New Delhi   Singapore   Sydney   Toronto

1 2 3 4 5 6 7 8 9   LCR   27 26 25 24 23 22

ISBN   978-1-264-27775-9
MHID   1-264-27775-X

e-ISBN   978-1-264-27776-6
e-MHID   1-264-27776-8

Interior design by Steve Straus of Think Book Works.
Cover and letter art by Kate Rutter.

McGraw-Hill books are available at special quantity discounts to use as premiums and sales promotions or for use in corporate training programs. To contact a representative, please visit the Contact Us pages at www.mhprofessional.com.

McGraw Hill is committed to making our products accessible to all learners. To learn more about the available support and accommodations we offer, please contact us at accessibility@mheducation.com. We also participate in the Access Text Network (www.accesstext.org), and ATN members may submit requests through ATN.

Contents

10 Writing to Inform 213

11 Writing to Analyze 237

Introduction

Welcome to your new *Must Know Middle School English Language Arts* book! You've probably had your fill of books asking you to memorize lots of terms (such as in school). This book isn't going to do that—although you're welcome to memorize anything you take an interest in. You may also have found that many books make a lot of promises about all the things you'll be able to accomplish by the time you reach the end of a given chapter. In the process, those books can make you feel as though you missed out on the building blocks that you actually need to meet those goals.

With *Must Know Middle School English Language Arts*, we've taken a different approach. When you start a new chapter, right off the bat you will see one or more **must know** ideas. These are the essential concepts behind what you are going to study, and they will form the foundation of what you will learn throughout the chapter. With these **must know** ideas you will have what you need to hold it together as you study, and they will be your guide as you make your way through each chapter.

To build on this foundation, you will find easy-to-follow discussions of the topic at hand, accompanied by comprehensive examples that will increase your ability to communicate successfully today and in the future. Each chapter ends with review questions—nearly 400 throughout the book—designed to instill confidence as you practice your new skills.

This book has other features that will help you on your English language arts (ELA) journey. It has a number of sidebars that will either provide helpful information or just serve as a quick break from your studies. The **BTW** ("by the way") sidebars point out important information as well as tell you what to be careful about English-wise. Every once in a while, an **IRL** ("in real life") sidebar will tell you what you're studying has to do with the real world; other IRLs may just be interesting factoids.

In addition, this book is accompanied by a flashcard app that will give you the ability to test yourself at any time. The app includes more than a hundred flashcards with a review question on one side and the answer on the other. You can either work through the flashcards by themselves or use them alongside the book. To find out where to get the app and how to use it, go to the next section, The Flashcard App.

Before you get started, however, we also want to introduce you to your guide throughout this book. Kelly Scardina is an experienced educator in ELA. With twenty-two years of experience in both high school and middle school ELA, Kelly knows what students need to improve their reading, writing, and speaking abilities in order to showcase their critical thinking and communication skills in the future. As a passionate reader and writer herself, Kelly knows the pitfalls ELA students can face, and she can show you how to avoid these pitfalls. She is an experienced mentor who can help you grow academically and find your own voice.

Before we leave you to the author's sure-footed guidance, let us give you one piece of advice. While we know that saying something "is the *worst*" is a cliché, if anything *is* the worst in ELA, it might be knowing how to cite research in an academic paper correctly. Let Kelly clear up that confusion so you can always feel confident about your English skills!

Good luck with your studies!

The Flashcard App

This book features a bonus flashcard app to help you test yourself on what you have learned as you worked through the chapters. The app includes more than a hundred flashcards, both front and back, featuring exercises covering topics in the book. The book gives you two options on how to use it. You can jump right into the app and start from any point, or you can take advantage of the handy QR codes near the end of each chapter in the book, which will take you directly to the flashcards related to what you're studying at the moment.

To access the flashcard feature, follow these simple steps:

Search for the **Must Know High School** App from
either Google Play or the App Store.

↓

Download the app to your smartphone or tablet.

↓

Once you've got the app,
you can use it in either of two ways.

Just open the app and you're ready to go.	Use your phone's QR code reader to scan any of the book's QR codes.
You can start at the beginning, or select any of the chapters listed.	You'll be taken directly to the flashcards that match the chapter you chose.

**Be ready to test your
ELA knowledge!**

Author's Note

Must Know Middle School English Language Arts is not just another drills and skills book but rather a guide to developing real communication skills you will need in the future, not just for high school or for college, but for life. No matter what path you pursue in the future, you will always need a strong handle on reading, writing, and speaking skills. In grade school, you concentrated on learning how to read, how to write, and how to present yourself. Now it is time to sharpen these basic skills. You will learn how to read, write, and speak with purpose.

There are two primary goals of this book. First, you will understand that being an avid reader will also improve your writing skills. There is a proven correlation between good readers and strong writers. When you immerse yourself in literature and read with an attentive eye, you will recognize author "moves" that you would like to emulate; notice the ways authors play with words, sentences, and structures to create meaning; and begin to take risks and experiment with your work. When you read, you also learn the nuances of language, grammar, and conventions.

The second goal is for you to realize the power having these reading, writing, and speaking skills can afford you. Plato once said, "Rhetoric is the art of ruling the minds of men." When you can express yourself in an effective way, people notice, pay attention, and listen. From Abraham Lincoln arguing to abolish slavery, to Martin Luther King Jr. fighting for civil rights, to Greta Thunberg persuading us to care for the environment, these leaders all understood that words can change the world, influence future generations, and alter the course of history. With social media and the latest technology at your fingertips, today you have overwhelming opportunities to make a difference. From witty memes to sarcastic tweets, young people more than ever can express their opinions to millions with a few taps at a keyboard! Your voice matters.

Close-Reading Skills

MUST KNOW

 Good readers are active readers.

 Strategies help you read a text closely.

 Annotations help readers make meaning of a text.

What Is the Difference between an Active Reader and a Passive Reader?

Active Readers: There are many times when we read for pleasure. However, there are some texts that require readers to think critically about the text. Some texts ask us to dig deeper, to uncover the author's purpose, to slow down, to pause, and to reflect.

Strong readers are *active readers*: they make predictions, connections, observations, and inferences. In addition, they pay attention to language, defining unknown words and examining word choice. They may often stop in parts and think about character choices, problems, motivations, and actions. Active readers may pause when they see a beautifully constructed sentence. They may even linger and reread parts to make sure they understand what exactly is happening.

Most importantly, when strong readers are confused they go back and try to make sense of what they are reading. They ask questions in their heads, and they look closely at the text to find the answers. In essence, they use their tools to comprehend the text, not just read the words on the page.

In my classroom, I often find there are two types of readers: *passive readers* and *active readers*. Passive readers often read the text; however, they may not remember what they read; they may not be able to discuss the text deeply because they did not absorb what they read. They didn't pay attention to important details or think too much about the character, the conflict, or the pressures the characters face. Sometimes my passive readers can't even recall the characters' names! Yes, they read the text, literally, but they didn't use strategies to help them make meaning of the text.

What Strategies Do Active Readers Use?

Reading Strategies: Oftentimes when I give reading checks or hold class discussions or one-on-one reading conferences, some of the students who struggle will *swear* that they did, in fact, complete the reading—even though they couldn't remember details or answer the questions about the reading insightfully. Do I believe them? Of course I do! Most likely when they read, however, they were reading passively and were not using reading strategies to help them make meaning from the text.

Active reading goes beyond just reading the words on the page. It goes beyond just finishing a text. It calls for you to take time and digest it. How does the reading make you feel? What emotions are stirred? How are you left unsatisfied? What makes you hunger for more?

Active reading calls on students to utilize close-reading skills:

- Reacting

- Observing

- Inferring

- Questioning

- Connecting

Sharing Reactions: This strategy should be as natural as breathing. You are reacting all day to stimuli around you. Your parents ask you to clean your room, and you react with an eye roll or a loud slam of the door in frustration. You watch a TikTok video and you laugh out loud and share it with a friend. You see a beautiful sunset at the beach and you take a picture. You eat an ice cream cone and lick your lips, savoring the flavor. It is normal to react to art too. A painting can make us reminiscent of our childhood; a poem can bring us to tears; a play can make us angry. When you read, feelings usually emerge. Sometimes you relate to characters and worry about them after you finish a chapter. Sometimes you really hate how the character responded to a friend. Sometimes you find a scene predictable or unrealistic. Sometimes you hate the ending or are left with many lingering questions.

Good readers react to the text in ways too numerous to mention. The more you react to text, the more you will have to share. When I read a book, many times, I am driven to text or call a friend immediately, a friend who has also read the same book. I want to know what my friend thought about certain parts, and I want to compare notes! These notes are mostly mental notes, but on many occasions I often keep track of my reactions in the margins of my book so that I won't forget all the details I want to discuss!

Making Observations: As you read, pay attention to details. Small details often go unnoticed. Active readers notice the little clues that authors leave in the text to convey character, setting, and conflict. Sometimes authors will also use these small details to foreshadow future events. Many times, after I complete a fiction book, I will reread places where the author led me, as the reader, to the outcome all along. It's fun to go back, reread, and uncover these details that you might have missed in the beginning. Good observation looks like this:

- Something I noticed...

- It seems like...

- I can tell that...

- I see this pattern...

- It looks like...

- A surprising detail is...

- A closer look at the text shows

- It appears that...

- I am seeing...

Making Inferences: When you read, you are encouraged to read between the lines. Use author clues in the text to draw conclusions about what you have read. Make reasonable guesses based on textual evidence as support. Too often, students jump to conclusions or make judgments about characters and their situations without proper evidence from the text. A student may come to the conclusion that a character is lazy; however, there should be clear examples that support this inference. The author may not directly tell the reader that the character is lazy. More likely, the author will provide details to show the reader. Maybe the character never cleans his room when he is asked. Maybe he copies homework from a friend. Maybe he puts dishes in the sink instead of in the dishwasher. Here are a few ways to begin an inference:

- From the clues in the text, I think...

- Based on evidence from the passage, I know...

- This evidence suggests...

- Words such as _____ make me think...

- This is true because in the text...

Asking Questions: Have you ever met someone new? A new classmate? A new team member? A partner for a group project? At first, conversation can be awkward because you don't know much about each other. What do you do to break the ice and forge forward in the beginning of a relationship? Well, most likely you will ask each other questions! You might ask, "Where do you live?", "Do you have siblings?", or "What are your interests?" The questions will come easily because there is so much to learn, so much you don't know about the individual.

The same applies to a new text. Starting a new text is equally challenging, simply because readers do not have a lot of information yet. In the beginning, an active reader will have many questions because the author is releasing details to the readers slowly. Asking questions to yourself or writing them in the margins is a critical reading strategy that will help you get to know the new text better and make sense of the incoming information. When I begin a text, I ask questions about characters

BTW

Strong writers "show, don't tell." Writers don't often tell readers what to think. Instead, they use details, language, and other clues in order for readers to draw conclusions.

Tell: Dan is tall.

Show: Dan had to duck before he entered the room.

Readers should infer that Dan was so tall he had to duck when he entered the room. This is a good inference.

Tell: The teacher was furious!

Show: Her face was red, her hands shook, her foot tapped, and her voice became loud.

Readers can infer that the teacher is angry because of her body language and appearance.

I'm meeting. I ask questions about the dialogue, the emerging conflicts, the setting. Why is this character alone? Where is she? Why is she alone? Why is she holding a torn jacket?

Sometimes you may have questions because you are simply confused. Imagine you are on a road trip, and your parents find themselves in an unfamiliar area. What are the signals that indicate your family is lost? Maybe you don't recognize the surroundings. Maybe a popular landmark that used to be there no longer exists. Maybe they missed the exit. Maybe they went too far ahead. Maybe they were arguing and not paying attention to the signs on the freeway.

Just like drivers may find themselves in unknown territory, readers, when navigating a text, might suddenly find themselves in a different and more challenging section of the text. While they might have had smooth sailing a few moments ago, readers can suddenly find themselves in a place in that text that feels obscure, unclear, or uncertain. This sudden weighing down of the text is done intentionally by the author to make you pause, slow down, and think. When this happens, consider what *it is* about the section that you are finding puzzling. Be aware of what makes a certain passage challenging, so you can choose the right tool to help you make meaning. Here are some questions to ask:

- Did the setting change?

- Was there a shift in time, such as a flashback or flash-forward?

- Did a new character emerge?

- Are there difficult words you don't know?

- Is there a new narrator?

- Is a symbol or theme emerging?

- Is the author revealing a message here?

When drivers get lost, there are resources they turn to for help: Perhaps they ask a passerby for directions; perhaps they use their GPS; perhaps they look on Google Maps to find their way.

Fortunately, readers also have tools to navigate a challenging part in the text.

Making Connections: I love reading the most when I can relate to what I read. Sometimes a character reminds me of my grandmother. Sometimes I have faced a similar situation that the character is experiencing, and I understand. One book may remind me of a movie I've just seen. A poem may transport me back to my childhood. When readers make connections, they create meaning with the text. They engage with the text on an emotional level. This strategy is always helpful when interacting with any written work. Keep in mind the most common ways to make connections: Make connections to your own life, make connections to the world around you, and make connections to other work mediums you have experienced (books, poems, films, plays, etc.). To make connections, use some of these starters:

> BTW
>
> *Readers should ask questions before, during, and after they read. Asking insightful questions can help a reader make meaning of the text, analyze the author's purpose, and understand character actions, motivations, and responses.*

- I remember when...

- This reminds me of...

- I felt this way once...

- I had a similar experience when...

There are three kinds of connections readers can make to the text they are reading:

> **Text-to-text:** How does this book, poem, essay remind me of others I have read?
>
> **Text-to-self:** How does this book, poem, essay remind me of my own life?
>
> **Text-to-word:** How does this book, poem, essay remind me of world events, the news, or history?

Making Predictions: My son and I were recently watching a movie together and, based on the first half hour of the film, he started to tell me what he thought would happen next. He proceeded to give me examples and little details throughout the film that made him think this way. Amazingly, he was right! Although I was annoyed that he spoiled the ending for me, I was happy to see that he was using a combination of his inferences, observations, and critical-thinking skills to put the pieces together to predict the ending. We can make predictions in books too. Authors also plant clues, leaving seeds for us to follow. If readers follow closely, they will often pick up foreshadowing details, patterns in word choice, and other examples in the text that can predict the outcome.

- Considering these examples, I think _____ will happen because _____.

- Looking back at the author's clues, I think the character will _____.

- Analyzing the title, I think the text will be about _____.

- Based on the headings/subheadings, I think the text will be about _____.

- Because I know that _____, I predict that _____.

- Based on what I know about _____, my guess is _____.

You can make predictions before you read any text by considering the title, looking at any pictures or images on the cover, and using your preexisting knowledge of the text subject.

You can also make predictions as you read. Make decisions about what will come next in the story by considering all the details you have already read. Authors often leave clues in the text to help you predict what is coming.

Defining New Words: Recently, I was reading an essay by Indian-American author Jhumpa Lahiri called "Indian Takeout." As a person who loves to travel and eat, I was intrigued by the food from Calcutta that Lahiri fondly describes: *Jalebi* and *Mughlai parathas*. As much of a foodie as I consider myself to be, I had never had the opportunity to try either of these culinary treats: a mango and a flatbread that both sound as good as Lahiri promises. My curiosity got the better of me, and I had to Google both foods in order to learn more about these Indian treats.

If you want to improve your reading, one strategy is to take time to look up new words or terms. These unfamiliar words may be more challenging vocabulary, technical terms, or even those that come from another country or are part of another culture. Taking the time to look up these words on the Internet or in a standard dictionary will increase your reading comprehension and also will add to your overall appreciation of a text.

IRL Did you know that learning vocabulary improves your reading comprehension? Research has shown that kids need to understand ninety-eight percent of the words they read to understand what they are reading.

When you read, be sure to underline or highlight words or terms you don't recognize. Sometimes you can figure out the meaning through context clues. For example, from the context of Lahiri's essay and from the title, "Indian Takeout," I could tell that Jalebi and Mughlai parathas were types of food. When I looked these words up in Google, I was able to confirm my guess and also find out more!

BTW

One of the most effective strategies to learn a new word is to learn through the context of the sentence in which the word appears. Context means the situation. Use clues within the sentence to make an educated guess about the word's definition.

What Does Annotation Mean? Why Is It Useful?

Annotation: As an active reader, I cannot help myself from marking up a text. Obviously, I never deface a book that is not mine, a library book, or a borrowed book from a friend. But books I own, articles I read in the Sunday paper, and poems I come across in a literary journal are all at the mercy of my pen! I am always highlighting, underlining, starring, and writing in the margins. When I have to read a text for class or I see a piece that I may want to teach, I am actively taking notes. These notes may be on the side of the page or on top of separate notes.

What Should You Mark When You Annotate?

You might ask. Sometimes I underline a beautifully structured sentence that I love. Sometimes I circle words that seem to work in a pattern. Sometimes I note a crafty move an author makes that is interesting or surprising or feels intentional. Sometimes I write notes in the margins about what I'm thinking as I read, questions I may have, or what I might be wondering at the time. I circle lines I want to remember and passages that require a second read or more focus. These markings help me engage with the text in a more meaningful way. Sticker notes are also good tools to use on a text that is not your own. Place those notes all over the page to keep track of your thinking!

 **IRL** In his essay "How to Mark a Book," Mortimer J. Adler suggests not only to "read between the lines," but also to "write between the lines." After all, he warns, "it's not an act of mutilation but of love." Overall, the most proficient readers think about their own reading. Making annotations, taking notes, and writing responses about the text can help readers explore the text more insightfully.

What Are Some Effective Ways to Annotate?

Here is a passage from Lucy Maud Montgomery's novel *Anne of Green Gables*, written in 1908. Read the passage, and then note the ways I make notes to track my thinking.

Mrs. Rachel Lynde lived just where the Avonlea main road dipped down into a little hollow, fringed with alders and ladies' eardrops and traversed by a brook that had its source away back in the woods of the old Cuthbert place; it was reputed to be an intricate, headlong brook in its earlier course through those woods, with dark secrets of pool and cascade; but by the time it reached Lynde's Hollow it was a quiet, well-conducted little stream, for not even a brook could run past Mrs. Rachel Lynde's door without due regard for decency and decorum; it probably was conscious that Mrs. Rachel was sitting at her window, keeping a sharp eye on everything that passed, from brooks and children up, and that if she noticed anything odd or out of place she would never rest until she had ferreted out the whys and wherefores thereof.

There are plenty of people in Avonlea and out of it, who can attend closely to their neighbor's business by dint of neglecting their own; but Mrs. Rachel Lynde was one of those capable creatures who can manage their own concerns and those of other folks into the bargain. She was a notable housewife; her work was always done and well done; she "ran" the Sewing Circle, helped run the Sunday-school, and was the strongest prop of the Church Aid Society and Foreign Missions Auxiliary. Yet with all this Mrs. Rachel found abundant time to sit for hours at her kitchen window, knitting "cotton warp" quilts—she had knitted sixteen of them, as Avonlea housekeepers were wont to tell in awed voices—and keeping a sharp eye on the main road that crossed the hollow and wound up the steep red hill beyond. Since Avonlea occupied a little triangular peninsula jutting out into the Gulf of St. Lawrence with water on two sides of it, anybody who went out of it or into it had to pass over that hill road and so run the unseen gauntlet of Mrs. Rachel's all-seeing eye.

Following is a model of my annotation. As I read, I used my pen to circle, star, underline, and write ideas, jot questions, and keep track of thoughts. If the text is yours, it is often the easiest way to annotate. I often encourage

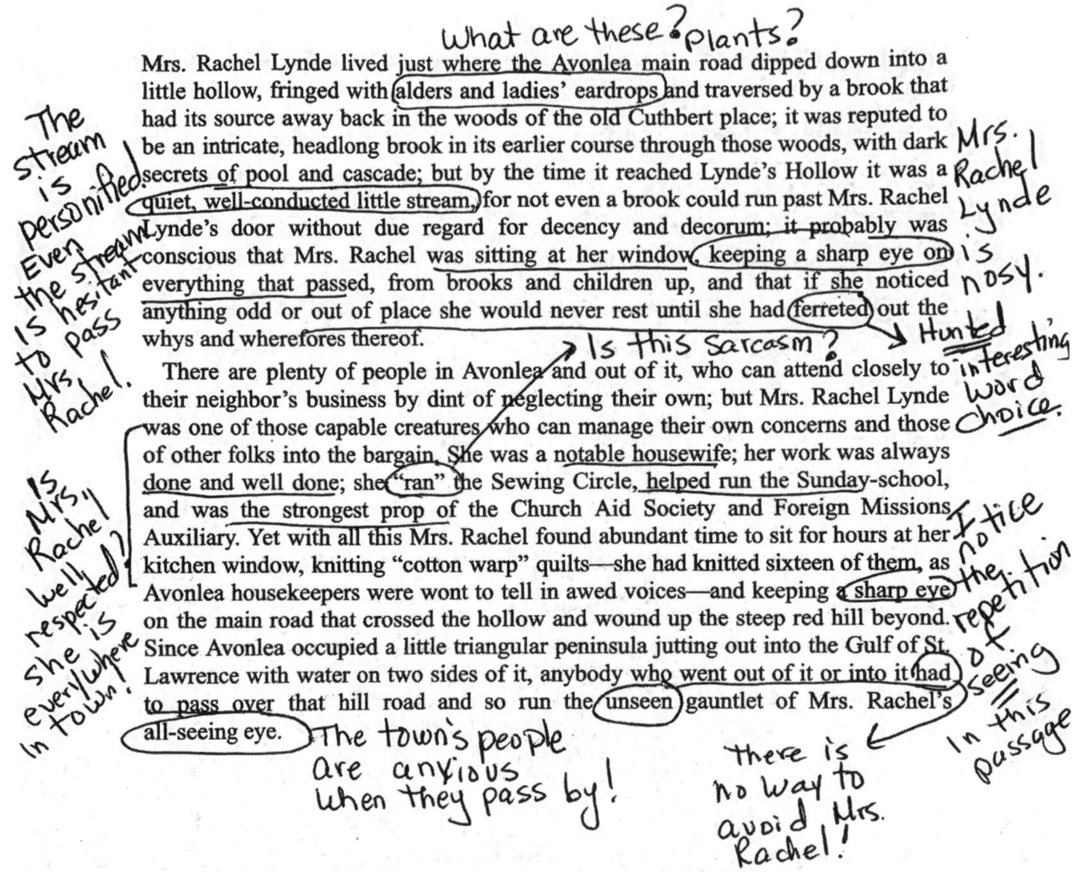

What are these? plants?

Mrs. Rachel Lynde lived just where the Avonlea main road dipped down into a little hollow, fringed with alders and ladies' eardrops and traversed by a brook that had its source away back in the woods of the old Cuthbert place; it was reputed to be an intricate, headlong brook in its earlier course through those woods, with dark secrets of pool and cascade; but by the time it reached Lynde's Hollow it was a quiet, well-conducted little stream, for not even a brook could run past Mrs. Rachel Lynde's door without due regard for decency and decorum; it probably was conscious that Mrs. Rachel was sitting at her window, keeping a sharp eye on everything that passed, from brooks and children up, and that if she noticed anything odd or out of place she would never rest until she had ferreted out the whys and wherefores thereof.

There are plenty of people in Avonlea and out of it, who can attend closely to their neighbor's business by dint of neglecting their own; but Mrs. Rachel Lynde was one of those capable creatures who can manage their own concerns and those of other folks into the bargain. She was a notable housewife; her work was always done and well done; she "ran" the Sewing Circle, helped run the Sunday-school, and was the strongest prop of the Church Aid Society and Foreign Missions Auxiliary. Yet with all this Mrs. Rachel found abundant time to sit for hours at her kitchen window, knitting "cotton warp" quilts—she had knitted sixteen of them, as Avonlea housekeepers were wont to tell in awed voices—and keeping a sharp eye on the main road that crossed the hollow and wound up the steep red hill beyond. Since Avonlea occupied a little triangular peninsula jutting out into the Gulf of St. Lawrence with water on two sides of it, anybody who went out of it or into it had to pass over that hill road and so run the unseen gauntlet of Mrs. Rachel's all-seeing eye.

Margin annotations:
- The stream is personified!
- Even the stream is hesitant to pass Mrs. Rachel.
- Is Mrs. Rachel well respected? She is everywhere in town.
- Mrs. Rachel Lynde is nosy.
- Is this sarcasm?
- Hunted
- Interesting word choice.
- I notice the repetition of seeing in this passage
- The town's people are anxious when they pass by!
- there is no way to avoid Mrs. Rachel!

my students to purchase their own copies of books we read in class so they can write on the pages freely.

Sticker Notes: Notes that can stick are one of my favorite ways to mark up a text because they make note taking easy and convenient.

Often when I want to take notes, the text is not mine, and I want to be respectful by not writing on it, especially a library book, a school text, or a text I borrow from a friend. The

BTW

Don't be afraid to draw illustrations when you annotate! Drawings, pictures, and images increase comprehension and understanding too.

beauty is that sticker notes can go anywhere on the page and can be removed easily. Look at the types of notes I took to mark up the following passage:

Anne of Green Gables

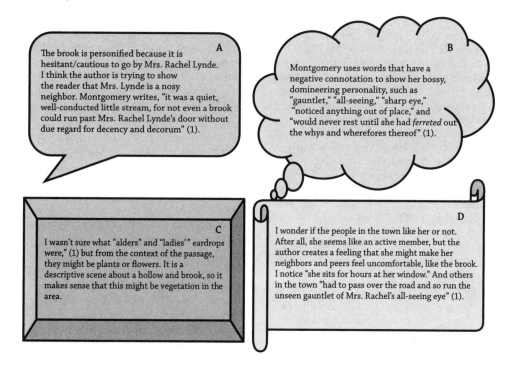

A The brook is personified because it is hesitant/cautious to go by Mrs. Rachel Lynde. I think the author is trying to show the reader that Mrs. Lynde is a nosy neighbor. Montgomery writes, "it was a quiet, well-conducted little stream, for not even a brook could run past Mrs. Rachel Lynde's door without due regard for decency and decorum" (1).

B Montgomery uses words that have a negative connotation to show her bossy, domineering personality, such as "gauntlet," "all-seeing," "sharp eye," "noticed anything out of place," and "would never rest until she had *ferreted* out the whys and wherefores thereof" (1).

C I wasn't sure what "alders" and "ladies'" eardrops were," (1) but from the context of the passage, they might be plants or flowers. It is a descriptive scene about a hollow and brook, so it makes sense that this might be vegetation in the area.

D I wonder if the people in the town like her or not. After all, she seems like an active member, but the author creates a feeling that she might make her neighbors and peers feel uncomfortable, like the brook. I notice "she sits for hours at her window." And others in the town "had to pass over the road and so run the unseen gauntlet of Mrs. Rachel's all-seeing eye" (1).

The brook is personified because it is hesitant/cautious to go by Mrs. Rachel Lynde. I think the author is trying to show the reader that Mrs. Lynde is a nosy neighbor. Montgomery writes, "it was a quiet, well-conducted little stream, for not even a brook could run past Mrs. Rachel Lynde's door without due regard for decency and decorum."

Montgomery uses words that have a negative connotation to show her bossy, domineering personality, such as *gauntlet, all-seeing, sharp eye, noticed anything out of place*, and "would never rest until she had *ferreted* out the whys and wherefores thereof."

I wasn't sure what *alders* and *ladies' eardrops* were, but from the context of the passage, I thought they might be plants or flowers. It is a descriptive scene about a hollow and brook, so it makes sense that this might be vegetation in the area.

I wonder if the people in the town like her or not. After all, she seems like an active member, but the author creates a feeling that she might make her neighbors and peers feel uncomfortable, like the brook. I notice "she sits for hours at her window." And others in the town "had to pass over the road and so run the unseen gauntlet of Mrs. Rachel's all-seeing eye."

Margin Notes: If you have room in your text, like a teacher-provided photocopy of the text, you can squeeze notes on the side of the text as well. In this model, I take notes on the side of a text:

Mrs. Rachel Lynde lived just where the Avonlea main road dipped down into a little hollow, fringed with *alders and ladies' eardrops* and traversed by a brook that had its source away back in the woods of the old Cuthbert place; it was reputed to be an intricate, headlong brook in its earlier course through those woods, with dark secrets of pool and cascade; but by the time it reached Lynde's Hollow it was a quiet, well-conducted little stream, for *not even a brook could run past Mrs. Rachel Lynde's door without due regard for decency and decorum*; it probably was conscious that Mrs. Rachel was *sitting at her window*, keeping a *sharp eye on everything that passed*, from brooks and children up, and that if she *noticed anything odd or out of place she would never rest* until she had ferreted out the whys and wherefores thereof.

There are plenty of people in Avonlea and out of it, *who can attend closely to their neighbor's business* by dint of neglecting their own; but *Mrs. Rachel Lynde was one of those capable creatures who can manage their own concerns and those of other folks into the bargain.* She was a *notable housewife; her work was always done and well done; she "ran" the Sewing Circle, helped run the Sunday-school, and was the strongest prop of the Church Aid Society and Foreign Missions Auxiliary.* Yet with all this Mrs. Rachel found abundant time to sit for hours at her kitchen window, knitting "cotton warp" quilts—she had knitted sixteen of them, as Avonlea housekeepers were wont to tell in awed voices—and keeping a sharp eye on the main road that crossed the hollow and wound up the steep red hill beyond. Since Avonlea occupied a little triangular peninsula jutting out into the Gulf of St. Lawrence with water on two sides of it, anybody who went out of it or into it had to pass over that hill road and so run the unseen gauntlet of Mrs. Rachel's all-seeing eye.

I wasn't sure what *alders* and *ladies' eardrops* were, but from the context of the passage, I thought they might be plants or flowers. It is a descriptive scene about a hollow and brook, so it makes sense that this might be vegetation in the area.

From some of the details in the passage, I'm noticing that Mrs. Rachel Lynde seems to be nosy and a busybody! I see phrases like "sharp eye," "closely to their neighbor's business," and "capable creatures who can manage their own concerns and those of other folks."

She appears to be very busy and also active in her town: She runs the "Sewing Circle" and "Sunday-school" and participated in "the Church Aid Society and Foreign Missions Auxiliary."

I wonder if the people in the town like her or not. After all, she seems like an active member, but the author creates a feeling that she might make her neighbors and peers feel uncomfortable, like the brook.

I notice "she sits for hours at her window." And others in the town "had to pass over that hill road and so run the unseen gauntlet of Mrs. Rachel's all-seeing eye."

I can tell by the context of the sentence that *gauntlet* has a negative connotation. It must not be good. When I looked it up, to "run the gauntlet" means "a public trial one must overcome." It seems that it is a form of torture to pass by Mrs. Rachel at her window.

Journal Writing: One common way that middle school English teachers will have you think deeply about your reading will be through journal writing or personal responses. A literary journal is used to respond to your reading in a way that you control. Teachers usually give fewer guidelines so you can express yourself freely. Sometimes teachers even allow you to include drawings, illustrations, doodles, charts, and other structures to share your ideas about the text.

In a journal entry, you don't have to create paragraphs, and you don't have to begin with an introduction or end with a conclusion. In many cases, teachers will say do not worry about grammar and conventions. They just want to see your thoughts about the reading. So you can let your hair down and just share!

In a journal response, synthesize some of the notes you took on your reading. Share reactions, connections, confusions, questions, observations, and inferences.

Look at the following journal response as a model on the popular young adult novel by Gae Polisner, *The Summer of Letting Go*:

So far I am really enjoying Gae Polisner's novel *The Summer of Letting Go* although it is really sad. Although it is almost summer vacation and Francesca should be excited about the end of school, the completion of finals, and the freedom summer entails, she is dreading it. Right now, her life seems to be so complicated. She is still grieving over her younger brother's death in which she feels she "let Simon die" (19) because she should have been watching him swim. In addition, she is having intense feelings for her best friend's boyfriend, and she believes her father is having an affair with a neighbor. That's enough for anyone to feel less enthusiastic about summer and to lead someone to feel very much "alone" (29).	Notice the informality of the response. The writer shares genuine feelings about the book. The writer includes the title and author of the book she has read. Watch how the author provides context here. The writer helps the reader follow her idea by giving the background of the book. The writer shares information, such as who, what, when, where, why, and how so that the reader understands. Who: Francesca, a teenager When: the summer What: She blames herself for her younger brother's death.

It seems like Francesca might be drawn to Bradley because she has more in common with Bradley than Lisette. Bradley is pretty hot, but he also seems to have similar interests to Francesca. Lisette thinks Bradley is "weird" at times, because he likes to save bugs and won't kill them because they might "have souls." Although Lisette thinks this is "goofy," Francesca thinks a boy she met at the pool might be her brother Simon "reincarnated." This is a crazy thought, but someone like Bradley might just understand without being judgmental. Even though Bradley is off limits to her, she can't help but wonder if there is some "karmic connection between us" (31).

I wonder if these feelings for Bradley will ultimately strain the girls' friendship? Already Francesca notices that their relationship isn't the same lately. Normally Francesca would tell Lisette everything, but lately, even though she wants to share, she can't. She thinks, "there's a wall between [them]" (31). Between the weird encounter with a young boy at the pool that eerily reminds her of her deceased brother and her father's strange behavior, Francesca has a lot she could tell Lisette, but she's holding back because she "feels overwhelmed by the need to be like [they] used to be, just the two of [them]" (29).

Francesca also is overwhelmed by the situation with her father. He's been acting so strange lately. He's parking at the end of the block, leaving work early, and dressing differently. Another reason is that he seems much happier of late ... happier than he's been since her brother drowned a few years back. Could he really be having an affair with her neighbor as Francesca thinks?

Why: She is supposed to be watching Simon when he drowns.

How: She goes to fill a pail of water when they are building sandcastles. She has a hard time forgiving herself.

Notice how the writer includes supporting details from the reading and also quotations from the text to support her ideas.

The writer uses sentence starters such as "I wonder," "I noticed," "It seems like," and "Perhaps" to share her ideas.

Review more sentence starters in chapter one.

I noticed that Francesca seems closer with her father than her mother, who's always volunteering at the Foundation for Prevention. For example, her father still calls her by her nickname "Beans," while her mother doesn't anymore. Also, Francesca seems to notice these subtle changes in her father while her mother doesn't. The death of a child can really drive a couple apart. *Perhaps* the grief has pulled her parents apart from each other.

Could her father be finding happiness with Mrs. Merrill? Is she helping him escape the pain of his son's death? I feel terrible that Francesca has so many problems to deal with right now. I am interested in finding out more: Will she catch her father with Mrs. Merrill? Who is this boy Frankie Sky? Will he help her with her grief over her brother? What will happen with Lisette once Francesca starts getting closer to Bradley?

Authors choose their words with care. In the *Anne of Green Gables* passage, Lucy Maud Montgomery's *intention* is to show Mrs. Rachel Lynde in a negative light: She is a person who meddles in the lives of others. She is intrusive.

Montgomery uses words that have a negative *connotation* to show her bossy, domineering personality, such as *gauntlet, all-seeing, sharp eye, noticed anything out of place*, and "would not rest until she had *ferreted* out the whys and wherefores thereof."

Author's Intention: The author's plan or purpose

Denotation: The actual dictionary definition of a word. *Home* is defined as "the place where one lives permanently, especially as a member of a family or household."

Connotation: An idea or feeling that a word communicates. *Home* seems comfy and warm. A hovel is also a home, but it has a negative connotation. Abode, dwelling, residence: all have different connotations.

EXERCISES

EXERCISE 1.1

Let's practice being active readers with the continuation of the passage from Anne of Green Gables.

She was sitting there one afternoon in early June. The sun was coming in at the window warm and bright; the orchard on the slope below the house was in a bridal flush of pinky-white bloom, hummed over by a myriad of bees. Thomas Lynde—a meek little man whom Avonlea people called "Rachel Lynde's husband"—was sowing his late turnip seed on the hill field beyond the barn; and Matthew Cuthbert ought to have been sowing his on the big red brook field away over by Green Gables. Mrs. Rachel knew that he ought because she had heard him tell Peter Morrison the evening before in William J. Blair's store over at Carmody that he meant to sow his turnip seed the next afternoon. Peter had asked him, of course, for Matthew Cuthbert had never been known to volunteer information about anything in his whole life.

And yet here was Matthew Cuthbert, at half-past three on the afternoon of a busy day, placidly driving over the hollow and up the hill; moreover, he wore a white collar and his best suit of clothes, which was plain proof that he was going out of Avonlea; and he had the buggy and the sorrel mare, which betokened that he was going a considerable distance. Now, where was Matthew Cuthbert going and why was he going there?

Had it been any other man in Avonlea, Mrs. Rachel, deftly putting this and that together, might have given a pretty good guess as to both questions. But Matthew so rarely went from home that it must be something pressing and unusual which was taking him; he was the shyest man alive and hated to have to go among strangers or to any place where he might have to talk. Matthew, dressed up with a white collar and driving in a buggy, was something that didn't happen often. Mrs. Rachel, ponder as she might, could make nothing of it and her afternoon's enjoyment was spoiled.

"I'll just step over to Green Gables after tea and find out from Marilla where he's gone and why," the worthy woman finally concluded. "He doesn't generally go to town this time of year and he *never* visits; if he'd run out of turnip seed he wouldn't dress up and take the buggy to go for more; he wasn't driving fast enough to be going for a doctor. Yet something must have happened since last night to start him off. I'm clean puzzled, that's what, and I won't know a minute's peace of mind or conscience until I know what has taken Matthew Cuthbert out of Avonlea today."

1. Thomas Lynde—a meek little man whom Avonlea people called "Rachel Lynde's husband"—was sowing his late turnip seed on the hill field beyond the barn.

   From the context of this sentence, what do you think the word *meek* means?

   a. Bossy

   b. Strong

   c. Quiet

   d. Talented

2. What can you infer about Mr. Thomas Lynde from the following details?
   Thomas Lynde—a meek little man whom Avonlea people called "Rachel Lynde's husband"—

   a. The people of Avonlea admired his farming.

   b. Rachel Lynde is the dominant person in the marriage.

   c. Rachel Lynde does not like her husband.

   d. Thomas Lynde does not like his wife.

3. What is the author's intention for including these details in the text?

   Matthew Cuthbert ought to have been sowing his on the big red brook field away over by Green Gables. Mrs. Rachel knew that he ought because she had heard him tell Peter Morrison the evening before in William J. Blair's store over at Carmody that he meant to sow his turnip seed the next afternoon.

   a. To further develop Mrs. Lynde as a nosy character
   b. To criticize Matthew Cuthbert for being a lazy farmer
   c. To show the reader that Peter Morrison is not a trustworthy character
   d. To illustrate that Mrs. Lynde is a thoughtful person

4. According to the text, "Matthew Cuthbert had never been known to volunteer information about anything in his whole life." What is revealed about Matthew Cuthbert?

   a. Matthew Cuthbert is not an interesting character in the book.
   b. Matthew Cuthbert is a private person.
   c. Matthew Cuthbert does not like anyone in Avonlea.
   d. Matthew Cuthbert is sneaky.

5. What observations does Mrs. Lynde make that arouse her suspicions regarding Mr. Matthew Cuthbert?

   a. Matthew Cuthbert is not "busy" when he should be.
   b. Matthew Cuthbert is dressed in "a white collar and his best suit of clothes."
   c. Matthew Cuthbert is driving his buggy.
   d. All of the above

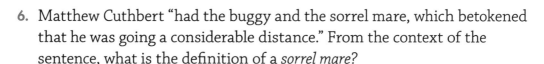

6. Matthew Cuthbert "had the buggy and the sorrel mare, which betokened that he was going a considerable distance." From the context of the sentence, what is the definition of a *sorrel mare?*

    a. A tan suitcase
    b. A bunch of flowers
    c. A rare-colored horse
    d. A map of the area

7. As an active reader, what do you learn about Mr. Matthew Cuthbert's character?

    a. He does not like to leave home much.
    b. He enjoys dressing up.
    c. He looks forward to picking up more seeds.
    d. He is sickly.

8. "I won't know a minute's peace of mind or conscience until I know what has taken Matthew Cuthbert out of Avonlea today." What does this sentence reveal about Mrs. Rachel Lynde?

    a. Mrs. Lynde is patient.
    b. Mrs. Lynde is a helpful person.
    c. Mrs. Lynde is jealous of Mr. Cuthbert's travels.
    d. Mrs. Lynde is snooping.

9. And yet here was Matthew Cuthbert, at half-past three on the afternoon of a busy day, placidly driving over the hollow and up the hill; moreover, he wore a white collar and his best suit of clothes, which was plain proof that he was going out of Avonlea; and he had the buggy and the sorrel mare, which *betokened* that he was going a considerable distance.

    From the context of the sentence, what do you think is the best definition of *betokened*?

    a. Indicated
    b. Denied
    c. Caused
    d. Rejected

10. Which of the following words has a *negative* connotation in the text?

    a. Hummed
    b. Pressing
    c. Myriad
    d. Peace

EXERCISE 1.2

Identify each of the reading strategies in the following examples.

1. I once had a friend who loved to gossip about everyone in class. It made me uncomfortable.

    a. Inference
    b. Question
    c. Observation
    d. Connection

2. I do not think Marilla Cuthbert will be happy to see Mrs. Rachel Lynde when Rachel arrives to question her about Matthew's travels.
    a. Prediction
    b. Reaction
    c. Connection
    d. Observation

3. I think good neighbors mind their own business.
    a. Observation
    b. Connection
    c. Reaction
    d. Question

4. Matthew Cuthbert reminds me of another character I read in a book called *Ethan Frome* because both men were reticent and reserved. *What kind of connection is being made here?*
    a. Text-to-self
    b. Text-to-text
    c. Text-to-world
    d. All of the above

5. Because she cannot figure out where Matthew Cuthbert is going, Mrs. Rachel Lynde seems agitated by the lack of information. I think she is frustrated when she says, "I won't know a minute's peace of mind or conscience until I know what has taken Matthew Cuthbert out of Avonlea today."
    a. Inference
    b. Text-to-self connection
    c. Prediction
    d. Reaction

6. I was surprised that Mrs. Rachel Lynde could declare that her whole day was spoiled because she didn't know where Mr. Matthew Cuthbert was heading.
    a. Question
    b. Text-to-world connection
    c. Reaction
    d. Using context to define a word

7. What could be so important to draw Matthew Cuthbert from Green Gables and get dressed up for the occasion?
    a. Reaction
    b. Observation
    c. Inference
    d. Question

8. Mrs. Rachel, ponder as she might, could make nothing of it, and her afternoon's enjoyment was spoiled. I am assuming that *ponder* means *to think about.*
    a. Question
    b. Inference
    c. Text-to-world connection
    d. Using sentence context for meaning

9. Which reading strategy is being applied in the following note?
    After reading this line, "for not even a brook could run past Mrs. Rachel Lynde's door without due regard for decency and decorum," I think the author, Lucy Maud Montgomery, mocks Mrs. Lynde's meddlesome nature. Even the brook is cautious when passing her home.
    a. Connection
    b. Inference
    c. Reaction
    d. Observation

10. If someone dresses in his best set of clothes, it must mean that the person is going to an important event or may want to make a good first impression.
    a. Inference
    b. Reaction
    c. Connection
    d. Definition

EXERCISE 1.3

Directions: Match the correct term in the box with the appropriate definition.

Connection, denotation, observation, reaction, inference, question, prediction, context, annotation, connotation

1. The literal meaning of a word	
2. A note-taking strategy to read a text closely	
3. Guessing what will happen next based on prior reading	
4. The feeling a word evokes	
5. Noticing something in the text	
6. Responding to the text with feeling and emotion	
7. Reaching a conclusion based on text evidence	
8. Drawing parallels between a text and the world or another text or to life experiences	
9. Asking for more information	
10. Learning a word through the sentence's meaning	

NOTES

 # Components of Fiction

MUST KNOW

 A genre is a type of literature.

 Setting, plot, character, and conflict are components of fiction.

 Characterization is the description of how a character looks, feels, acts, thinks, and behaves.

What Is a Genre?

A *genre* is a type of literature, and for middle school readers, there are many! When you think about your reading life, you might notice that you tend to favor one genre over others. It's great to have a favorite genre that you are particularly drawn to; however, if you've never stepped outside of your reading comfort zone, you are missing out!

J. K. Rowling, the author of the Harry Potter series, reminds us, "If you don't like reading, you haven't found the right book." Exploration into other types of reading can expose you to tons of exciting new titles and authors that you didn't know previously, thus widening your choices. Be open to giving another genre a try! You may be pleasantly surprised.

As a reader today, there are so many contemporary authors writing for the teenage audience. These books deal with issues and topics that appeal specifically to young readers. Following are some of the genres that appeal most to teens.

Types of Fiction

Realistic Fiction: When I was a tween back in the '80s, there didn't seem to be a large selection of books that featured characters my age. I was often stuck choosing books with characters that felt too juvenile or that were too mature, outside my realm of experience. Luckily for you, young adult (YA) fiction has exploded over the years, offering middle schoolers overwhelming options of realistic fiction titles. Realistic fiction is a genre where characters, their settings, and conflicts feel relatable to you. The characters face situations you might have also experienced yourself. The characters share feelings you have felt and deal with similar issues as you.

Dystopia: As a middle school teacher, I have noticed that my students are obsessed with dystopia. Teens have always wondered about the future, imagining the problems that people will eventually face and questioning whether or not the human race will endure. However, with the COVID-19 pandemic challenges and the bleak picture global warming paints, teenage readers have been gravitating to dystopian titles more than ever. This genre features a future society where problems arise, and people suffer. In this world, characters often face injustice and must find ways to survive the impossible.

Fantasy: Teens who are looking for ways to escape the struggles and drudgery of the real world can choose to immerse themselves in fantasy, books filled with magic and the supernatural. Although humans may appear in the story, they may cohabit the fictional worlds with elves, gnomes, fairies, and other fantastical creatures. In these imaginary worlds, characters have powers that can help them solve their problems and break free from the restraints of reality.

Graphic Novel: If you enjoy reading comics, a graphic novel tells a story through illustrations and visuals. However, don't dismiss the genre because it includes mostly pictures. Most graphic novels are sophisticated texts, often exploring complex topics such as racism, war, mental illness, and addiction. Graphic novels can be fiction or nonfiction. They are highly entertaining for both avid and reluctant readers.

IRL The first book to be considered young adult (YA) was titled *Seventeenth Summer.* The book, written by Maureen Daly, was published in 1942.

"The term 'young adult' was coined by the Young Adult Library Services Association during the 1960s to represent the 12–18 age range."

Ashley Strickland, *CNN*

What Makes a Work of Fiction?

Components of Fiction

How do you know when you are reading a work of fiction? There are some ways to identify fiction. As you read, you will experience plots, explore settings, meet characters, and learn about the conflicts they face.

Plot: I was reading a book at the beach when my son, noticing the vivid cover, curiously asked me, "Mom, what is that book about?" When authors write, they have a storyline in mind or a sequence of events they want to bring together to tell a story. This is known as the plot. The plot is the glue that secures all the parts of a text together. When a teacher asks you to provide a brief summary of what you read, this task will require you to discuss (in writing or in speech) the most memorable parts of the text chronologically from beginning to end. Following are a few terms to help you in the discussion of plot.

IRL A nineteenth-century German playwright named Gustav Freytag established a story arc known as Freytag's Pyramid. It is a dramatic structure outlining the steps of successful storytelling: exposition, rising action, climax, falling action, and resolution.

Exposition: In this part of the text, the author takes time to provide a bit of background, establish the setting, and introduce characters. Picture this: A family is setting up camp by their favorite vacation spot at Sunshine Lake. They are excited to finally start their week of camping. As Mom starts pitching the tent, the kids begin by emptying the truck, removing their sleeping bags, supplies and gear. Viking, their year-old goldendoodle, is running amok in joy, barking happily in a new environment and sniffing around the area.

In this section, readers learn that the family has been coming to the same site for the past five years. We learn that Mom and the kids love fishing, canoeing, and hiking. We learn that Dad can't attend this year because he is stuck at a work conference, so this is the first year Mom and her three sons will be camping alone. It's a beautiful day. It's sunny, and there was no traffic during the three-hour ride to the campsite. Despite their disappointment, Marc, Leon, and Walter are in good spirits while they help Mom unload the truck. They are looking forward to getting the site set up so they can have an afternoon swim at the lake. Okay! We learn a bit about the setting, a bit about the family dynamics, and some information about the characters is revealed.

Rising Action: Welcome to the exciting part of the story! After establishing the background for the reader, the author will begin to develop the conflict. This is where a problem or an issue arises that piques the reader's interest. The camping trip seems to be going without a hitch, when suddenly, nine-year-old Walter notices that Viking is nowhere to be found. After looking inside the truck and checking out the immediate area, Walter starts to panic and call after Viking. Mom and his brothers also stop their work and start hollering his name. *He has to be close by*, they think. *He will hear us soon and come running back.* They comfort each other. *He probably just found something interesting to sniff in the woods.* They agree and decide to take a break and go look for him.

Here is where the conflict begins. Readers will begin to get anxious for the family and the dog. Readers will certainly have questions now: *Will they find Viking easily? To where did he wander? Is the dog okay? How will this intriguing event affect the camping trip? What will happen to the family as they search for their beloved dog?* This section will be the longest part of the text. The plot will thicken, and suspense will capture the reader's attention as the tension builds. Many twists and turns may occur to propel the story forward. As Mom and the boys start searching, they begin to find mysterious notes that reveal more information about Viking's whereabouts. It appears that the dog did not wander away but has been taken to a safe location. If they want their dog returned, they must find him. The messages, which contain clues, lead them on a scavenger hunt throughout the campgrounds. As they search and try to make sense of the situation, they face a series of challenges.

Climax: Here is the highest point of tension in the story. It is the moment readers have been waiting to reach. It is the most exciting part of the story, the moment when readers may learn the truth! The family finds their dog at last. The last clue leads them to their original campsite. Exhausted and frustrated, they return to where they started, but to their surprise, Dad, friends, and family are waiting for them. Five tents are fully set, including theirs.

Falling Action: Here, readers learn the truth. The conflict is resolved. Viking is safe and sound. It turns out that Dad didn't have a work conference at all. It is a surprise party for Leon, who is turning 18 and leaving for college in a few weeks! Mom was in on the dognapping from the start. She played along with Dad's sneaky plan. There is a huge dinner spread waiting for them, and the group tells them all the details as they drink lemonade and fill up on steak and sides. It seems like Dad had a lot of help from the rest of the group to coordinate the messages and to make the scavenger hunt work. Everyone explains their parts.

Resolution: It's the end of the story. All is resolved. In this story, the family has a happy ending. Even Viking is gnawing on a big steak bone! However, in some texts, readers may find a tragic ending. Characters may face terrible consequences for their actions or change, learn, and grow from their mistakes.

Maybe in a different scenario, Mom might have repeatedly warned the youngest, Marc, to keep an eye on Viking while she and his older brothers did the heavy work at the campsite. Marc had been too distracted watching YouTube videos on his cell phone (even though he was told to leave it home for the trip) and didn't see Viking wander off. Full of remorse and regret, Marc helps his family find Viking after days of searching, and Mom has broken her ankle while they hiked. The trip is ruined, and they all suffer from thirst, hunger, and the outdoor elements before the rangers find them. Marc has learned to be more responsible. Leon and Walter learn to resolve long-held sibling rivalry issues and work together. Finally, Dad shares his guilt about choosing work over family.

Character

One of the most important parts to a successful plot is interesting characters who move the plot along. A *character* is an individual in a story. In most stories, there is at least one *main character*, the central person, animal, or object that is the focus of the story. The story may be experienced through the main character's eyes. Aside from the main character, works of fiction may also include *side*, or *secondary*, *characters* who support the main character. These characters are not the primary focus, and they may appear significantly less than a main character.

Following are a few other types of characters you should know.

Protagonist: The main character in a work of fiction is sometimes referred to as the *protagonist* of the story. This character is center stage, prominent to the story, and the one who faces the situation head-on. If you think about superhero movies you've seen, your protagonist is Superman,

Batman, and Spiderman. The plot centers around them. They are the ones with the struggles. They drive the story.

Antagonist: The *antagonist* directly opposes the protagonist. In many cases, this is the bad guy/woman in the story. Think of your villains: the Joker, the Penguin, Catwoman. In some cases, the antagonist is not even a character. The antagonist could be a thing that opposes the protagonist, such as nature. The antagonist can even exist inside of the protagonist as an internal struggle the character faces.

> **IRL**   In Greek, *proto* means *first.* Protagonist means *first character.*
>
> Here are some familiar protagonists from pop culture: Harry Potter and Luke Skywalker.
>
> In Greek, the word *antagonist* means *opponent or rival.* It comes from the word antagnistés.
>
> Here are some other popular antagonists in pop culture: Darth Vader and Voldemort.

Round Character: A *round character* is often an interesting one. This character is often the main character and is engaging to readers because they can relate to the complex feelings and emotions this character shares. There is a deep connection to this character because the reader cares about what happens to this character. The opposite is a *flat character*, one who lacks personality and is simplistic in nature.

Dynamic Character: Most round characters are also *dynamic*, meaning they change throughout the story. The character grows as a person, learns valuable lessons, and transforms by the end. The opposite is a *static character*, one who demonstrates little to no change in the story. The character is the same at the beginning and at the end.

Characterization: Consider one of your most recent teachers. On the first day of class, you probably make a lot of quick judgments about the teacher based on the way he looked, dressed, spoke, and acted. Maybe after the teacher greeted you at the door, you decided he was friendly. Maybe after you looked at the syllabus for the year, you came to the conclusion that this teacher was strict. (After all, no late work will be accepted!) Maybe after he made a few jokes, you snickered, thinking he was not funny at all, even though he tried. Finally, after assessing his elephant tie, you thought to yourself, this teacher has no taste. Whether these assumptions are right or wrong in the long run, we always make judgments about those around us based on their behaviors, actions, speech, and appearance.

IRL In Disney's film *Beauty and the Beast*, the beast would be an example of a *round and dynamic character*. The Beast is a main character who is interesting to the audience. Why does he live the way he does alone in his castle? Why is he so angry? Why are people afraid of him? In addition, he transforms throughout the story. Not only does he turn into a handsome prince by the end, he also learns to feel love when he meets Belle.

Belle, on the other hand, is an example of a *static character*. She is good, kind, and loving throughout the film. Her good nature does not change. She is thoughtful in the beginning of the film, and, even when she encounters the beast and is held captive, she remains compassionate in the circumstances.

Finally, Gaston is a *flat character*. He is two-dimensional: mean and chauvinistic. He tries to impress Belle with his strength and good looks. He is not developed any further.

Readers do the same for the characters they meet in the texts they read. *Characterization* is a strategy readers use to make sense of a character through context clues. Authors often use small details to reveal a character's attitude, personality, and mannerisms. Basically, it helps readers get to know a character well.

BTW

When characters speak, it is known as dialogue. Active readers pay attention to the words the characters say. Their speech reveals how they are feeling, what they intend to do next, and what they want and desire. Notice what Mrs. Lynde's dialogue to Marilla reveals:

"We're all pretty well," said Mrs. Rachel. "I was kind of afraid you weren't, though, when I saw Matthew starting off today. I thought maybe he was going to the doctor's."

Mrs. Rachel is being nosy. She has come to visit Marilla only to find out where Matthew was headed. Mrs. Rachel is prying into the Cuthberts' lives and trying to get Marilla to share her personal life with her. It is obvious to the reader, and it is obvious to Marilla!

Marilla's lips twitched understandingly. She had expected Mrs. Rachel up; she had known that the sight of Matthew jaunting off so unaccountably would be too much for her neighbor's curiosity.

When I first get to know characters in a new text, I pay close attention to the way characters speak, what characters say, how they dress, what they think, what actions they take (or don't take), and how they treat others. It's not very different from how we get to know real-life people.

When you are asked to discuss characterization, here are a few ways to begin. Consider the following questions:

- How does the character act?

- How does the character look or dress?

- How does the character speak?

- How does the character react?

- How do others react to the character?

BTW

When you describe a person or a character, you will have to use adjectives. Adjectives, one of the nine parts of speech, give us more information about nouns and pronouns.

For example: Middle school is often a challenging and confusing time in young-adult life.

The adjectives challenging and confusing tell us more about the time (noun).

The adjectives young-adult tell us more about the life (noun).

Nouns are persons, places, things, or ideas.

Person: student
Place: school
Thing: book
Idea: religion

A noun can be concrete, something easily seen: pen, paper, hat.
A noun can be abstract: something that exists but is not seen: love, hate, freedom.

Here is a list of go-to adjectives to help you describe the characters you meet in fiction. You may use these words for reference.

absent-minded	awful	cold	energetic	guarded
adventurous	balanced	competent	enthusiastic	hateful
affectionate	beautiful	composed	evasive	hearty
agile	blue	conceited	even-tempered	helpful
agreeable	blunt	condescending	excitable	hesitant
alert	boisterous	confident	ferocious	hot-headed
amazing	brave	confused	fiery	naughty
ambitious	bright	conscientious	flabby	nice
amiable	brilliant	considerate	flaky	obedient
amusing	buff	content	frank	picky
analytical	candid	dainty	friendly	pleasant
angelic	cantankerous	decisive	funny	plain
apathetic	capable	deep	fussy	repulsive
apprehensive	careful	dependent	generous	rich
ardent	careless	delightful	gentle	respectful
artificial	cautious	depressed	gloomy	rude
artistic	charming	devoted	good	shy
assertive	childish	direct	grave	silly
attentive	childlike	dirty	great	successful
average	cheerful	disagreeable	groggy	stylish
awesome	civil	discreet	grouchy	troubled

Let's try this using the two characters we met from *Anne of Green Gables*, Mrs. Rachel Lynde and Matthew Cuthbert. What would be a characteristic of each? How did you draw those conclusions? What evidence from the text supports your thinking?

She was sitting there one afternoon in early June. The sun was coming in at the window warm and bright; the orchard on the slope below the house was in a bridal flush of pinky-white bloom, hummed over by a myriad of bees. Thomas Lynde—a meek little man whom Avonlea people called "Rachel Lynde's husband"—was sowing his late turnip seed on the hill field beyond the barn; and Matthew Cuthbert ought to have been sowing his on the big red brook field away over by Green Gables. Mrs. Rachel knew that he ought because she had heard him tell Peter Morrison the evening before in William J. Blair's store over at Carmody that he meant to sow his turnip seed the next afternoon. Peter had asked him, of course, for Matthew Cuthbert had never been known to volunteer information about anything in his whole life.

And yet here was Matthew Cuthbert, at half-past three on the afternoon of a busy day, placidly driving over the hollow and up the hill; moreover, he wore a white collar and his best suit of clothes, which was plain proof that he was going out of Avonlea; and he had the buggy and the sorrel mare, which betokened that he was going a considerable distance. Now, where was Matthew Cuthbert going and why was he going there?

Had it been any other man in Avonlea, Mrs. Rachel, deftly putting this and that together, might have given a pretty good guess as to both questions. But Matthew so rarely went from home that it must be something pressing and unusual which was taking him; he was the shyest man alive and hated to have to go among strangers or to any place where he might have to talk. Matthew, dressed up with a white collar and driving in a buggy, was something that didn't happen often. Mrs. Rachel, ponder as she might, could make nothing of it and her afternoon's enjoyment was spoiled.

"I'll just step over to Green Gables after tea and find out from Marilla where he's gone and why," the worthy woman finally concluded. "He doesn't generally go to town this time of year and he *never* visits; if he'd run out of turnip seed he wouldn't dress up and take the buggy to go for more; he wasn't driving fast enough to be going for a doctor. Yet something must have happened since last night to start him off. I'm clean puzzled, that's what, and I won't know a minute's peace of mind or conscience until I know what has taken Matthew Cuthbert out of Avonlea today."

Character	Characteristic	Method of Analysis	Supporting Evidence
Thomas Lynde	Submissive (obedient/ passive)	How people respond to him	He is described as a meek little man whom Avonlea people called "Rachel Lynde's husband."
Mrs. Rachel Lynde	Nosy	What she thinks	"Now, where was Matthew Cuthbert going and why was he going there?" She sees Matthew leaving and she is determined to find out where he is going.
Matthew Cuthbert	Reticent	How he behaves	Matthew hardly leaves home.

Character Complexity: Characters are often complicated and show more than one trait. When you read a work of fiction, you often sympathize with and defend characters. We tend to see only the positive character traits. Perceptive readers acknowledge the parts of a character that are less likable. Although characters may at times appear extremely bright and knowledgeable, they can also be immature, childish, and defensive. In order to analyze a character fully, readers must remove their rose-colored glasses and examine characters' less-appealing sides.

Let's practice: As we continue to read our mentor text, *Anne of Green Gables*, try to keep track of each character's complex nature. Try to identify positive characteristics and negative or less likable characteristics of Mrs. Rachel Lynde and Marilla Cuthbert.

With this Mrs. Rachel stepped out of the lane into the backyard of Green Gables. Very green and neat and precise was that yard, set about on one side with great patriarchal willows and the other with prim Lombardies. Not a stray stick nor stone was to be seen, for Mrs. Rachel would have seen it if there had been. Privately she was of the opinion that Marilla Cuthbert swept that yard over as often as she swept her house. One could have eaten a meal off the ground without over-brimming the proverbial peck of dirt.

Mrs. Rachel rapped smartly at the kitchen door and stepped in when bidden to do so. The kitchen at Green Gables was a cheerful apartment—or would have been cheerful if it had not been so painfully clean as to give it something of the appearance of an unused parlor. Its windows looked east and west; through the west one, looking out on the back yard, came a flood of mellow June sunlight; but the east one, whence you got a glimpse of the bloom white cherry-trees in the left orchard and nodding, slender birches down in the hollow by the brook, was greened over by a tangle of vines. Here sat Marilla Cuthbert, when she sat at all, always slightly distrustful of sunshine, which seemed to her too dancing and irresponsible a thing for a world which was meant to be taken seriously; and here she sat now, knitting, and the table behind her was laid for supper.

Mrs. Rachel, before she had fairly closed the door, had taken a mental note of everything that was on that table. There were three plates laid, so that Marilla must be expecting someone home with Matthew to tea; but the dishes were everyday dishes and there was only crab-apple preserves and one kind of cake, so that the expected company could not be any particular company. Yet what of Matthew's white collar and the sorrel mare? Mrs. Rachel was getting fairly dizzy with this unusual mystery about quiet, unmysterious Green Gables.

"Good evening, Rachel," Marilla said briskly. "This is a real fine evening, isn't it? Won't you sit down? How are all your folks?"

Something that for lack of any other name might be called friendship existed and always had existed between Marilla Cuthbert and Mrs. Rachel, in spite of—or perhaps because of—their dissimilarity.

Marilla was a tall, thin woman, with angles and without curves; her dark hair showed some gray streaks and was always twisted up in a hard little knot behind with two wire hairpins stuck aggressively through it. She looked like a woman of narrow experience and rigid conscience, which she was; but there was a saving something about her mouth which, if it had been ever so slightly developed, might have been considered indicative of a sense of humor.

"We're all pretty well," said Mrs. Rachel. "I was kind of afraid *you* weren't, though, when I saw Matthew starting off today. I thought maybe he was going to the doctor's."

Marilla's lips twitched understandingly. She had expected Mrs. Rachel up; she had known that the sight of Matthew jaunting off so unaccountably would be too much for her neighbor's curiosity.

"Oh, no, I'm quite well although I had a bad headache yesterday," she said. "Matthew went to Bright River. We're getting a little boy from an orphan asylum in Nova Scotia and he's coming on the train tonight."

If Marilla had said that Matthew had gone to Bright River to meet a kangaroo from Australia, Mrs. Rachel could not have been more astonished. She was actually stricken dumb for five seconds. It was unsupposable that Marilla was making fun of her, but Mrs. Rachel was almost forced to suppose it.

"Are you in earnest, Marilla?" she demanded when voice returned to her.

"Yes, of course," said Marilla, as if getting boys from orphan asylums in Nova Scotia were part of the usual spring work on any well-regulated Avonlea farm instead of being an unheard of innovation.

Mrs. Rachel felt that she had received a severe mental jolt. She thought in exclamation points. A boy! Marilla and Matthew Cuthbert of all people adopting a boy! From an orphan asylum! Well, the world was certainly turning upside down! She would be surprised at nothing after this! Nothing!

"What on earth put such a notion into your head?" she demanded disapprovingly.

This had been done without her advice being asked, and must perforce be disapproved.

Character	Positive or Likable/Supporting Evidence from the Text	Negative or Less Likable Supporting Evidence from the text
My example: Marilla Cuthbert *Notice my strategy: I consider Marilla's actions and what others think about her to characterize her.*	It seems that Marilla Cuthbert is neat and organized. When Mrs. Rachel Lynde visits Green Gables, she notices that the yard is "very green and neat ... Not a stray stick nor stone was to be seen" (2). Keeping her property tidy is important to Marilla. Mrs. Rachel Lynde notices it and thinks, "Marilla Cuthbert swept that yard over as often as she swept her house."	Is Marilla Cuthbert lonely or too strict or stringent? The house is very clean; however, Mrs. Lynde thinks "it had not been so painfully clean as to give it something of the appearance of an unused parlor." The home seems still and lifeless.

Point of View: As you read, it's always important to identify who is telling the story. Is it the narrator? Is it a particular character? So much depends on the storyteller. For example, if there were a terrible car accident on the road and a police officer wanted to know what happened, the story might be told differently depending on who was giving the details.

Conflict: Although you are only in middle school, I can bet that over the years you have had some struggles along the way. Life isn't easy for anyone! We all have obstacles we have to face, and sometimes problems can be challenging to overcome. Some issues you face may be easier: Your two best friends are in an argument, and you are caught in the middle. Maybe all your friends have been invited to hang out but you. Or the dilemma can be more testing: Your friend has a copy of tomorrow's math quiz, and you have to decide whether or not you will accept the answers and cheat. Maybe your situation is very serious: Someone in your family is sick, your parents are separating, or you have faced a life-changing crossroad in your life. Literature can mirror life in that way.

> **BTW**
>
> When you try to determine the point of view, there are three types you **must know.**
>
> First-person: The narrator is telling the story and is also a character who participates in the story. Often, "I" will be used.
>
> Second-person: The story is told as if it were happening to you.
>
> Third-person: The story is told through he, she, them, him, or her.

Characters, too, face *conflicts* large and small. These conflicts are the interesting hooks that draw readers into the text. They create the tension that builds in the work. Conflicts also serve other purposes. They highlight social issues in the world. They help us learn empathy. They make us think: What would I do if I were in this situation? Would I be a leader or a follower? Would I stand up to a bully or for a cause? Would I react similarly or take a different path?

There are different types of conflicts to look for as you read and analyze a text. You'll notice that conflicts come from two opposing forces.

- **Conflict with the self:** This conflict happens internally. Consider the previous example: A character has a copy of the test. Do they cheat or stay honest? On one hand, if the character does well, they will have the opportunity to move into an advanced class. However, they have been taught that cheating is wrong. If they are caught, there will be consequences to face, and they will be disappointed in themselves.

- **Conflict with other people:** As you have surely experienced, most of our conflicts are caused when we clash with others. The characters are upset because their parents won't let them stay out past curfew. A character is hurt because a friend is avoiding them. The coach benched the main character for no reason even though they are the star of the team.

- **Conflict with society:** Some of the most difficult conflicts to endure are those created by government, culture, or traditions. If you watch or read the news, each day you will see individuals who are facing struggles against society. Perhaps it is a woman fleeing her homeland to avoid an arranged marriage. Maybe it is a refugee being refused asylum. Maybe it is an Olympian fighting an outdated dress code. Maybe it is an actress arguing to be paid the equivalent of her male counterpart. In many works of literature, characters also face injustice and bias in the society in which their stories are set. In Harper Lee's *To Kill a Mockingbird*, Tom Robinson, a black man in the Great Depression, is arrested and jailed for a crime he did not commit. In John Steinbeck's *Of Mice and Men*, Lenny and George are two migrant workers who struggle to find and maintain work during the Depression because of George's disability.

- **Conflict with nature:** Some conflicts are in our control. You can listen to your parents and play it safe. You can choose not to cheat on an exam. You can confront a friend who has been acting strange and heal the relationship. However, not all forces can be successfully opposed. Nature, for example, is a force that is more powerful than we are. Many characters in literature have learned this lesson the hard way: Nature is in charge. Storms, tornadoes, hurricanes, jungles, oceans, and mountains are not forces to be reckoned with. In the short story "To Build a Fire" by Jack London, an older man and his dog venture out into frigid terrain along the Yukon River despite the warnings about hiking alone in such freezing conditions. This area is unfamiliar to him, yet he dismisses the potential danger. He faces harsh consequences when he doesn't heed the advice. Animals and other living creatures can also be threats to people. Can you imagine being overrun with ants? In another short story, "Leiningen Versus the Ants" by Carl Stephenson, a plantation owner in Brazil is warned to flee his land because an army of soldier ants is en route and will overrun his fields, destroying and eating everything in sight. He is overconfident and refuses to leave. You can predict the outcome!

Setting: Imagine this: You just returned home from summer camp, and your grandparents ask you about your experience. Most likely if you share any stories about your time away, you will include details such as the time and the place in which the event happened. You will probably say something like this: "The first day of camp we were all in the cabin telling ghost stories when..." or "On the last night of color wars, a bunch of us went down to the lake and saw..." The time and place of the story is what readers call the *setting*. Details such as the time of day, location, season, month, or place are very important to the story. These details provide more than just a backdrop for the story to unfold.

A work of literature can take place in one setting the entire time. For example, in the classic book *One Flew Over the Cuckoo's Nest* by Ken Kesey, the setting takes place in a mental institution in Oregon. The setting *never* changes. However, settings can shift to multiple locations or jump time. In *The Catcher in the Rye* by J.D. Salinger, the teenage protagonist, Holden Caulfield, flees his private school, Pency Prep in Pennsylvania, and goes to New York City. Settings can span generations, such as in the popular YA book *Holes* by Louis Sacher. Although most of the story takes place in Green Lake, Texas, there are many flashbacks that jump back into the past in Latvia, which provide important family history. In some works of literature, the setting is not external but rather internal. This is known as a psychological setting. Yes, a book can actually take place in a character's mind! In this internal setting, the thoughts and feelings of the character are reflected.

In many cases, the setting is so important that *if changed*, the story would be entirely different in a new location. For example, the classic book *Lord of the Flies* by William Golding is set on a deserted island. A group of British boys have been stranded there after a plane crash. Without any parents or adults to help them, they must govern themselves, which leads to chaos and violence. If the boys did not find themselves on the island alone and instead on a class trip to Disney World, the story, including its outcome, would not have been the classic it is. In most cases, the setting affects the characters, their perspectives, and their actions. Setting can also reveal themes. A character from a small town might think very differently than a character in a big city. A character who grows up during the 1980s will behave very differently than one who grew up during the Great Depression.

 IRL Writer Frank Norris once said, "Things can happen in some cities and the tale of them will be interesting: the same story laid in another city would be ridiculous." Basically, in some works of literature the setting is more significant than in other works.

Let's examine the setting in Richard Connell's classic short story "The Most Dangerous Game." Watch how I use my close-reading strategies to analyze the setting.

"OFF THERE to the right—somewhere—is a *large island*," said Whitney. "It's rather a *mystery*—"	I notice that there is an island to the right. Is the setting on a ship?
"What island is it?" Rainsford asked.	The island is described as a mystery. I wonder why.
"The old charts call it '*Ship-Trap Island*,'" Whitney replied. "A suggestive name, isn't it? Sailors have a *curious dread* of the place. I don't know why. Some *superstition*—"	Ship-Trap Island is an interesting name. I think this name might be foreshadowing something ominous.

"Can't see it," remarked Rainsford, trying to peer through the dank tropical night that was palpable as it pressed its *thick warm blackness* in upon the *yacht.*

"You've good eyes," said Whitney, with a laugh, "and I've seen you pick off a moose moving in the brown fall bush at four hundred yards, but even you can't see four miles or so through a moonless Caribbean night."

"Nor four yards," admitted Rainsford. "Ugh! It's like moist black velvet."

"It will be light enough in Rio," promised Whitney.

"We should make it in a few days. I hope the jaguar guns have come from Purdey's. We should have some good hunting up the Amazon. Great sport, hunting."

"The best sport in the world," agreed Rainsford. "For the hunter," amended Whitney. "Not for the jaguar."

"Don't talk rot, Whitney," said Rainsford.

"You're a big-game hunter, not a philosopher. Who cares how a jaguar feels?"

"Perhaps the jaguar does," observed Whitney.

"Bah! They've no understanding."

"Even so, I rather think they understand one thing—fear. The fear of pain and the fear of death."

"Nonsense," laughed Rainsford.

"This *hot weather* is making you soft, Whitney. Be a realist. The world is made up of two classes—the hunters and the huntees. Luckily, you and I are hunters. Do you think we've passed that island yet?"

"I can't tell in the dark. I hope so."

"Why?" asked Rainsford.

"The place has a *reputation—a bad one.*"

"Cannibals?" suggested Rainsford.

"Hardly. Even *cannibals wouldn't live in such a God-forsaken place.* But it's gotten into sailor lore, somehow. Didn't you notice that the crew's nerves seemed a bit *jumpy* today?"

I notice the word choice the writer uses to describe this island: *dread* and *superstition.* These words have negative connotations to them.

It is interesting that Rainsford can't see the island through the *dank* night. There are also more eerie word choices: *thick, warm, blackness.*

Now I see, the characters are indeed on a yacht!

This simile sounds negative and gloomy too: the night is like *moist black velvet.* I wonder why there is so much imagery regarding sight? Perhaps the characters are blinded to the reality of the island?

The weather is uncomfortable. The setting so far is described in a way that makes me predict that something unfortunate will happen soon in the story.

The author has given readers a lot of clues regarding the setting.

The island has a bad reputation that even keeps cannibals away and makes the yacht crew nervous as the ship approaches.

EXERCISES

EXERCISE 2.1

Use your knowledge about fiction to answer the following questions.

1. Which of the following texts would be considered a work of fiction?
    a. A newspaper article
    b. A young adult novel
    c. A book review
    d. A science textbook

2. Which of the following features would belong in a work of fiction?
    a. Setting
    b. Characters
    c. Conflicts
    d. All of the above

3. Which line would reveal indirect characterization?
    a. Matthew Cuthbert had never been known to volunteer information about anything in his whole life.
    b. She was sitting there one afternoon in early June.
    c. Now, where was Matthew Cuthbert going and why was he going there?
    d. The sun was coming in at the window warm and bright.

4. In what part of the plot does an author take time to provide a bit of background, establish the setting, and introduce characters?
    a. Exposition
    b. Rising action
    c. Falling action
    d. Resolution

5. What type of character would most likely be a villain?
    a. The main character
    b. The antagonist
    c. The narrator
    d. A flat character

6. When working on characterization, you should do which of the following?
    a. Look for details about the character's appearance.
    b. Notice the character's behavior.
    c. Pay attention to the character's dialogue.
    d. All of the above

7. Had it been any other man in Avonlea, Mrs. Rachel, deftly putting this and that together, might have given a pretty good guess as to both questions. But Matthew so rarely went from home that it must be something pressing and unusual which was taking him; he was the shyest man alive and hated to have to go among strangers or to any place where he might have to talk. Matthew, dressed up with a white collar and driving in a buggy, was something that didn't happen often.

    This passage is an example of which of the following techniques?
    a. Direct characterization
    b. Conflict
    c. Indirect characterization
    d. Resolution

8. And yet here was Matthew Cuthbert, at half-past three on the afternoon of a busy day, placidly driving over the hollow and up the hill; moreover, he wore a white collar and his best suit of clothes, which was plain proof that he was going out of Avonlea; and he had the buggy and the sorrel mare, which betokened that he was going a considerable distance. Now, where was Matthew Cuthbert going and why was he going there?

This passage is written from which point of view?

a. First-person
b. Second-person
c. Third-person
d. None of the above

9. The setting of *Anne of Green Gables* is most likely which of the following?

a. A big city
b. A rural community
c. Aboard a ship
d. A boarding school

10. Which of the following would be considered an internal conflict?

a. Two men quarreling over a parking space
b. A student debating whether or not to cheat on a math test
c. A hunter fighting a wild beast
d. A hurricane during a camping trip

EXERCISE 2.2

Continue reading the next excerpt from "The Most Dangerous Game" and answer the following questions using the lessons you learned in this chapter.

"They were a bit strange, now you mention it. Even Captain Nielsen—"

"Yes, even that tough-minded old Swede, who'd go up to the devil himself and ask him for a light. Those fishy blue eyes held a look I never saw there before. All I could get out of him was 'This place has an evil name among seafaring men, sir.' Then he said to me, very gravely, 'Don't you feel anything?'—as if the air about us was actually poisonous. Now, you mustn't laugh when I tell you this—I did feel something like a sudden chill."

There was no breeze. The sea was as flat as a plate-glass window. We were drawing near the island then. What I felt was a—a mental chill; a sort of sudden dread.

"Pure imagination," said Rainsford. "One superstitious sailor can taint the whole ship's company with his fear."

"Maybe. But sometimes I think sailors have an extra sense that tells them when they are in danger. Sometimes I think evil is a tangible thing—with wave lengths, just as sound and light have. An evil place can, so to speak, broadcast vibrations of evil. Anyhow, I'm glad we're getting out of this zone. Well, I think I'll turn in now, Rainsford."

"I'm not sleepy," said Rainsford. "I'm going to smoke another pipe up on the afterdeck."

"Good night, then, Rainsford. See you at breakfast."

"Right. Good night, Whitney."

There was no sound in the night as Rainsford sat there but the muffled throb of the engine that drove the yacht swiftly through the darkness, and the swish and ripple of the wash of the propeller. Rainsford, reclining in a steamer chair, indolently puffed on his favorite brier. The sensuous drowsiness of the night was on him.

"It's so dark," he thought, "that I could sleep without closing my eyes; the night would be my eyelids—"

An abrupt sound startled him. Off to the right he heard it, and his ears, expert in such matters, could not be mistaken. Again he heard the sound, and again. Somewhere, off in the blackness, someone had fired a gun three times.

Rainsford sprang up and moved quickly to the rail, mystified. He strained his eyes in the direction from which the reports had come, but it was like trying to see through a blanket. He leaped upon the rail and balanced himself there, to get greater elevation; his pipe, striking a rope, was knocked from his mouth. He lunged for it; a short, hoarse cry came from his lips as he realized he had reached too far and had lost his balance. The cry was pinched off short as the blood-warm waters of the Caribbean Sea dosed over his head. He struggled up to the surface and tried to cry out, but the wash from the speeding yacht slapped him in the face and the salt water in his open mouth made him gag and strangle.

Desperately he struck out with strong strokes after the receding lights of the yacht, but he stopped before he had swum fifty feet. A certain coolheadedness had come to him; it was not the first time he had been in a tight place. There was a chance that his cries could be heard by someone aboard the yacht, but that chance was slender and grew more slender as the yacht raced on. He wrestled himself out of his clothes and shouted with all his power. The lights of the yacht became faint and ever-vanishing fireflies; then they were blotted out entirely by the night.

1. How would a reader know this passage is fiction?
    a. It has interesting characters.
    b. There is a plot.
    c. A setting is established.
    d. All of the above

2. Which adjective would best characterize Rainsford in this passage?
    a. Lazy
    b. Quarrelsome
    c. Arrogant
    d. Anxious

3. Which of the following words from the passage is an adjective?

    a. Pipe

    b. Deck

    c. Lights

    d. Poisonous

4. "Yes, even that tough-minded old Swede, who'd go up to the devil himself and ask him for a light." How is Captain Nielsen characterized in this line?

    a. Brave

    b. Sickly

    c. Hesitant

    d. Dangerous

5. Which line best contributes to Rainsford's characterization?

    a. "One superstitious sailor can taint the whole ship's company with his fear."

    b. Those fishy blue eyes held a look I never saw there before.

    c. "I'm not sleepy," said Rainsford.

    d. The lights of the yacht became faint and ever-vanishing fireflies; then they were blotted out entirely by the night.

6. Where in Freytag's Pyramid would this passage fall?

    a. Rising action

    b. Exposition

    c. Falling action

    d. Resolution

7. "They were a bit strange, now you mention it. Even Captain Nielsen—"

   "Yes, even that tough-minded old Swede, who'd go up to the devil himself and ask him for a light. Those fishy blue eyes held a look I never saw there before. All I could get out of him was 'This place has an evil name among seafaring men, sir.' Then he said to me, very *gravely*, 'Don't you feel anything?'—as if the air about us was actually poisonous. Now, you mustn't laugh when I tell you this—I did feel something like a sudden chill."

   From the context of these lines, *gravely* most likely means:

   a. Seriously

   b. Studiously

   c. Critically

   d. Courageously

8. What is the point of view in the story?

   a. First-person

   b. Second-person

   c. Third-person

   d. Switches between first-person and third-person

9. "Pure imagination," said Rainsford. "One superstitious sailor can taint the whole ship's company with his fear." "Maybe. But sometimes I think sailors have an extra sense that tells them when they are in danger. Sometimes I think evil is a tangible thing—with wave lengths, just as sound and light have. An evil place can, so to speak, broadcast vibrations of evil. Anyhow, I'm glad we're getting out of this zone. Well, I think I'll turn in now, Rainsford."

   What does the dialogue reveal here?

   a. Rainsford and the sailor have different opinions about the island.

   b. Rainsford does not believe the rumors about the island.

   c. The sailor's warnings about the island should be taken seriously.

   d. All of the above

10. As the passage ends, what conflict is developing?
    a. A conflict between Rainsford and Captain Nielsen
    b. A conflict between Rainsford and himself.
    c. A conflict between Rainsford and nature.
    d. A conflict between Rainsford and the entire crew.

EXERCISE 2.3

Continue reading the next excerpt from "The Most Dangerous Game" and answer the following questions using the lessons you learned in this chapter.

Rainsford remembered the shots. They had come from the right, and doggedly he swam in that direction, swimming with slow, deliberate strokes, conserving his strength. For a seemingly endless time he fought the sea. He began to count his strokes; he could do possibly a hundred more and then—

Rainsford heard a sound. It came out of the darkness, a high screaming sound, the sound of an animal in an extremity of anguish and terror.

He did not recognize the animal that made the sound; he did not try to; with fresh vitality he swam toward the sound. He heard it again; then it was cut short by another noise, crisp, staccato.

"Pistol shot," muttered Rainsford, swimming on.

Ten minutes of determined effort brought another sound to his ears— the most welcome he had ever heard—the muttering and growling of the sea breaking on a rocky shore. He was almost on the rocks before he saw them; on a night less calm he would have been shattered against them. With his remaining strength he dragged himself from the swirling waters. Jagged crags appeared to jut up into the opaqueness; he forced himself upward, hand over hand. Gasping, his hands raw, he reached a flat place at the top. Dense jungle came down to the very edge of the cliffs. What perils that tangle of trees and underbrush might hold for him did not concern Rainsford just then. All he knew was that he was safe from his enemy, the sea, and that utter weariness was on him. He flung himself down at the jungle edge and tumbled headlong into the deepest sleep of his life.

When he opened his eyes he knew from the position of the sun that it was late in the afternoon. Sleep had given him new vigor; a sharp hunger was picking at him. He looked about him, almost cheerfully.

"Where there are pistol shots, there are men. Where there are men, there is food," he thought. But what kind of men, he wondered, in so forbidding a place? An unbroken front of snarled and ragged jungle fringed the shore.

He saw no sign of a trail through the closely knit web of weeds and trees; it was easier to go along the shore, and Rainsford floundered along by the water. Not far from where he landed, he stopped.

Some wounded thing—by the evidence, a large animal—had thrashed about in the underbrush; the jungle weeds were crushed down and the moss was lacerated; one patch of weeds was stained crimson. A small, glittering object not far away caught Rainsford's eye and he picked it up. It was an empty cartridge.

"A twenty-two," he remarked. "That's odd. It must have been a fairly large animal too. The hunter had his nerve with him to tackle it with a light gun. It's clear that the brute put up a fight. I suppose the first three shots I heard was when the hunter flushed his quarry and wounded it. The last shot was when he trailed it here and finished it."

He examined the ground closely and found what he had hoped to find— the print of hunting boots. They pointed along the cliff in the direction he had been going. Eagerly he hurried along, now slipping on a rotten log or a loose stone, but making headway; night was beginning to settle down on the island.

Bleak darkness was blacking out the sea and jungle when Rainsford sighted the lights. He came upon them as he turned a crook in the coast line; and his first thought was that he had come upon a village, for there were many lights. But as he forged along he saw to his great astonishment that all the lights were in one enormous building—a lofty structure with pointed towers plunging upward into the gloom. His eyes made out the shadowy outlines of a palatial chateau; it was set on a high bluff, and on three sides of it cliffs dived down to where the sea licked greedy lips in the shadows.

1. Which details characterize Rainsford as observant?

    a. [The shots] had come from the right, and doggedly he swam in that direction, swimming with slow, deliberate strokes, conserving his strength.

    b. He examined the ground closely and found what he had hoped to find—the print of hunting boots.

    c. "A twenty-two," he remarked. "That's odd. It must have been a fairly large animal too."

    d. All of the above

2. Which details continue to develop the setting?

    a. Not far from where he landed, he stopped.

    b. His eyes made out the shadowy outlines of a palatial chateau; it was set on a high bluff, and on three sides of it cliffs dived down to where the sea licked greedy lips in the shadows.

    c. He did not recognize the animal that made the sound; he did not try to; with fresh vitality he swam toward the sound.

    d. He examined the ground closely and found what he had hoped to find—the print of hunting boots.

3. "A twenty-two," he remarked. "That's odd. It must have been a fairly large animal too. The hunter had his nerve with him to tackle it with a light gun. It's clear that the brute put up a fight. I suppose the first three shots I heard was when the hunter flushed his quarry and sounded it. The last shot was when he trailed it here and finished it."

    These lines best characterize Rainsford as:

    a. Strong

    b. Determined

    c. Stubborn

    d. Skilled

4. Some wounded thing—by the evidence, a large animal—had thrashed about in the underbrush; the jungle weeds were crushed down and the moss was lacerated; one patch of weeds was stained crimson. *A small, glittering object not far away caught Rainsford's eye and he picked it up. It was an empty cartridge.*

   Which type of conflict might the lines in italics develop?

   a. Man vs. man

   b. Man vs. society

   c. Man vs. nature

   d. Man vs. self

5. Ten minutes of determined effort brought another sound to his ears—the most welcome he had ever heard—the muttering and growling of the sea breaking on a rocky shore. He was almost on the rocks before he saw them; on a night less calm he would have been shattered against them. With his remaining strength he dragged himself from the swirling waters. Jagged crags appeared to jut up into the opaqueness; he forced himself upward, hand over hand. Gasping, his hands raw, he reached a flat place at the top. Dense jungle came down to the very edge of the cliffs. What perils that tangle of trees and underbrush might hold for him did not concern Rainsford just then.

   What can you infer about the setting based on the word choice in the passage?

   a. The island is densely populated.

   b. The island is dangerous.

   c. The island is barren.

   d. The island is small.

6. How does the author depict Rainsford as a resourceful hunter?
   a. Through Rainsford's inner thinking
   b. Through Rainsford's actions
   c. Through Rainsford's reactions
   d. All of the above

At first Rainsford thought it could not be real, but the stone steps were real enough, the massive door was real enough, and the creak of the knocker as he lifted it was also real enough. The knocker startled him with its booming loudness. The door opened suddenly and Rainsford was face to face with the largest man he had ever seen. In his hand the man held a long-barreled revolver, and he was pointing it straight at Rainsford's heart.

"Don't be alarmed," said Rainsford, with a smile which he hoped was disarming. "I'm no robber. My name is Sanger Rainsford of New York City. I fell off a yacht. I am hungry."

The man's only answer was to raise with his thumb the hammer of his revolver. Then the man's free hand went to his forehead in a military salute, he clicked his heels together and stood at attention. Another man was coming down the broad marble steps. He advanced to Rainsford and held out his hand.

"It is a very great pleasure and honor to welcome you Mr. Sanger Rainsford, the celebrated hunter, to my home."

Automatically Rainsford shook the man's hand.

"I've read your book about hunting snow leopards in Tibet, you see," explained the man. "I am General Zaroff." At this, the giant put away his pistol, saluted, and withdrew.

"Ivan is an incredibly strong fellow," remarked the general, "but he has the misfortune to be deaf and dumb. A simple fellow, but I'm afraid, a bit of a savage. Come, we can talk later. Now you want clothes, food, rest. You shall have them. This is a most restful spot." Ivan reappeared. Follow Ivan, if you please, Mr. Rainsford," said the general. "I was about to have my dinner, but I'll wait for you."

After changing, Rainsford returned downstairs to a magnificent dining room. About the hall were the mounted heads of many animals—lions, tigers, elephants, moose, bears; larger or more perfect specimens Rainsford had never seen. At the great table the general was sitting, alone.

"Perhaps," said General Zaroff, "you were surprised that I recognized your name. You see, I read all books on hunting. I have but one passion in my life, Mr. Rainsford, and it is the hunt. Here in my preserve on this island," he said in a slow tone, "I hunt more dangerous game."

Rainsford expressed his surprise. "Is there big game on this island?" The general nodded. "The biggest."

"Really?"

"Oh, it isn't here naturally, of course. I have to stock the island. I have hunted every kind of game in every land. It would be impossible for me to tell you how many animals I have killed. But when I too easily surmounted each new animal I hunted, I had to invent a new animal to hunt," he said.

"A new animal? You're joking."

"Not at all," said the general. "I never joke about hunting. I needed a new animal. I found one. So I bought this island, built this house, and here I do my hunting. The island is perfect for my purposes—there are jungles with a maze of trails in them, hills, swamps—"

"But the animal, General Zaroff?"

"I wanted the ideal animal to hunt," explained the general. "So I said: 'What are the attributes of an ideal quarry?' And the answer was, of course: 'It must have courage, cunning, and, above all, it must be able to reason.'"

"But no animal can reason," objected Rainsford. "My dear fellow," said the general, "there is one that can."

"I can't believe you are serious, General Zaroff," gasped Rainsford. "This is a grisly joke."

"Why should I not be serious? I never joke about hunting."

"Hunting? Good God, General Zaroff, what you speak of is murder. They are men!" The general laughed with entire good nature and quite unruffled. "That is why I use them. It gives me pleasure. They can reason, after a fashion. So they are dangerous."

7. After changing, Rainsford returned downstairs to a magnificent dining room. About the hall were the mounted heads of many animals—lions, tigers, elephants, moose, bears; larger or more perfect specimens Rainsford had never seen. At the great table the general was sitting, alone.

   What do these lines reveal about General Zaroff?

   a. General Zaroff is an experienced hunter.

   b. General Zaroff enjoys solitude.

   c. General Zaroff is a famous decorator.

   d. General Zaroff enjoys company.

8. "Oh, it isn't here naturally, of course. I have to stock the island. I have hunted every kind of game in every land. It would be impossible for me to tell you how many animals I have killed. But when I too easily surmounted each new animal I hunted, I had to invent a new animal to hunt," he said. "A new animal? You're joking."

   How do these lines characterize General Zaroff?

   a. General Zaroff is cordial.

   b. General Zaroff is humble.

   c. General Zaroff is arrogant.

   d. General Zaroff is charming.

9. "Hunting? Good God, General Zaroff, what you speak of is murder. They are men!" The general laughed with entire good nature and quite unruffled. "That is why I use them. It gives me pleasure. They can reason, after a fashion. So they are dangerous."

   What type of character is General Zaroff based on this passage?

   a. Protagonist

   b. Antagonist

   c. A flat character

   d. None of the above

10. What type of conflict is established in the lines quoted in question #9?

    a. Man vs. man

    b. Man vs. society

    c. Man vs. nature

    d. Internal conflict

Flashcard App

3 Analyzing Fiction

MUST KNOW

 The theme is the message the author is trying to convey.

 Literary devices include flashback, foreshadowing, irony, and suspense.

 Being insightful goes beyond identifying strategies: Consider how these devices work to support the author's purpose.

In this chapter, we will focus on literary devices readers of fiction notice when they read this genre. Besides being able to read carefully, it is also important to read deeply. In middle school, teachers will expect you to provide *insight* into the reading. They will ask you to share your thoughts about the theme or to analyze the text. What they expect is not a summary but rather a discussion about the author's techniques, literary devices, or craft moves. You will learn some ways you can delve into your reading to show your thinking.

Reading a book on the beach is one of my favorite summertime activities. When I am reading solely for pleasure, I may not annotate my book formally with a pencil or a sticky note. However, my mind is always busy and active making mental notes: thinking about the themes that emerge in the text, thinking about *why* the authors choose the moves they do, and thinking about how these devices support the work as a whole.

As a lifelong reader, these habits come naturally to me. Professional swimmers may take laps for fun and not for competition, but even then, they will stick to correct form. Chefs may cook for their families once they leave the restaurant kitchen, but they are still going to use best practices in their home preparation. Active readers, too, begin to use deep reading strategies they learn and practice in school—even when they step away from the classroom. After time, these strategies become embedded in our brains, and it feels normal and natural to keep reading actively.

What Is a Theme?

Theme: One of the greatest gifts one can get from reading is the author's messages from the text. Most likely these messages will be subtle or implied. That means the author will not come out directly and say what the message is, but rather will use literary devices (characterization, conflict, setting, symbolism, irony) to reveal the messages through the course of the text. When teachers ask you to discuss a theme, first consider big ideas. Then ask yourself: *What message does the author have about that big idea? What does* *the author want you to know? What life lessons can be imparted from the text? What does the author say about the subject? What is the writer whispering to you?* A work of literature can have many themes.

Possible life lessons:

- Never give up.

- Judge others by their character.

- Work hard for success.

- Be yourself.

- Think before you act.

- Be proud of who you are.

- Speak up when injustice occurs.

Motif: Oftentimes in literature, important ideas repeat throughout the text. It may not be the same word over and over, but variations of the main idea. For example, in the short story "The Most Dangerous Game," there is a darkness motif that runs through the story. Right from the beginning, it is too dark for Rainsford and the crew to see the island. Rainsford "peers" but "can't see it." The night is compared to "a thick warm blackness." The night is soon again described as "moist black velvet." As the yacht passes by, Rainsford thinks he doesn't even have to close his eyes to sleep because it is just that dark: "The night would be my eyelids." His thoughts are interrupted by the sound of a gunshot "somewhere off in the blackness." These references to darkness continue throughout the text.

 IRL Just remember: A theme is a statement, not a single word.

For example, *revenge* is a big idea or a topic. Ask yourself, what does the author say about revenge? What is the message about revenge? What did I, the reader, learn about the nature of revenge?

Theme: When you seek revenge, you wind up hurting yourself.

Note how I turn some big ideas from "The Most Dangerous Game" to thematic statements:

Big Idea	Thematic Statement
Survival	It takes both strength and wit to survive a life-threatening experience.
Hunting	Hunting may seem like a civilized sport unless you are the one being hunted.
Killing	There is a difference between hunting, murder, and self-defense.

What Are Some Literary Devices to Know?

Foreshadowing: When you watch a scary movie, chances are you can predict what will happen next based on small details in previous scenes. For example, if you learn that anyone who has entered the woods at the edge of town has never returned, you will not be too surprised when a character and his friends also struggle to make it out in one piece! How did you know? Well, there was foreshadowing. Maybe an elderly gentleman warned the teenagers not to venture too deep. Maybe eerie sounds were heard nearby. Maybe a villager shared her story about her missing dog who wandered in and failed to come back. Foreshadowing is a fun device! Authors also leave subtle clues about what may happen later in the text. If you pay attention closely, you may recognize these hints in the dialogue, descriptions, and word choice.

Let's look back at the passage from "The Most Dangerous Game." A good reader will detect foreshadowing in the opening lines of the story. Ship-Trap Island is a perfect example of foreshadowing. If I were on that yacht, I would not want to approach an island with that name nor with the "bad reputation." Even the crew on board feels nervous and "jumpy" when the ship approaches. I can't help but feel that the author is trying to warn the reader that danger is approaching. After all, the night is so dark, like "moist velvet," that it is hard to see. I think ships get into danger when the captain and crew cannot see ahead. The author adds these details on purpose for the reader to notice and make predictions.

Flashback: As you mature as a reader, you will begin to read more complex texts. Be prepared for authors to use more sophisticated writer's moves, such as shifts in time known as flashbacks. We discussed how some plots move in chronological order. However, in many texts, authors jump around and include multiple flashbacks, which may include events that happened in the past that provide more information for the present. For example, a flashback may explain how prior experiences or history shaped the characters to who they are now. We might learn more about why the characters act, behave, and think the way they do.

For example, in the 2009 Pixar movie *Up*, Carl Fredricksen is an elderly widower who appears very cranky and crotchety. In the beginning of the film, he is not very friendly to a young wilderness explorer named Russell. Through a series of flashbacks, viewers learn the source of Carl's frustration and irritability. He has lost his wife Ellie, the love of his life, and has not been able to fulfill the dreams they had together, especially of exploring South America. Once viewers understand Carl's past, they feel more sympathy for Carl and come to see him as endearing. The flashbacks cast Carl in a whole new light.

Flashbacks can also reveal more about a setting. For example, if you've ever seen Pixar's *Cars*, the character Lightning McQueen is heading to California to compete in the final race of the Piston Cup when he gets held up against his will in a small town called Radiator Springs. McQueen hates the town, considering it backwards and shoddy, not worth his time. However, as he completes his community service for speeding and damaging the main road, he becomes fond of the other cars in the town, and to his amazement and surprise, he learns the history of this run-down town. In a flashback, Sally, a lawyer in the town, explains the history of Radiator Springs. Years before, the town had been a popular destination along U.S. Route 66. Cars, trucks, and other vehicles would make the stop and dine, shop, and rest. The town was a jewel until the interstate was built, and the cars traveling bypassed Radiator Springs altogether. The town lost business and went into a gradual decay. From the flashback, we learn the sad story, and like Lightning McQueen, we begin to feel sorry for the residents who were left behind. Our perspective of the town changes completely from contempt to empathy.

Irony: When my kids were little, they loved Disney's animation film *Frozen*. Their favorite character was Olaf, the snowman. He was super silly and made them giggle. One of his songs was especially funny. As a snowman, he couldn't wait for summer! In the lyrics, he imagines basking in the sun and swimming. My kids would crack up when he sang, "I'll be doing whatever snow does in summer!" Why is this so funny? Well, answer the question: What does snow do in the summer? It melts! Living in New York winters, I know that; my kids know that; in fact, everyone but Olaf knows that! But did you know that his fantasy about the summer life in the heat is a literary device known as irony? Irony is the difference between the way things are and the way things should be. Olaf mistakenly believes that in the summer he will be able to "put his head up to the burning sand" and get "gorgeously tanned," but, in fact, we all know he won't last in the sun's rays. In a matter of minutes, he will be a huge puddle. Irony at its finest. There are three types of irony you should get to know: *situational*, *verbal*, and *dramatic*.

Situational Irony: Your teacher says she will not tolerate spelling mistakes, and yet, in her syllabus, she has a few typos (words spelled incorrectly). A sign is taped to the front of a fence that states: No posting on public property. A store that advertises being open 24 hours a day is closed. These are all examples of situational irony: The opposite of what is expected occurs.

Verbal Irony: You yell at your parents, "Everything is just fine!" when you run up to your room and slam the door after a bad day. When you leave the house, you exclaim, "Wow, what a beautiful day!" when it's clearly pouring out. As you can see, verbal irony is when someone says something that is the opposite of what they actually mean.

Dramatic Irony: Sometimes an audience or reader is privy to more information than the character in a movie, play, or work of literature. For example, in a scary movie the audience knows that a murderer is inside the house, and the main character doesn't. In Disney's movie *Frozen*, Olaf the snowman sings a song about the joys of summer. He can't wait to experience the heat! The audience laughs because they know he won't get to enjoy it at all. In fact, he will melt.

Another place you will often encounter irony is in political cartoons. Political cartoons can be found in the editorial section of a newspaper or sometimes even in the comics section. Political cartoons reveal a cartoonist's opinion about politics or political subjects and even political figures themselves. The cartoon is humorous and, at times, mocking.

BTW

Don't be confused: Verbal irony and sarcasm are different even if they sound alike. Verbal irony occurs when a person says the opposite of what is intended. The intention of sarcasm is to criticize or mock someone or something.

Sarcasm: "This is a nice place you have here," the sister muttered as she entered her friend's messy apartment. (The sister is being sarcastic. The apartment is a wreck. She is being critical.)

Verbal Irony: "It's a great time to go for a swim," replied the man as he passed by the partially frozen lake. (Irony is the opposite: People swim in the summer, not the winter. No one is being criticized.)

Source: The U.S. National Archives

This political cartoon is titled "Snagged." It was published in the *Washington Post* on May 17, 1903.

In the cartoon, Governor Samuel Pennypacker of Pennsylvania is featured.

Irony is the opposite of what you expect to happen. In this cartoon, the governor is not catching fish; rather, he is snagging himself on the hook.

EXERCISES

EXERCISE 3.1

***Answer the following questions from the passage from "The Most Dangerous Game,"
this time testing yourself on literary devices.***

"They were a bit strange, now you mention it. Even Captain Nielsen—"

"Yes, even that tough-minded old Swede, who'd go up to the devil himself
and ask him for a light. Those fishy blue eyes held a look I never saw there
before. All I could get out of him was 'This place has an evil name among
seafaring men, sir.' Then he said to me, very gravely, 'Don't you feel anything?'—
as if the air about us was actually poisonous. Now, you mustn't laugh when I
tell you this—I did feel something like a sudden chill. There was no breeze. The
sea was as flat as a plate-glass window. We were drawing near the island then.
What I felt was a—a mental chill; a sort of sudden dread."

"Pure imagination," said Rainsford. "One superstitious sailor can taint the
whole ship's company with his fear."

"Maybe. But sometimes I think sailors have an extra sense that tells them
when they are in danger. Sometimes I think evil is a tangible thing—with
wave lengths, just as sound and light have. An evil place can, so to speak,
broadcast vibrations of evil. Anyhow, I'm glad we're getting out of this zone.
Well, I think I'll turn in now, Rainsford."

"I'm not sleepy," said Rainsford.

"I'm going to smoke another pipe up on the afterdeck."

"Good night, then, Rainsford. See you at breakfast."

"Right. Good night, Whitney."

There was no sound in the night as Rainsford sat there but the muffled
throb of the engine that drove the yacht swiftly through the darkness,
and the swish and ripple of the wash of the propeller. Rainsford, reclining
in a steamer chair, indolently puffed on his favorite brier. The sensuous
drowsiness of the night was on him.

"It's so dark," he thought, "that I could sleep without closing my eyes; the night would be my eyelids—"

An abrupt sound startled him. Off to the right he heard it, and his ears, expert in such matters, could not be mistaken. Again he heard the sound, and again. Somewhere, off in the blackness, someone had fired a gun three times.

Rainsford sprang up and moved quickly to the rail, mystified. He strained his eyes in the direction from which the reports had come, but it was like trying to see through a blanket. He leaped upon the rail and balanced himself there, to get greater elevation; his pipe, striking a rope, was knocked from his mouth. He lunged for it; a short, hoarse cry came from his lips as he realized he had reached too far and had lost his balance. The cry was pinched off short as the blood-warm waters of the Caribbean Sea dosed over his head. He struggled up to the surface and tried to cry out, but the wash from the speeding yacht slapped him in the face and the salt water in his open mouth made him gag and strangle.

Desperately he struck out with strong strokes after the receding lights of the yacht, but he stopped before he had swum fifty feet. A certain coolheadedness had come to him; it was not the first time he had been in a tight place. There was a chance that his cries could be heard by someone aboard the yacht, but that chance was slender and grew more slender as the yacht raced on. He wrestled himself out of his clothes and shouted with all his power. The lights of the yacht became faint and ever-vanishing fireflies; then they were blotted out entirely by the night.

1. Which of the following details from the story could be examples of foreshadowing?
    a. 'This place has an evil name among seafaring men, sir.'
    b. "It's so dark."
    c. The blood-warm waters of the Caribbean Sea dosed over his head.
    d. All of the above

2. What might be an example of irony?
   a. The island is called Ship-Trap Island.
   b. Rainsford isn't sleepy.
   c. The pipe was knocked from his mouth.
   d. An abrupt sound startled Rainsford.

3. "But sometimes I think sailors have an extra sense that tells them when they are in danger. Sometimes I think evil is a tangible thing—with wave lengths, just as sound and light have. An evil place can, so to speak, broadcast vibrations of evil. Anyhow, I'm glad we're getting out of this zone."
   Which literary device is being used here?
   a. Flashback
   b. Symbolism
   c. Irony
   d. Foreshadowing

4. "They were a bit strange, now you mention it. Even Captain Nielsen—"
   From these lines, what do you think Rainsford might have said if the sailor hadn't interrupted him?
   a. Even Captain Nielsen is going to bed early.
   b. Even Captain Nielsen doesn't want to dock on the island.
   c. Even Captain Nielsen seems anxious.
   d. Even Captain Nielsen is hot.

5. He leaped upon the rail and balanced himself there, to get greater elevation; his pipe, striking a rope, was knocked from his mouth. He lunged for it; a short, hoarse cry came from his lips as he realized he had reached too far and had lost his balance. The cry was pinched off short as the blood-warm waters of the Caribbean Sea dosed over his head. He struggled up to the surface and tried to cry out, but the wash from the

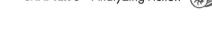

speeding yacht slapped him in the face and the salt water in his open mouth made him gag and strangle.

Which device is used in this passage?

   a. Foreshadowing

   b. Flashback

   c. Verbal irony

   d. All of the above

6. Which line from the text in question #5 builds suspense?

   a. "It's so dark," he thought, "that I could sleep without closing my eyes; the night would be my eyelids—"

   b. "Good night, then, Rainsford. See you at breakfast."

   c. "Pure imagination," said Rainsford.

   d. An abrupt sound startled him.

7. Which type of irony is found in the following lines?

"Yes, even that tough-minded old Swede, who'd go up to the devil himself and ask him for a light. Those fishy blue eyes held a look I never saw there before. All I could get out of him was 'This place has an evil name among seafaring men, sir.'

   a. Dramatic

   b. Verbal

   c. Situational

   d. All of the above

8. What is the mood of the excerpt?

   a. Idyllic

   b. Calm

   c. Foreboding

   d. Hopeful

9. Which words help establish the mood?
    a. Abrupt
    b. Startled
    c. Darkness
    d. All of the above

10. Rainsford falls overboard and the yacht leaves him behind struggling in the water. Why is this situational irony?
    a. Rainsford should have gone to bed instead of smoking a pipe.
    b. Rainsford should have been able to swim back to the boat easily.
    c. Rainsford should have known he would fall.
    d. Rainsford did not believe the rumors and superstitions of the crew.

EXERCISE 3.2

Continue reading the next excerpt from "The Most Dangerous Game" and answer the following questions, testing yourself on literary devices.

Rainsford remembered the shots. They had come from the right, and doggedly he swam in that direction, swimming with slow, deliberate strokes, conserving his strength. For a seemingly endless time he fought the sea. He began to count his strokes; he could do possibly a hundred more and then—

Rainsford heard a sound. It came out of the darkness, a high screaming sound, the sound of an animal in an extremity of anguish and terror.

He did not recognize the animal that made the sound; he did not try to; with fresh vitality he swam toward the sound. He heard it again; then it was cut short by another noise, crisp, staccato.

"Pistol shot," muttered Rainsford, swimming on.

Ten minutes of determined effort brought another sound to his ears— the most welcome he had ever heard—the muttering and growling of the sea breaking on a rocky shore. He was almost on the rocks before he saw them; on a night less calm he would have been shattered against them. With his remaining strength he dragged himself from the swirling waters. Jagged crags appeared to jut up into the opaqueness; he forced himself upward, hand over hand. Gasping, his hands raw, he reached a flat place at the top. Dense jungle came down to the very edge of the cliffs. What perils that tangle of trees and underbrush might hold for him did not concern Rainsford just then. All he knew was that he was safe from his enemy, the sea, and that utter weariness was on him. He flung himself down at the jungle edge and tumbled headlong into the deepest sleep of his life.

When he opened his eyes he knew from the position of the sun that it was late in the afternoon. Sleep had given him new vigor; a sharp hunger was picking at him. He looked about him, almost cheerfully.

"Where there are pistol shots, there are men. Where there are men, there is food," he thought. But what kind of men, he wondered, in so forbidding a place? An unbroken front of snarled and ragged jungle fringed the shore.

He saw no sign of a trail through the closely knit web of weeds and trees; it was easier to go along the shore, and Rainsford floundered along by the water. Not far from where he landed, he stopped.

Some wounded thing—by the evidence, a large animal—had thrashed about in the underbrush; the jungle weeds were crushed down and the moss was lacerated; one patch of weeds was stained crimson. A small, glittering object not far away caught Rainsford's eye and he picked it up. It was an empty cartridge.

"A twenty-two," he remarked. "That's odd. It must have been a fairly large animal too. The hunter had his nerve with him to tackle it with a light gun. It's clear that the brute put up a fight. I suppose the first three shots I heard was when the hunter flushed his quarry and wounded it. The last shot was when he trailed it here and finished it."

He examined the ground closely and found what he had hoped to find— the print of hunting boots. They pointed along the cliff in the direction he had been going. Eagerly he hurried along, now slipping on a rotten log or a loose stone, but making headway; night was beginning to settle down on the island.

Bleak darkness was blacking out the sea and jungle when Rainsford sighted the lights. He came upon them as he turned a crook in the coast line; and his first thought was that he had come upon a village, for there were many lights. But as he forged along he saw to his great astonishment that all the lights were in one enormous building—a lofty structure with pointed towers plunging upward into the gloom. His eyes made out the shadowy outlines of a palatial chateau; it was set on a high bluff, and on three sides of it cliffs dived down to where the sea licked greedy lips in the shadows.

1. Which device is used in these lines?

    Rainsford heard a sound. It came out of the darkness, a high screaming sound, the sound of an animal in an extremity of anguish and terror.

    a. Setting
    b. Characterization
    c. Flashback
    d. Foreshadowing

2. Which word does the author use to foreshadow?

    But as he forged along he saw to his great astonishment that all the lights were in one enormous building—a lofty structure with pointed towers plunging upward into the gloom.

    a. Enormous
    b. Gloom
    c. Lofty
    d. Astonishment

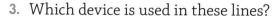

3. Which device is used in these lines?

    Some wounded thing—by the evidence, a large animal—had thrashed about in the underbrush; the jungle weeds were crushed down and the moss was lacerated; one patch of weeds was stained crimson. *A small, glittering object not far away caught Rainsford's eye and he picked it up. It was an empty cartridge.*

    a. Suspense
    b. Foreshadowing
    c. Words that convey mood
    d. All of the above

4. Which words in the following passage most likely contribute to foreshadowing?

    Ten minutes of determined effort brought another sound to his ears— the most welcome he had ever heard—the muttering and growling of the sea breaking on a rocky shore. He was almost on the rocks before he saw them; on a night less calm he would have been shattered against them. With his remaining strength he dragged himself from the swirling waters. Jagged crags appeared to jut up into the opaqueness; he forced himself upward, hand over hand. Gasping, his hands raw, he reached a flat place at the top. Dense jungle came down to the very edge of the cliffs. What perils that tangle of trees and underbrush might hold for him did not concern Rainsford just then. All he knew was that he was safe from his enemy, the sea, and that utter weariness was on him. He flung himself down at the jungle edge and tumbled headlong into the deepest sleep of his life.

    a. Shattered
    b. Perils
    c. Enemy
    d. All of the above

5. What theme is most likely emerging at this point in the story?

    a. Man cannot survive alone.

    b. Nature can be man's enemy.

    c. Man should avoid the jungle.

    d. Man is the weakest creature.

6. What might Rainsford's question foreshadow to the readers?

    "Where there are pistol shots, there are men. Where there are men, there is food," he thought. But what kind of men, he wondered, in so forbidding a place?

    a. He will find food to eat eventually.

    b. He will not find other people on the island.

    c. The men he encounters later on in the story will be questionable.

    d. He will enjoy his stay on the island.

7. What is the significance of the following line?

    Rainsford heard a sound. It came out of the darkness, a high screaming sound, the sound of an animal in an extremity of anguish and terror.

    a. The line builds suspense.

    b. The line foreshadows ominous events later in the story.

    c. The words *darkness, screaming, anguish*, and *terror* contribute to the mood.

    d. All of the above

8. What might the jungle symbolize in the story?

    a. Entrapment

    b. Civilization

    c. Madness

    d. Oppression

9. Through the context of this sentence, what is the definition of chateau?

   But as he forged along he saw to his great astonishment that all the lights were in one enormous building—a lofty structure with pointed towers plunging upward into the gloom. His eyes made out the shadowy outlines of a palatial chateau...

   a. Mountain

   b. Town

   c. Mansion

   d. Beast

10. What might the chateau symbolize to Rainsford in the sentence from question #9?

    a. Freedom

    b. Civilization

    c. Industry

    d. Knowledge

EXERCISE 3.3

Read each example and identify the type of irony used: verbal, situational, or dramatic.

1. The police station got robbed last night. _____

2. A math teacher makes a mistake with an equation. _____

3. A customer is dissatisfied and yells at the cashier, "Thanks for the great service!" _____

4. In the play *Romeo and Juliet*, the audience knows that Juliet is only sleeping. Romeo thinks she is dead, and he kills himself. _____

5. The spelling bee trophy has a spelling mistake. _____

6. In the play *Macbeth*, the king trusts Macbeth even though the audience knows that Macbeth is considering killing the king to secure the throne.

   _____

7. The woman has a flat tire, and she exclaims, "Well, this is turning out to be a great day!" _____

8. A girl in the sitcom thinks everyone forgot her birthday, but the audience knows her friends are planning a surprise party. _____

9. A travel agent is a homebody and hates to travel. _____

Source: The U.S. National Archives

10. _____

4 Components of Poetry

MUST KNOW

 Poetry is writing that expresses emotion.

 Poems can be identified by their informal style, rhyme, and rhythm.

 Poetry is different from prose, and there are many types.

Poetry is a special kind of writing. When you receive a birthday card, often the inside fold will contain a verse or two. When you listen to your favorite songs on the radio or stream from your phone, you might sing along to the lyrics you hear. Poetry moves us, inspires us, and touches us in ways that only a poem can.

The English Language Arts (ELA) classroom is another place you will encounter poetry. In the previous chapter, you learned about the components of fiction. In this chapter, you will learn about the basics of poetry: the definition of poetry, how it differs from prose, the types of poems you may encounter, and some of the ways to recognize poetry.

How Is Poetry Different from Prose?

Prose is the ordinary language that people use. It is written in traditional sentences and paragraphs. On the other hand, **poetry** is an artistic expression. It doesn't follow conventions. Lines can be long or short. Poetry can rhyme. Poetry can have line breaks. It can be written in any form a poet wants to capture the poet's intentions.

What Is Poetry?

When it comes to poetry, there are dozens of definitions! It is hard to boil it down to one definition. Poetry touches the heart and is so personal that it means something completely different to anyone you ask. It is written from the heart. Poetry can be written about any subject in the world; it is not limited to a particular topic. Poetry is one of the oldest forms of expression. Poets have used this medium to explore subjects ranging from love, nature, animals, and relationships to beauty. Poetry can also be a vehicle calling for change. Poetry can criticize war, demand justice, and question society.

The dictionary defines poetry as "literary work in which special intensity is given to the expression of feelings and ideas by the use of distinctive style and rhythm." However, over time, many authors and poets have tried to express what poetry means to them:

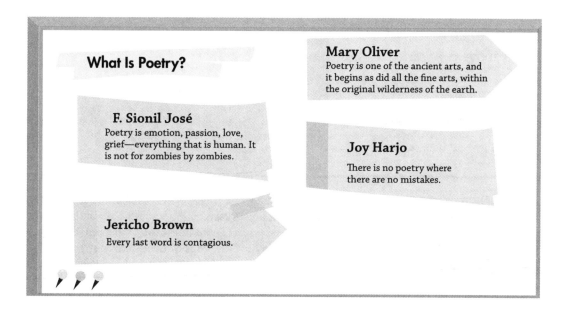

What Is Poetry?

Mary Oliver
Poetry is one of the ancient arts, and it begins as did all the fine arts, within the original wilderness of the earth.

F. Sionil José
Poetry is emotion, passion, love, grief—everything that is human. It is not for zombies by zombies.

Joy Harjo
There is no poetry where there are no mistakes.

Jericho Brown
Every last word is contagious.

What Are Some Components of Poetry?

Stanza: One way to identify poetry is by the way it looks. Many poems are composed of a group of words arranged in rows. The way the words and rows are delineated depends on the poet's purpose, what the poet hopes to convey. Groups of these lines are known as stanzas.

Rhyme: Another way you can recognize poetry is through rhyme. Rhyme adds a musical component to a poem. You can probably trace your first experiences with rhyme to your early childhood. When you heard bedtime stories, read picture books, or sang nursery rhymes like "Twinkle, Twinkle, Little Star," you were introduced to the pleasant sound of rhyme. Notice how the end of this popular poem uses rhyme: The word that ends each line rhymes with the word below it, *star* rhymes with *are*, etc.

Twinkle, Twinkle, Little Star

EXAMPLE

> Twinkle, twinkle, little **star,**

How I wonder what you **are.**

Up above the world so **high,**

Like a diamond in the **sky.**

Twinkle, twinkle, little **star**

> How I wonder what you **are!**

IRL "Twinkle, Twinkle, Little Star" is a poem written by the English author Jane Taylor. It was published in 1806 and wasn't set to music until much later in 1838. The poem was set to the melody of "Ah! vous dirai-je, maman" by Mozart. You know this tune: It's the same used for "The Alphabet Song" (or "The ABC Song").

Rhyme Scheme: The rhyme scheme is a pattern of repeating sounds at the end of lines or stanzas. Notice how "Twinkle, Twinkle, Little Star" uses rhyming words at the end of lines one and two, and three and four. However, each poem can have its own rhyme scheme. Look at this example in Robert Frost's poem "Neither Out Far nor in Deep":

EXAMPLE

> The people along the **sand** (A)

All turn and look one **way.** (B)

They turn their back on the **land**. (A)

> They look at the sea all **day.** (B)

This pattern is intentional: The first and third lines rhyme, and the second and fourth lines rhyme.

The ship was **cheer'd,** the harbor **clear'd,**
And every **day,** for food or **play,**
In mist or **cloud,** on mast or **shroud, . . .**
Whiles all the **Night,** through fog-smoke **white,**
Glimmer'd the white moonshine...

Rhythm: In the '80s, when I was a teen, there was a song by Gloria Estefan and the Miami Sound Machine titled "The Rhythm Is Gonna Get You." It was super catchy because of the sound. Chances are you might not know this classic dance song, but if you think of a popular song you love to dance to, you probably like it for the same reason: the rhythm. Rhythm occurs in music, in dance, in painting, in your heartbeat, in your brain, and in our language. Poetry can also have *rhythm*, which is a Greek word that means *measured motion*. Rhythm is beat and a pace, a device that demonstrates stressed and unstressed syllables. Here is an example from William Shakespeare's play *Macbeth*:

> **BTW**
>
> *Sometimes a poem can even have an internal rhyme scheme, a pattern of rhyming words inside the same line. This means that the words in a line rhyme inside instead of at the end.*

EXAMPLE

▸ *DOU-ble, / DOU-ble / TOIL and / TROU-ble;*

▸ *FI-re / BURN, and / CAL-dron / BUB-ble.*

What Are the Different Types of Poems?

From classical poems to rap lyrics, there are many types and styles of poems to enjoy. Poetry can be written or spoken or sung. Rap and song lyrics are also considered poetry. There are even contests for students who want to express themselves in poetry jams. The beauty of poetry is that it has many shapes and forms, giving poets many opportunities and ways to communicate.

 IRL One of the earliest poems ever written was the "Epic of Gilgamesh." It was written about 4,000 years ago. This poem is a story about a Sumerian king named Gilgamesh who goes on a hero's journey, fighting monsters and gods along the way. The overarching theme: No one can escape death. The word *epic* comes from the ancient Greek term *epos*, which means *story, word, poem*.

Epic Poem: This is a lengthy poem written in the past about a hero and the adventures he takes. In these poems, the hero often encounters supernatural forces or gods and goddesses. The hero might have to fight monsters and other creatures. The hero is usually brave and strong and outwits death many times on the journey. One of the most famous epic poems is "The Odyssey" by Homer, which is 15,000 lines long!

Characteristics of an epic poem:

- Includes heroes

- Features gods and goddesses

- Features conflicts with monsters and other creatures

- Includes long journeys

Excerpt from "The Odyssey," Book One	Characteristics of an Epic Poem
Tell me, O Muse, of that ingenious hero who travelled far and wide after he had sacked the famous town of Troy. Many cities did he visit, and many were the nations with whose manners and customs he was acquainted; moreover he suffered much by sea while trying to save his own life and bring his men safely home; but do what he might he could not save his men, for they perished through their own sheer folly in eating the cattle of the Sun-god Hyperion; so the	Here is a hero named Odysseus. The hero travels long distances. The hero suffers on his journey and almost loses his life. The hero is brave and noble because he wants to save his crew and bring them home.

Excerpt from "The Odyssey," Book One	Characteristics of an Epic Poem
god prevented them from ever reaching home. Tell me, too, about all these things, oh daughter of Jove, from whatsoever source you may know them. So now all who escaped death in battle or by shipwreck had got safely home except Ulysses, and he, though he was longing to return to his wife and country, was detained by the goddess Calypso, who had got him into a large cave and wanted to marry him. But as years went by, there came a time when the gods settled that he should go back to Ithaca; even then, however, when he was among his own people, his troubles were not yet over; nevertheless all the gods had now begun to pity him except Neptune, who still persecuted him without ceasing and would not let him get home.	The hero encounters gods and goddesses during his journey. The hero will face multiple trials and ordeals before he finds his way back home.

 IRL   One of the first sonnets was written by an Italian poet named Petrarch. William Shakespeare also wrote 154 sonnets during his lifetime!

Sonnet: The sonnet is another famous genre of poetry that has a predictable structure. The sonnet consists of fourteen lines. The lines are broken into three *quatrains* and end with a *couplet*. It is written in *iambic pentameter*, ten beats per line, and contains a rhyme scheme. Every other line rhymes: the first and third, and the second and fourth.

Characteristics of the sonnet:

- Consists of fourteen lines

- Includes three quatrains

- Ends with couplet

- Written in iambic pentameter

- Expresses a question or problem to be solved

Sonnet 18 William Shakespeare		Notice the Rhyme Scheme
Shall I compare thee to a summer's **day?**	A	The sonnet is broken into three
Thou art more lovely and more **temperate:**	B	*quatrains:* lines of four.
Rough winds do shake the darling buds of **May,**	A	
And summer's lease hath all too short a **date:**	B	
Sometime too hot the eye of heaven **shines,**	C	The quatrains set up the problem
And often is his gold complexion **dimmed,**	D	or conflict.
And every fair from fair sometime **declines,**	C	
By chance, or nature's changing course **untrimmed:**	D	
But thy eternal summer shall not **fade,**	E	*Stanza:* Group of lines that
Nor lose possession of that fair thou **ow'st,**	F	compose a poem.
Nor shall death brag thou wand'rest in his **shade,**	E	
When in eternal lines to time thou **grow'st,**	F	
So long as men can breathe or eyes can **see,**	G	The sonnet ends in a *couplet:*
So long lives this, and this gives life to **thee.**	G	last two lines. The two lines rhyme.
		The couplet resolves the poem.

Iambic pentameter is a challenging form to write. Each line has only ten syllables! Sometimes poets have to choose each word with care in order to fit this pattern. Sometimes the poet must choose the structure over a word itself, hence altering the meaning.

There are just ten syllables in each of these famous lines by William Shakespeare. The last line has eleven. Sometimes Shakespeare needed a little wiggle room. It is very challenging to keep the ten syllables at times.

Here are some famous examples:

"All that glisters is not gold" (*The Merchant of Venice*, Act 2, Scene 7)

"The course of true love never did run smooth." (*A Midsummer Night's Dream*, Act 1, Scene 1)

"To be or not to be, that is the question." (*Hamlet*, Act 3, Scene 1)

BTW

Iamb *is a group of two syllables with an emphasis on the second.*

Pentameter *comes from the Greek root* pent, *which means* five.

The lines in iambic pentameter alternate between unstressed and stressed beats, creating this pattern: "de/DUM de/DUM de/DUM de/DUM de/DUM." It is a rhythm that is pleasing to the ear and is often described as a heartbeat.

Narrative Poem: These are long poems that tell a story and include a beginning, middle, and end. Some narrative poems can be several books long, such as "The Iliad" by Homer. Usually the narrator is the speaker.

Characteristics of a narrative poem:

- Has characteristics of a story

- Includes characters, plot, and conflict

- Told by a narrator/speaker

For example, look at the excerpt from the following poem, "Paul Revere's Ride," by Henry Wadsworth Longfellow:

Excerpt from "Paul Revere's Ride"	Characteristics of a Narrative Poem
Listen, my children, and you shall hear Of the midnight ride of Paul Revere, On the eighteenth of April, in Seventy-Five: Hardly a man is now alive Who remembers that famous day and year. He said to his friend, "If the British march By land or sea from the town to-night, Hang a lantern aloft in the belfry-arch Of the North-Church-tower, as a signal-light,— One if by land, and two if by sea; And I on the opposite shore will be, Ready to ride and spread the alarm Through every Middlesex village and farm, For the country-folk to be up and to arm." Then he said "Good night!" and with muffled oar Silently rowed to the Charlestown shore, Just as the moon rose over the bay, Where swinging wide at her moorings lay The Somerset, British man-of-war: A phantom ship, with each mast and spar Across the moon, like a prison-bar, And a huge black hulk, that was magnified By its own reflection in the tide.	A speaker narrates. Includes the character: Paul Revere. Includes a setting. Includes plot details. A conflict is included.

> **IRL** In history, many stories were passed down orally from one generation to the next. Narrative poetry grew out of these oral traditions. Rhythm, rhyme, and repetition helped speakers memorize the stories. Narrative poems were very popular, and the poem "Paul Revere's Ride" is a classic narrative poem about the American Revolution. Written in 1860, it is about Paul Revere, who rode through Boston to warn the colonists that the British were invading.

Haiku: The haiku also originated as an oral poem in thirteenth-century Japan. Original haikus were often very long—hundreds of stanzas—but over time, they became very short! The haiku is a three-line poem that consists of only seventeen syllables. The first line has five syllables, the second line has seven syllables, and the last line has five syllables. The goal of a haiku is to capture a very small, brief moment.

Characteristics of a haiku:

- Focuses on a brief moment

- Written in three lines

- Consists of seventeen syllables

"The Old Pond" by Matsuo Basho	Characteristics of a Haiku
An old pond! A frog jumps in— the sound of water.	Written in three lines. Includes seventeen syllables. Captures a small moment.

Note: In Japanese, this sonnet has 17 syllables. When translated into English, it has 12.

Limerick: Poetry is not always serious. Limericks are funny! In Irish, the word means *humorous* and *nonsensical*. They can be tough to write though, because they are only five lines long, and all the lines are in one stanza. The limerick also has an interesting rhyme scheme: The first, second, and last lines rhyme, and the third and fourth rhyme together.

IRL   Some of the oldest limericks can be found in *The Book of Nonsense* by Edward Lear, a British poet. Published in 1887, the book contained at least seventy-two limericks for children.

> There was an Old Derry down Derry,
>
> who loved to see little folks merry;
>
> So he made them a Book,
>
> and with laughter they shook
>
> At the fun of that Derry down Derry.

Characteristics of a limerick:

- Tries to be funny

- Has only five lines in one stanza

- Consists of a rhyme scheme: aabba

"There Was an Old Man with a Beard"	Characteristics of a Limerick
There was an Old Man with a beard, Who said, "It is just as I feared!— Two Owls and a Hen, Four Larks and a Wren, Have all built their nests in my beard!"	■ Consists of five lines ■ Written in one stanza ■ Humorous ■ Follows an aabba rhyme scheme

Elegy: On the flip side, some poems can be very sad because they express grief from death. Poetry can entertain us, and poetry can comfort us. In Greek, the word *elegy* means *song of mourning*. Poets write elegies to praise and honor those who have died. Sometimes they will show admiration of the person's life.

Characteristics of an elegy:

- Begins with a lament about loss

- Expresses anger or sorrow

- Honors and praises the deceased

- Poses questions about life and death

- Uses language that is formal and ceremonial

Excerpt from "An Elegy for D. H. Lawrence" by William Carlos Williams	
Green points on the shrub And poor Lawrence dead. The night damp and misty And Lawrence no more in the world To answer April's promise with a fury of labor Against waste, waste, and life's Coldness.	Laments the loss of life.
Once he received a letter— he never answered it—praising him: so English he had thereby raised himself to an unenglish greatness. Dead now and it grows clearer what bitterness drove him.	Often expresses anger or sorrow about death.
This is the time the serpent in the grotto water dripping from the stone into a pool.	Honors the life of the deceased.
Mediterranean evenings. Ashes of Cretan fires. And to the north Forsythia hung with yellow bells in the cold.	Praises the deceased.

EXERCISES

EXERCISE 4.1

For each question, choose the correct multiple-choice answer.

1. Which of the following statements is true about poetry?
    a. Poetry is an expression of feelings.
    b. There are multiple ways to define poetry.
    c. Poetry is different from prose.
    d. All of the above

2. What is one difference between poetry and prose?
    a. Poetry is longer than prose.
    b. Poetry is more enjoyable than prose.
    c. Poetry is constructed through lines and stanzas; prose is written in paragraphs.
    d. Poetry is more modern than prose.

3. In poetry, a group of words arranged in rows is known as a:
    a. Stanza
    b. Rhyme scheme
    c. Sonnet
    d. Couplet

4. Rhyme scheme is best defined as:
    a. A pattern of words that don't rhyme
    b. A pattern of rhymes that end at the end of each line
    c. A pattern of silly sounds that are pleasing to the ear
    d. A pattern of words that all start with the same letter

5. Which of the following statements is true about rhyme?
    a. All poems rhyme.
    b. Rhyme can only occur at the end of each sentence.
    c. Rhyme can occur anywhere in a line of a poem.
    d. Rhyme only occurs in poems for children.

6. Internal rhyme is best defined as:
    a. Rhyme that occurs at the end of each line
    b. Rhyme that occurs in the middle of a line
    c. Rhyme that is forced
    d. All of the above

7. Where can rhythm be found?
    a. In poetry
    b. In music
    c. In our heartbeat
    d. All of the above

8. If you wanted to laugh, which poem would most likely amuse you?
    a. Sonnet
    b. Limerick
    c. Elegy
    d. Epic poem

9. A poem that mourns and honors the deceased would be a(n):
    a. Elegy
    b. Limerick
    c. Narrative poem
    d. Epic poem

10. Which is true about a sonnet?

    a. It is written in iambic pentameter.

    b. It includes a couplet.

    c. It often sets up a problem with a resolution.

    d. All of the above

EXERCISE 4.2

Match each term in the box with its correct definition.

> sonnet, epic poem, narrative poem, elegy, limerick, haiku, iambic pentameter, quatrain, couplet, stanza

1. Two lines of a verse _____

2. A poem that features characteristics of a story: plot, character, conflict _____

3. A brief poem that originated in Japan and focuses on a single moment _____

4. A poem that features the journey of a hero _____

5. Shakespeare wrote 164 sixteen-line poems known by this name _____

6. A poem used to mourn and honor the deceased _____

7. A nonsensical poem that is humorous in nature _____

8. A group of lines in a poem _____

9. A line of verse with five metrical feet that contains a pattern of stressed and unstressed syllables _____

10. A stanza that contains four lines _____

EXERCISE 4.3

Match each term in the box with the following examples.

sonnet, narrative poem, quatrain, iambic pentameter, haiku, internal rhyme, couplet, epic poem, elegy, limerick

1. There was an old man on the Border,
    Who lived in the utmost disorder;
    He danced with the cat,
    And made tea in his hat,
    Which vexed all the folks on the Border.
                    —Edward Lear	

2. Let me not to the marriage of true minds
    Admit impediments; love is not love
    Which alters when it alteration finds,
    Or bends with the remover to remove.
    O no, it is an ever-fixed mark
    That looks on tempests and is never shaken;
    It is the star to every wandering bark,
    Whose worth's unknown, although his height be taken.
    Love's not Time's fool, though rosy lips and cheeks
    Within his bending sickle's compass come;
    Love alters not with his brief hours and weeks,
    But bears it out even to the edge of doom.
    If this be error and upon me proved,
    I never writ, nor no man ever loved.
                    —William Shakespeare	

3. So, lovers dream a rich and long delight,
    But get a winter-seeming summer's night.
                    —John Donne	

4. Tell me, O muse, of that ingenious hero who travelled far and wide after he had sacked the famous town of Troy. Many cities did he visit, and many were the nations with whose manners and customs he was acquainted; moreover he suffered much by sea while trying to save his own life and bring his men safely home; but do what he might he could not save his men, for they perished through their own sheer folly in eating the cattle of the Sun-god Hyperion; so the god prevented them from ever reaching home. Tell me, too, about all these things, O daughter of Jove, from whatsoever source you may know them.

—Homer

5. The outlook wasn't brilliant for the Mudville nine that day;
      The score stood four to two with but one inning more to play.
      And then when Cooney died at first, and Barrows did the same,
      A sickly silence fell upon the patrons of the game.

      A straggling few got up to go in deep despair. The rest
      Clung to that hope which springs eternal in the human breast;
      They thought if only Casey could but get a whack at that—
      We'd put up even money now with Casey at the bat.

      But Flynn preceded Casey, as did also Jimmy Blake,
      And the former was a lulu and the latter was a cake;
      So upon that stricken multitude grim melancholy sat,
      For there seemed but little chance of Casey's getting to the bat.

—Ernest Lawrence Thayer

6. Thought I, the fallen flowers
    Are returning to their branch;
    But lo! they were butterflies.
               —Arakida Moritake	

7. While I nodded, nearly **napping,** suddenly there came a **tapping,**
    As of someone gently **rapping, rapping** at my chamber door.
               —Edgar Allan Poe	

8. O Captain! my Captain! our **fearful trip is done,**
    The ship has weather'd every rack, the prize we sought is won,
    The port is near, the bells I hear, the people all exulting,
    While follow eyes the steady keel, the vessel grim and daring;
    But O heart! heart! heart!
    O the bleeding drops of red,
    Where on the deck my **Captain lies,**
    Fallen cold and **dead.**
               —Walt Whitman	

9. Friends, Romans, countrymen, lend me your ears. —William Shakespeare	

10. My candle burns at both ends;
    It will not last the night;
    But ah, my foes, and oh, my friends—
    It gives a lovely light!
               —Edna St. Vincent Millay	

Flashcard App

5 Analyzing Poetry

MUST ⚡ KNOW

⚡ Poetic devices are intentional words, phrases, and sounds that poets use to create poems.

⚡ Figurative language is when you describe something by comparing it to something else.

⚡ Sound devices are special tools poets use to create meaning through sound.

In the previous chapter, you learned about the definition of poetry, the components of a poem, and the types of poems. In this chapter, we will continue our study of poetry by focusing on the poetic devices poets use to convey their poem's meaning.

Learning to recognize poetic devices goes beyond doing well on your class assignments and state exams. When you notice the devices in the poem and how they are used intentionally, you develop a deeper meaning of the poem and also an appreciation for the poet's craft. Recognizing the poet's talent and skill can help you improve your own writing! When we watch the masters, we learn how to apply these moves to our own work.

What Are Poetic Devices and Why Are They Used?

Poetic Devices: I am a teacher because I've always loved reading and writing, but as the years have passed, I have found a new passion for cooking. Unfortunately, I do not have the time to go back to school while I teach, but through YouTube videos, social media sites, cookbooks, and the occasional lesson, I have learned a lot about cooking.

Chefs have tools they use to make great food. When they start any dish, they gather knives, spoons, graters, cutting boards, zesters, tongs, thermometers, and spatulas. These tools help them with culinary techniques such as broiling, roasting, grilling, baking, searing, sautéing, panfrying, and stir-frying. Artists, athletes, and singers also have techniques to improve their craft.

Poets also have a toolbox. *Poetic devices* are the intentional use of words, phrases, sounds, and even shapes to create a poem and express meaning.

What Are Some Types of Figurative Language to Know?

Figurative language is a device that uses words in ways that are not literal. There are different types of figurative language to know when reading and writing poems: personification, metaphor, simile, and hyperbole.

Personification: I bet when you see commercials or ads on the Internet or on television, there are animals that talk, pieces of candy that dance, cars that sing, and toys that cry. If you have watched the Disney movie *Toy Story*, you have seen toys like Woody and Buzz doing all sorts of things that only humans can do. The toys talk on phones, chase cars, fight villains, and interact with each other. Giving inanimate qualities humanlike characteristics is known as *personification*, and poets rely on personification to convey meaning.

Consider the nursery rhymes you heard growing up. They are filled with examples of personification.

Hey, Diddle, Diddle, The cat and the fiddle, The cow jumped over the moon; The little dog laughed To see such sport, And the dish ran away with the spoon.	Can a cow jump over the moon? Can a dog laugh? Can a dish run away?	Humpty Dumpty sat on a wall, Humpty Dumpty had a great fall, All the king's horses and all the king's men Couldn't put Humpty together again.

Let's examine the personification in an excerpt of Emily Dickinson's poem "Because I Could Not Stop for Death."

Because I could not stop for Death, He kindly stopped for me; The Carriage held but just Ourselves And Immortality. We slowly drove, he knew no haste And I had put away My labor and my leisure too, For His Civility.	Notice how death is acting like a person: Death is courteous and kind. He stops and waits patiently for the speaker. Death takes on human qualities. The speaker and death drive along together.

Metaphor: If you ever heard a mother say her child is "the light of her life" or "apple of my eye," she is using a metaphor. In our everyday speech, we use metaphors all the time to express ourselves. Metaphors are comparisons between two things that aren't alike but may have some similarities.

IRL As a culture, we use metaphors to express our feelings all the time! It is common to hear metaphors in day-to-day conversation.

How many of these popular metaphors have you heard?

Hard work is the key to success.

America is a melting pot.

It was music to my ears.

The world is your oyster.

Your room is a disaster!

William Shakespeare's "Sonnet 18," featured in the previous chapter, is a great example of metaphor.

Shall I compare thee to a summer's day?
Thou art more lovely and more temperate:
Rough winds do shake the darling buds of May,
And summer's lease hath all too short a date;
Sometime too hot the eye of heaven shines,
And often is his gold complexion dimm'd;
And every fair from fair sometime declines,
By chance or nature's changing course untrimm'd;
But thy eternal summer shall not fade,
Nor lose possession of that fair thou ow'st;
Nor shall death brag thou wander'st in his shade,
When in eternal lines to time thou grow'st:
So long as men can breathe or eyes can see,
So long lives this, and this gives life to thee.

In this sonnet, the loved one is like a summer's day: The loved one is good-natured, beautiful, and at the mercy of fate, to "fade away."

Here is another quick example by Emily Dickinson, the poem "Hope is the Thing with Feathers."

Hope is the thing with feathers—
That perches in the soul—
And sings the tune without the words—
And never stops—at all—
And sweetest—in the Gale—is heard—
And sore must be the storm—
That could abash the little Bird
That kept so many warm—
I've heard it in the chillest land—
And on the strangest Sea—
Yet—never—in Extremity,
It asked a crumb—of me.

In this poem, Dickinson compares hope to a bird, two unlike things. However, she finds ways they are similar: Both hope and birds can touch the soul, can provide comfort, and ask little in return.

Simile: Madonna sings "Like a Prayer." Nirvana jammed to "Smells Like Teen Spirit." Gatorade reminds us to "Float like a butterfly. Sting like a bee." Similes are one of the most popular literary devices. We hear them in song lyrics. We see them in commercials and in advertisements. A simile creates similar comparisons as a metaphor; however, a simile is more direct, using the words *like* or *as*. Similes are much easier to recognize!

Let's examine the use of simile in William Wordsworth's classic poem "I Wandered Lonely as a Cloud."

BTW

A metaphor can be a phrase, a full sentence, or several sentences in length, as in an extended metaphor. An extended metaphor can stretch for the entire length of a poem. Notice how the metaphor runs all the way through Carl Sandburg's poem "Fog."

The fog comes
on little cat feet.
It sits looking
over harbor and city
on silent haunches
and then moves on.

In this short poem, Sandburg compares the fog to a cat. A fog and a cat are two different things, but they do have some commonalities. A cat and a fog both move in a similar manner. If you've ever seen a fog, you know it moves slowly just like a cat. Neither a fog nor a cat linger around long. They may sit for a bit and then disappear.

I wandered lonely as a cloud
That floats on high o'er vales and hills,
When all at once I saw a crowd,
A host, of golden daffodils;
Beside the lake, beneath the trees,
Fluttering and dancing in the breeze.

Continuous as the stars that shine
And twinkle on the milky way,
They stretched in never-ending line
Along the margin of a bay:
Ten thousand saw I at a glance,
Tossing their heads in sprightly dance.

The waves beside them danced; but they
Out-did the sparkling waves in glee:
A poet could not but be gay,
In such a jocund company:
I gazed—and gazed—but little thought
What wealth the show to me had brought:

For oft, when on my couch I lie
In vacant or in pensive mood,
They flash upon that inward eye
Which is the bliss of solitude;
And then my heart with pleasure fills,
And dances with the daffodils.

The speaker directly compares himself to a cloud as he takes his solitary walk.

Being alone, he is able to experience the beauty of nature all around him.

Hyperbole: This term is probably a new one for you, but believe me, you are well-acquainted with these expressions! If your parents have told you a "million times" to clean your room, you'll recognize hyperbole, an outrageous exaggeration that emphasizes a point. These statements are not meant to be taken literally. Other common examples include "I was so hungry, I could eat a horse," "I slept like a rock," and "It's a jungle out there!"

Let's examine the use of hyperbole in an excerpt from Robert Burns's poem "A Red, Red Rose."

Till a' the seas gang dry, my dear,
And the rocks melt wi' the sun;
I will love thee still, my dear,
While the sands o' life shall run.

The speaker claims his love will last beyond a dry sea and until rocks melt by the sun, all examples of exaggerations.

Idiom: Each year, my school has new students from all over the world. Besides transitioning to a new culture, they also have to learn a new language. One challenge to learning a new language is mastering the idioms, the nonliteral phrases and expressions that have meaning that are different from their individual parts. For example, if you were learning to speak English, what would you think if someone said to you, "It's raining cats and dogs"? That idiom would be very confusing indeed!

Let's take a close look at the idiom used in the excerpt from Robert Frost's poem "Mending Wall."

BTW

Not all exaggeration is considered hyperbole. Hyperbole is extreme, often unrealistic, and used to embellish or accentuate details in a text.

Complaining that you waited over half an hour when you actually waited 15 minutes would be exaggeration.

Claiming your shoes are killing you would be hyperbole.

He will not go behind his father's saying,
And he likes having thought of it so well
He says again, "Good fences make good neighbors."

Good fences make good neighbors is an idiom. It is not literal.

IRL Here are some more popular idioms:

- Break a leg.
- Call it a day.
- Better late than never.
- We'll cross that bridge when we come to it.
- I'm under the weather.

Pun: One of my favorite types of figurative language is the pun because it is so punny! Okay, that was a bad attempt at humor, but, hopefully, you see the nature of a pun. A pun is a play on words. Typically, the humor occurs when two words sound the same but have different meanings. Puns appear in everyday speech. Lots of jokes are silly simply because of the pun. For example, "A bike can't stand on its own because it is two-tired" or "I like whiteboards because they are re-markable."

Look at this pun used in *Romeo and Juliet* by William Shakespeare:

"Ask for me tomorrow, you shall find me a grave man."	In this line, the meaning of the word *grave* is *serious*. But Mercutio dies, and so the word acts as a pun in the scene.

What Are Sound Devices in Poetry?

Repetition: As a teacher, my biggest pet peeve is repeating myself over and over again. I don't mind clarifying directions for a student when needed, but when students ignore me while I am speaking, the repetition can be frustrating. However when it comes to learning a new skill, research shows we learn by repetition when we repeat steps over and over.

Writers also rely on repetition, repeating a word or phrase over and over to emphasize a point in a text. In addition, the repetition of sounds are not only pleasing, but it can also convey ideas.

Let's look at how Edgar Allan Poe uses repetition in his poem "The Raven" to create meaning.

Once upon a midnight dreary, while I pondered, weak and weary, Over many a quaint and curious volume of forgotten lore— While I nodded, nearly napping, suddenly there came a tapping, As of someone gently rapping, rapping at my chamber door. "'Tis some visitor," I muttered, "tapping at my chamber door—	For example, in "The Raven" the word *nevermore* repeats at the end of each stanza to emphasize the speaker's sorrow. He will never see his love Lenore again. In addition, the repetition of the knocking at his door reveals the speaker's distress.

Only this and nothing more."

Ah, distinctly I remember it was in the bleak December;

And each separate dying ember wrought its ghost upon the floor.

Eagerly I wished the morrow;—vainly I had sought to borrow

From my books surcease of sorrow—sorrow for the lost Lenore—

For the rare and radiant maiden whom the angels name Lenore—

Nameless *here* for evermore.

Alliteration: Have you ever experienced a tongue twister? A tongue twister is a phrase that is difficult to articulate. Some people enjoy the challenge of saying a line that is difficult. Usually tongue twisters are hard to master because of the alliteration that appears. Alliteration is the repetition of the first letter sound in each word or in words that are adjacent or close by.

While I nodded, nearly napping, suddenly there came a tapping, As of someone gently rapping, rapping at my chamber door.	In "The Raven," the words "weak and weary" and "nodded *nearly* napping" repeat the same letter sound to create a dark effect.

IRL

One of the first tongue twisters dates back to nineteenth-century England. A woman named Mary Anning used to collect shells on the beach to sell and make money: "She sells seashells by the seashore."

Here are some popular tongue twisters using alliteration. Try saying them out loud quickly!

- I scream, you scream, we all scream for ice cream!
- Peter Piper picked a peck of pickled peppers.
- How much wood would a woodchuck chuck if a woodchuck could chuck wood?

Assonance: The repetition of vowel sounds in words that appear close together is called assonance.

> Once upon a midnight dreary, while I pondered, *weak and weary*,
>
> Over many a quaint and curious volume of forgotten lore—

For example, in "The Raven" the speaker says "while I pondered *weak* and *weary*." Notice how the *ea* sound repeats.

Consonance: Another example of sound repetition that is focused on consonant sounds is consonance. In addition, these sounds do not have to appear only at the beginning of a word. These sounds can appear at the beginning, middle, or end of words.

> While I *nodded, nearly napping*, suddenly there came a tapping,
>
> As of someone gently rapping, rapping at my chamber door.
>
> "'Tis some visitor," I muttered, "tapping at my chamber door—
>
> Only this and nothing more."

Notice how the *n* sound repeats in all three words.

Onomatopoeia: When I was young, one of my favorite television shows was *Batman*. I don't remember much about the show now, but one thing I never forgot was the fight scenes. It wasn't necessarily the punches, kicks, or jabs Batman and Robin gave to the villains who tested them, but rather the flashy words that would appear at the top of the screen as they fought. Words such as *BAM* or *THUNK* or *POW* would appear colorfully with every aggressive action.

BTW

Here are some more examples of onomatopoeia: chop, ticktock, ring-ring, moo.

Onomatopoeia words like flutter, croaking, tinkled, and shrieked appear in "The Raven."

This device is onomatopoeia, a figure of speech in which words evoke the actual sound of the thing they refer to or describe. Onomatopoeia gives the language a sensory effect, making readers feel as if they are actually hearing the sound for themselves.

EXERCISES

EXERCISE 5.1

Match the definition with the correct term.

onomatopoeia, simile, metaphor, pun, hyperbole, personification, idiom, extended metaphor, alliteration, repetition

1. Repeating a word or phrase over and over to emphasize a point in a text	
2. Creates a sensory effect, making readers feel as if they are actually hearing the sound for themselves	
3. Over-the-top exaggeration	
4. A comparison using *like* or *as*	
5. The repetition of sounds that only appear in the beginning of words	
6. Giving humanlike qualities to inanimate objects or nonhuman things	
7. A play on words	
8. A version of a metaphor that carries on over multiple lines	
9. An expression that is not meant to be taken literally; it is figurative	
10. A poetic device that makes a comparison between two things for effect	

EXERCISE 5.2

Use what you've learned about poetry to analyze the following poem.

Stopping by Woods on a Snowy Evening
by Robert Frost

1 Whose woods these are I think I know.
2 His house is in the village though;
3 He will not see me stopping here
4 To watch his woods fill up with snow.
5 My little horse must think it queer
6 To stop without a farmhouse near
7 Between the woods and frozen lake
8 The darkest evening of the year.

9 He gives his harness bells a shake
10 To ask if there is some mistake.
11 The only other sound's the sweep
12 Of easy wind and downy flake.

13 The woods are lovely, dark and deep,
14 But I have promises to keep,
15 And miles to go before I sleep,
16 And miles to go before I sleep.

1. Which device is used in line 13, "The woods are lovely, dark and deep"?

   a. Personification

   b. Simile

   c. Repetition

   d. Alliteration

2. What device is used in the following lines?
   He gives his harness bells a shake
   To ask if there is some mistake.
   a. Personification
   b. Symbol
   c. Allusion
   d. Simile

3. Which of the following devices is used in the last two lines of the poem?
   a. Assonance
   b. Onomatopoeia
   c. Simile
   d. Repetition

4. What idea is emphasized in line 14, "But I have promises to keep"?
   a. The village is far away.
   b. The horse is too tired to continue.
   c. There is much more life ahead.
   d. The speaker is eager to leave.

5. What device is used in line 11 when the speaker says, "The only other sound's the sweep"?
   a. Repetition
   b. Assonance
   c. Metaphor
   d. Alliteration

6. What device is used in line 4 when the speaker stops "To watch his woods fill up with snow"?

    a. Personification

    b. Simile

    c. Hyperbole

    d. Pun

A Red, Red Rose
by Robert Burns

> O my Luve is like a red, red rose
> That's newly sprung in June;
> O my Luve is like the melody
> That's sweetly played in tune.
>
> So fair art thou, my bonnie lass,
> So deep in luve am I;
> And I will luve thee still, my dear,
> Till a' the seas gang dry.
>
> Till a' the seas gang dry, my dear,
> And the rocks melt wi' the sun;
> I will love thee still, my dear,
> While the sands o' life shall run.
>
> And fare thee weel, my only luve!
> And fare thee weel awhile!
> And I will come again, my luve,
> Though it were ten thousand mile.

7. What poetic device is used in lines 1 and 3?
    a. Simile
    b. Metaphor
    c. Pun
    d. Idiom

8. Which of the following lines contains hyperbole?
    a. O my Luve is like the melody
    b. Till a' the seas gang dry
    c. And I will come again, my luve
    d. That's newly sprung in June

9. Which of the following devices are used in the poem?
    a. Repetition
    b. Simile
    c. Alliteration
    d. All of the above

10. When the poet claims his love will last until "the rocks melt wi' the sun," he is using which device?
    a. Simile
    b. Metaphor
    c. Hyperbole
    d. Pun

EXERCISE 5.3

Explain the meaning of the following idioms.

1. Tina got revenge on him, and Charlie got a taste of his own medicine. _____

2. Good things come to those who wait. _____

3. Sally felt like she was on a wild goose chase. _____

4. The homework was a piece of cake. _____

5. The children had a blast at the arcade. _____

6. Once in a blue moon, an opportunity like this comes along.

   _____

7. It took Liza a few weeks to get a handle on her new job.

   _____

8. When his teacher confronted Ethan, he began to beat around the bush.

   _____

9. The program fell apart because the administrators tried to cut corners.

   _____

10. Even though Ethan lied, the teacher let him off the hook this time.

    _____

6 Components of Nonfiction

 Nonfiction and fiction have different characteristics.

 There are many different types of nonfiction.

 Text features can help readers navigate the text and reveal the main idea.

In the first few chapters, you learned strategies to read and analyze fiction, including poetry. In the next two chapters, you will learn some **must know** strategies to navigate nonfiction texts. Nonfiction texts make up the bulk of your reading in school. If you have been given a textbook to study, a news article to read, or a documentary to watch, then you will need to know some essential skills that apply to this genre. Nonfiction is usually the foundation of academic reading, and it is important to know how to read this genre carefully because much of your learning as you enter high school and college will depend on your ability to read nonfiction successfully. You must be an active reader when it comes to nonfiction.

Being an informed citizen is more important than ever. Reading nonfiction can help you understand and navigate the world around you. From fast food to global warming, nonfiction covers many interesting subjects that shed light on an array of topics.

What Is Nonfiction?

Believe it or not, you encounter nonfiction reading *all the time*. Think about it: You wake up in the morning, and perhaps you glance at the copy of the newspaper on the kitchen table. A headline grabs your attention, and you begin to read. You eat breakfast, and as you look around you, the back of the cereal box catches your eye. You start reading the nutritional value chart. "Wow," you think, "I can't believe there are this many calories in one individual serving!" It is obvious that your portion of cereal contains much more. As you make your way out the door, you might grab the mail from your mailbox and leaf through the fliers, take-out menus, pamphlets, and other leaflets in the mix of mail before you hand the pile to your parents. You may even pull out a letter you received from your school with information such as your schedule or updated school policies.

Slowly you make your way to the bus stop, and as you cross the street, you may see advertisements on the sides of buildings, on the backs of trucks, and maybe even an ad being written in the sky! When you get on the bus, you might begin scrolling through your phone, where articles, news, blogs, recipes, and other nonfiction posts surface. If you are traveling somewhere far, you might read travel guides to give you information about your destination: How long does it take to get there? What sights should you visit? What is the weather like? What is its history? A majority of reading that we consume is nonfiction, and these materials are widely available to us.

IRL The earliest record of nonfiction writing can be traced back to the Bronze Age. In 740 BC, the *Babylonian Chronicles* were being written on tablets, recording information about Babylonian kings and history.

What Are the Differences between Nonfiction and Fiction?

Unlike fiction, nonfiction is fact based. Nonfiction writers try to teach us about the world: They write about real events, real people, and real places. Whereas fiction is made up, nonfiction is the truth. The main difference between the two genres, though, is the purpose of each. Authors of fiction strive to entertain readers, while nonfiction writers strive to educate, explain, or inform.

As a student, you will encounter a great deal of nonfiction writing in science, social studies, and health classes. Your teacher may give you a textbook, journals, or articles to read. In other classes, you may read a memoir, autobiography, biography, or essay collection. Visual nonfiction may also include TED Talks, presentations, documentaries, and learning videos from YouTube or other educational channels. In many cases, nonfiction may also include an author's opinion; however, it is the author's responsibility to support the presented argument with facts and evidence.

Fiction	Nonfiction
Created by imagination	Based on fact
Made-up events	True events
Fabricated people, places, things	Real people, places, things
Tells a story	Shares truth
Read to enjoy	Read to learn
Must be read in order	Can read in any order
Characters, setting, plots	Statistics, expert testimony, polls
Chapters	Charts, graphs
Illustrations	Table of contents
Literary devices	Text features
Figurative language	Glossary
Theme	Academic vocabulary
Plot	Time lines

IRL More students are gravitating toward nonfiction!

Here are some reading trends, according to U.S. Book Statistics 2021:

"Adult fiction and nonfiction showed modest increases of 6% and 4.8%, respectively."

"Young adult nonfiction jumped 38.3% as students sought academic support for online courses."

Source: *Publishers Weekly*

What Are Some Types of Nonfiction?

When I was younger, I always gravitated toward fiction when reading.
I never thought I would enjoy nonfiction. However, as I matured as a reader,
I discovered a love for the genre. As a student, I never knew there were
so many types of nonfiction to explore. Now more than ever, I realize
how much I was missing! Any chance I can, I choose to read nonfiction.

I especially enjoy literary nonfiction, an overlap between the two. Nonfiction is prose based on fact.

Literary Nonfiction: John Glenn and Neil Armstrong were the first men to land on the moon, but their great achievement was not accomplished without the help of brilliant black women who made this famous moon landing possible. Margot Lee Shetterly's best-selling book, *Hidden Figures*, tells the remarkable story of the black women who worked for NASA behind the scenes as mathematicians and engineers during the space race between the United States and the Soviet Union in 1969. In a combination of facts and literary devices, the readers are pulled into the lives of those who made the Apollo mission possible. Literary nonfiction is prose that uses literary techniques to report on persons, places, and events without altering facts.

Memoir: In 2012, Malala Yousafzai, a Pakistani teenage girl, was shot in the head as she made her way to school. The Taliban made an example of her, hoping to deter other young girls from seeking an education. Malala survived and went on to be a champion of women's education and was the youngest recipient of the Nobel Peace Prize. She wrote a memoir entitled *I am Malala: How One Girl Stood Up for Education and Changed the World*. If you are intrigued by real-life stories, then a memoir is for you! Memoirs do not include the entire life of the author, just the most important memories. Memoirs are self-written and focus on the author's life. The word *memoir* comes from the French word *memorie*.

Biography: World War II veteran Louis Zamperini was an Olympic runner before he was captured by the Japanese. From a plane crash to floating on a raft surrounded by hungry sharks, Zamperini survived extraordinary feats, including two years in a prisoner of war camp. *Unbroken* is an example of a biography. It is written by Laura Hillenbrand. The book tells the story of Zamperini's remarkable life. A biography is different from a memoir because it focuses on the entire life story and not just specific moments or events. A biography can be written about a person who is still alive or is dead. A biography could even be about an animal! Check out Laura Hillenbrand's biography about a champion American racehorse named Seabiscuit.

Autobiography: Anne Frank was a young Jewish girl who lived during the Holocaust. In 1942, she and her family hid for two years in the Netherlands before they were taken by the Nazis. Anne died in a concentration camp, but her diary was found and later published for the world to remember the millions who perished. *The Diary of Anne Frank* is an autobiography. It is a type of biography written by the person whose life story is told.

Journalism: If you have read the news, reported on a current event for class, or watched the evening broadcast, then you are very familiar with this type of nonfiction. Journalism is the art of creating news, the collection and gathering of fact, and the preparation and distribution of news to the people. Whether it is a front-page news story about the most recent local event or a news anchor reporting on world events, journalism is a prime example of nonfiction. Reporters tell the audience the who, what, when, where, and why about events happening locally and around the world to keep us informed.

Documentary: When you watch a movie at the cinema or view one from Netflix, you are mostly looking to be entertained. A documentary is also a film, but its purpose is to educate and teach. Sometimes documentaries are created to persuade. Using facts, statistics, and expert testimony, documentaries can explore any topic—from fast food and global warming to spelling bee competitions.

IRL If you're looking to watch some interesting documentaries, check these titles out!

Bully: A film about bullying and its effects on children

Supersize Me: A film documenting one man's experiment with eating fast food for a month

Food, Inc.: A film that explores where and how our food is manufactured

The Social Dilemma: A film that explores the dangers that social media poses

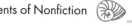

What Are Some Strategies to Help Readers Navigate Nonfiction?

When it comes to reading nonfiction, you must use different strategies than when you read fiction. Think of the sports you may play. You would need different equipment to play lacrosse versus what you would need to play tennis or basketball. Although all the sports would require similar skills—dexterity, agility, speed, coordination—the sports use different equipment to help you play the game. Both fiction and nonfiction may ask you to ask questions, make connections, have reactions, and look up new words. Nonfiction requires readers to use new equipment: Nonfiction readers look for text features, graphs, charts, time lines, and illustrations to make sense of the text.

In addition, nonfiction writers also use different strategies to help develop their purpose. It is just as important to be able to read and understand the visuals as the words in a text.

What Are Text Features?

Text features: Some students consider nonfiction reading more challenging than fiction. Nonfiction can be harder because it lacks much of the exciting twists and turns of fiction. After all, there are no characters to relate to, no plots to drive suspense, and no conflicts to entertain us. However, there are tools that nonfiction readers use to stay focused. Once you recognize that you are reading nonfiction, there are many features there to help you navigate the reading.

One of the clearest ways to recognize nonfiction texts is by their text features. Think about the textbooks you use in school or the visual resources you might read online in social studies and science. They do not include characters or dialogue; instead, you will see charts, graphs, and timelines.

BTW

Because readers do not have to read a nonfiction book in order, and they may not intend to read the entire book, there are two main purposes of a table of contents. The table of contents can show the reader all of the topics to be covered in the book, and it can also direct a reader quickly to the exact information they need.

Text features are not always included in the main body of the text. Instead, you may see this information on the first page, the last page, or on the sides of the page. This book is nonfiction. Look at the pages. Do you see all the features that appear outside of the writing?

Titles, Book Covers, and Tables of Content

So many of my readers completely ignore three of the most helpful features: titles, book covers, and tables of contents. These three text features provide initial information that can help you as a nonfiction reader.

Some authors consider the title to be the most difficult to write because it really has to capture the essence of their writing. Therefore, thinking about

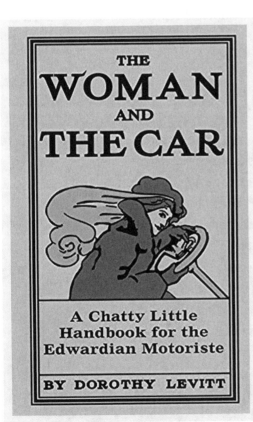

If you were to begin this nonfiction book, what would you learn from your observations of the title and the cover?

As a reader, I am wondering, why would women need a manual on how to drive a car?

From the picture on the cover, I notice that the woman at the wheel doesn't look like a woman today. Instead, she looks like a woman from the past.

By recalling prior knowledge, I remember that in the 1920s, some women were called flappers. These women were recognized by their fashion style. Flappers wore their hair in short bobs or flowy curls, as the picture depicts. Flappers flouted conventions of the day. At the turn of the century, women were fighting for rights and more independence. Driving a car gave women more freedom.

The cover and title make me think of more questions I'd like answered: When did women start driving? What kinds of rules will this book present? Were the rules for women different than the rules for men? I can't wait to find out more!

THE WOMAN
AND THE CAR
A CHATTY LITTLE HANDBOOK
FOR ALL WOMEN WHO MOTOR
OR WHO WANT TO MOTOR
BY DOROTHY LEVITT & &
EDITED WITH INTRODUCTORY
ARTICLES BY C. BYNG-HALL
ILLUSTRATED BY PHOTOGRAPHS
SPECIALLY TAKEN & & &

LONDON: JOHN LANE, THE BODLEY HEAD
NEW YORK: JOHN LANE COMPANY, MCMIX

Photo by Foulsham & Banfield, Ltd. https://publicdomainreview.org/collection/the-woman -and-the-car

the title before you read is essential. The title may reveal more than meets the eye. The title not only grabs the reader's attention, it also can give the reader a glimpse into the content matter, set an expectation of what is to come in the reading, and establish a tone and purpose. The illustrations on the cover also give vital information to the reader about the content.

A title and a cover can help a nonfiction reader to make meaning of the information that will be presented. Let's look at a book entitled *The Woman and the Car* by Dorothy Levitt (1909).

 In 1909, Alice Ramsey, a twenty-two-year-old, became the first woman to drive across the United States.

A table of contents is an organized list of topics or subjects covered in a nonfiction text that the reader can locate in the opening pages of the book. It usually lists topics along with their coordinating page numbers.

CONTENTS

From the Table of Contents in *The Woman and the Car*, I see the topics that will be covered in the chapters. In this book, readers can learn the price of a car, the cost to maintain it, and the accessories a driver will need. A female reader would learn how to dress appropriately when driving a car and also good manners when it comes to the road. Female readers will also learn how to drive, how to avoid trouble, and what to do in case of trouble.

A reader could decide to read the entire book from cover to cover or just the chapters that they feel necessary.

Source: https://publicdomainreview.org/collection/the-woman-and-the-car

When you peruse the table of contents, you can preview what content and subjects will be presented in the book. If you are looking for specific information, you can find the page to go directly to the topic immediately.

Headings and *subtitles* help the reader identify the main ideas in a certain section of text. They are text features that organize the content for the reader and most often appear in the beginning of a page or section. For example, if you look through this book, you will notice headings and subheadings indicating what information each chapter will cover and what topics will be featured in each section. You can consider them to be short titles within the overarching titles, main titles, or chapters of the book.

Illustrations are pictures, decorations, or visual aids that help readers comprehend the text. Illustrations go beyond making a text more attractive.

THE WOMAN AND THE CAR

CHAPTER I

THE CAR—ITS COST, UP-KEEP AND ACCESSORIES

Motoring as a Pastime for Women—Patience of more Value than Nerve—Selection of a Car—Single-cylinder the best for Women who are going to drive themselves and attend to the Mechanism—Cost of a Small Car—Necessary Accessories and their Cost—Expense of Up-keep—The necessary Licences and the Cost

PATIENCE, the capacity for taking pains, is of more value than the most ponderous nerve. You may be afraid, as I am, of driving in a hansom through the crowded streets of town —you may be afraid of a mouse, or so nervous that you are startled at the slightest of sudden sounds—yet you can be a skilful motorist, and enjoy to the full the delights of this greatest of out-door pastimes, if you possess patience —the capacity for taking pains.

Motoring is a pastime for women : young,

15

◄ In chapter one of *The Woman and the Car*, the heading tells readers that the upcoming chapter will include information about Cost, Up-Keep and Accessories.

Source: https://publicdomainreview.org/collection/the-woman-and-the-car

The caption reads:

Photo. H. W. Nicholls

One of the most important articles to wear is a scarf or muffler for the neck.

Source: https://publicdomainreview.org/collection/the-woman-and-the-car

Visuals support the information in the text and can help students make sense of the reading. Many textbooks include illustrations to make the material more accessible to students.

Captions usually appear under an illustration or visual. They are usually short, only a few sentences in length. They usually provide background information on the visual, draw the reader's attention to something interesting or important, or clarify an idea. They also might include the name of the artist, photographer, or illustrator.

Bold, Italics, Underlines, Font Size, and Color

When you are reading a nonfiction text, you might see the font size or color of text change. You may notice words in **bold,** a darker shade of text, or *italics*, slanted letters. Perhaps words or phrases are even underlined.

The Woman and the Car

they begin to have a hard, stiff feeling which is far from comfortable. I have, however, seen very pretty costumes, coats and skirts, made of thin glove kid, or *suède*, but these are luxuries, as they cost from twenty-five to thirty guineas each.

As to head-gear, there is no question : the round cap or close-fitting turban of fur are the most comfortable and suitable, though with the glass screen up it is possible to wear an ordinary hat, with a veil round it. However, if you go in for caps, see that they fit well—there is nothing more uncomfortable than the cap that does not fit. It is a good plan to have caps made to match your costumes. When fixing the cap, pin it securely, and over it put a *crêpe-de-chine* veil, of length a-plenty. These can be obtained from most of the leading drapers, and it is quite a simple matter to make them yourself with a length of *crêpe* or washing silk. Before tying the veil, twist the ends. This prevents the knot working loose and is very necessary, as the veil, in addition to protecting the hair, helps to keep the hat securely in place.

26

In the second paragraph, the word *crêpe-de-chine* is offset with italics. Perhaps this word was most likely italicized to provide the female audience with a definition of the fine fabric.

Crêpe is also bolded to provide the definition of a "washing silk."

Source: https://publicdomainreview.org/collection/the-woman-and-the-car

Pay attention!

Writers often switch the font to bold or italics to signal important information, ideas, or concepts.

The bold, italicized, or underlined words could be important definitions to know, an idea that the writer wants to emphasize, or important titles to recognize.

Bullets: Nonfiction writers often use bullets to give the reader information quickly and simply. Bullets simplify the information, giving readers the important ideas they need to know. You can use bullets to review information or to get a general idea of what's included in the passage, chapter, or book. Bullets improve the text's readability, highlighting key facts, terms, directions, or instructions.

Index: Another useful tool in nonfiction books, especially research books, is an index. The index appears in the back of the book, and it includes

INDEX

If a reader wants to know the definition and function of an accelerator, the reader can find that information on page 111.

If a reader is looking for information regarding coats for motoring, the reader can turn to page 25.

Source: https://publicdomainreview.org/collection/the-woman-and-the-car

a list of important words or terms with the corresponding pages. Nonfiction readers can find the exact topic they need in a book by browsing an index. Conveniently, the index is in alphabetical order.

Glossary: A nonfiction book may also include a glossary, a dictionary of important **must know** terms mentioned in the text. The words/terms will appear in alphabetical order for the reader to find easily. The glossary typically appears at the end of the book for quick reference. It will usually include unknown words or specialized words.

Readers of nonfiction will also encounter other helpful tools such as *graphs, charts,* and *diagrams* to help them interpret the text.

Graph: A graph is a drawing that presents information in a visual way.

Chart: A chart is a visual that organizes information in a way that makes sense to the reader.

THE MOTOR WOMAN'S DICTIONARY

ACCELERATOR.—A device, operated by a pedal, for increasing the speed of the engine, either by suspending the controlling action of the governor or opening the throttle.

ACCUMULATOR.—An apparatus for storing electricity. *See* Battery.

ACETYLÈNE.—An inflammable gas giving a brilliant light. It is commonly produced by adding water to carbide of calcium.

AMMETER.—An instrument used for measuring the number of ampères in an electrical circuit. *See* Ampère.

AMPÈRE.—The unit of measure of the quantity of current flowing through an electrical circuit. *See* Volt.

AXLES.—The horizontal shafts or girders by which the weight of carriage is transferred to the road wheels and at the ends of which

III

For example, in *The Motor Woman's Dictionary*, a reader could find a definition for unknown and specialized words regarding driving and car mechanics:

Accelerator

Ammeter

Axles

Source: https://publicdomainreview.org/collection/the-woman-and-the-car

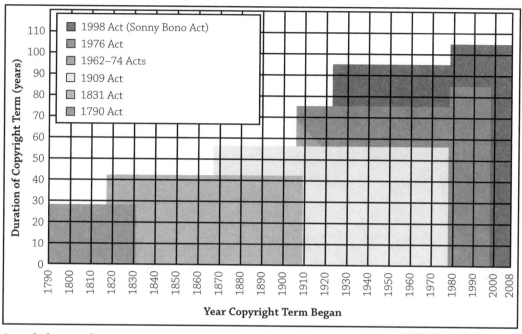

A graph showing the expansion of U.S. copyright law over time (assuming works created 35 years before their authors' death)

The Coming of the Small Car

car has found the cost of running 3400 miles to be as follows:

	£	s.	d.
Tyre Repairs	2	13	0
Petrol	6	19	0
Oil and Grease	2	6	0
Sundry Repairs	1	10	0
Charging Accumulators . .		18	0
Brushes and Waste.		10	0
Total	14	16	0

In the chart to the left, readers can see the breakdown of how much it will cost to drive a car 3400 miles. Listing the costs in a chart is easier to understand than listing them in paragraph form.

Source: https://publicdomainreview.org/collection/the-woman-and-the-car

Diagram: A diagram is a drawing that shows or explains information to the reader.

Time Line: In textbooks and other works of nonfiction, it is common to see time lines, a tool that outlines important dates, events, or activities in chronological order, following one another in time.

> **BTW**
>
> *When you understand the purpose of text features, you will take away a deeper understanding of the text than you would without. In fact, a text box often provides more information than the text about a topic, and often a text box contains information that does not even appear in the text. Don't skip!*

IRL According to Haig Kouyoumdjian, Ph.D., in *Psychology Today*, "A large body of research indicates that visual cues help us to better retrieve and remember information." Kouyoumdjian explains that "words are abstract and rather difficult for the brain to retain, whereas visuals are concrete and, as such, more easily remembered."

What Is the Main Idea?

Main Idea: Text features offer you support as you read a nonfiction text. However, as an active reader, you must also use close-reading skills to comprehend the material. When you begin to read nonfiction, it is important to look for the main idea. It is the first step you should take when reading.

The main idea is the primary point an author wants to make in the writing. Think of it as the most important idea of a piece, the reason the author is writing. Most writers will not reveal their main idea directly. Instead, active readers use the information given to infer the main idea. Just like we discussed in the "Reading Fiction" chapter, to make an inference is to make a reasonable guess.

Let's read an excerpt from the book *The Woman and the Car* and find the main idea.

Patience, the capacity for taking pains, is of more value than the most ponderous nerve. You may be afraid, as I am, of driving in a hansom through the crowded streets of town—you may be afraid of a mouse, or so nervous that you are startled at the slightest of sudden sounds—yet you can be a skillful motorist, and enjoy the delights of this greatest of out-door pastimes, if you possess patience—the capacity for taking pains.

Motoring is a pastime for women; young, middle-aged, and—if there are any—old. There may be pleasure in being whirled around the country by your friends and relatives, or in a car driven by your chauffeur; but the real, intense pleasure comes only when you drive your own car.

I have hunted—and was one with those who declare that the most glorious of all out-door life is in the saddle, on a fast, clean jumping hunter; but when, by accident, I took up motoring I found the exhilaration, the delights of the gallop doubled. It fascinated me, and it fascinates any woman who tries it.

From considering the title, examining the cover, browsing the table of contents, and reading the opening passage of the book, I will make an inference about the main idea.

The *main idea* is that women will love the freedom of driving a car once they get over their initial fear and learn some helpful tips.

Dorothy Levitt's purpose is to convince women that driving is a valuable skill, and it is possible for them to learn.

What Are Details in Nonfiction?

Details: Similar to reading fiction, nonfiction writers also pay attention to details. Details are important information that support the main idea. Details can be specific words, small phrases, or complete sentences that capture what the author is trying to convey.

- Details can provide more information: who, what, when, where, why, how.

- Details can answer some of your initial questions.

- Details can give the reader context/background.

- Details can provide definitions to new words and concepts.

- Details can clear up misconceptions.

- Details can help a reader visualize descriptions.

- Details keep the reader engaged and interested in the reading.

Now, as to ordinary garments, dress for the season of the year exactly as you would if you were not going motoring. I would advise shoes rather than boots as they give greater freedom to the ankles and do not tend to impede the circulation, as a fairly tightly laced or buttoned boot would do, but this is a matter of individual taste. In winter time it is advisable to wear high gaiters, have them specially made, almost up to the knee.

Regarding coats—there is nothing like a thick frieze, homespun, or tweed, lined with "Jaeger" or fur. The former has the advantage of being lighter in weight than the latter and is just as warm and much less expensive. In England in winter one can wear a coat of this description right up to the beginning of summer. For summer itself, the ideal coat is of thin cream serge. It retains its freshness and does not crease like alpaca, linen or silk. The serge looks, and feels, smart all the summer—the silk or alpaca, after its first hard day, begins to look creased and shabby.

As to head-gear, there is no question: the round cap or close-fitting turban of fur are the most comfortable and suitable, though with the glass screen up it is possible to wear an ordinary hat, with a veil round it. However, if you go in for caps, see that they fit well— there is nothing more uncomfortable than the cap that does not fit. It is a good plan to have caps made to match your costumes. When fixing the cap, pin it securely, and over it put a *crêpe-de-chine* veil, of length a-plenty. These can be obtained from most of the leading drapers, and it is quite a simple matter to make them yourself with a length of *crêpe* or washing silk. Before tying the veil, twist the ends. This prevents the knot working loose and is very necessary, as the veil, in addition to protecting the hair, helps to keep the hat securely in place.

Source: https://publicdomainreview.org/collection/the-woman-and-the-car
book p. 24, 25, 26

Main Idea of Chapter Two

EXAMPLE

> For a woman driving a car, it is important to consider what you wear.

Supporting Details

EXAMPLE

1. Consider the season when you dress.

2. For more flexibility when driving, wear shoes rather than boots.

3. When it comes to coats, tweed and frieze are lightweight and less expensive.

EXERCISES

EXERCISE 6.1

Choose the best answer to each of the following questions.

1. Which of the following is a characteristic of nonfiction?
    a. Nonfiction is based on imagination.
    b. Nonfiction is fact based.
    c. Nonfiction includes characters.
    d. Nonfiction must be read from cover to cover.

2. Which of the following is **NOT** an example of nonfiction?
    a. Bibliography
    b. Memoir
    c. Poetry
    d. Cookbook

3. What is one difference between fiction and nonfiction?
    a. Fiction is not true; nonfiction is true.
    b. Fiction must be read in order; nonfiction can be read out of order.
    c. Fiction is meant to entertain; nonfiction is meant to inform.
    d. All of the above

4. If you wanted to find a specific topic in a nonfiction book, you should go to the:
    a. Title
    b. Book cover
    c. Glossary
    d. Table of contents

5. If you wanted to look up the definition of a word or term in a nonfiction book, you should go to the:

    a. Table of contents

    b. Back cover

    c. Glossary

    d. All of the above

6. Which of the following text features would inform you about the content?

    a. Title

    b. Book cover

    c. Table of contents

    d. All of the above

7. From this table of contents from *The ABC of Bee Culture* (1817), what can you infer about the author's purpose?

Comb Basket 43
Comb Foundation 44
    Foundation Machine 44
    How to Make Wax Sheets 45
    Rolling the Wax Sheets. 46
    Trimming, Squaring/and Cutting the Sheets 46
    Carlin's Foundation Cutter. 47
    Sagging of the Foundation. 47
Comb Honey 48
    Clustering on the Outside of Hives 48
    How to Remove the Filled Sections 48
    Always Use the Tin Separators 48

Source: http://reader.library.cornell.edu/docviewer/digital?id=hivebees5017633#page/8
/mode/2up
first page of "Contents"

a. The book will explain how to get rid of bees.
b. The book will compare bees to other insects.
c. The book will argue why bees are necessary.
d. The book will teach readers how to care for bees.

8. What would be the author's purpose for including the following diagram?

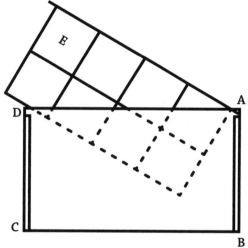

Source: https://libguides.niagaracc.suny.edu
/c.php?g=952880&p=6995214
book p. 40

a. To demonstrate how to cage the bees properly
b. To encourage the reader to take up beekeeping
c. To remind readers why bees are useful
d. All of the above

ANGER OF BEES. I confess I do not like the term "anger," when applied to bees, and it almost makes me angry when I hear people speak of their being "mad," as if they were always in a towering rage, and delight in inflicting exquisite pain on everything and everybody coming near them. Bees are, on the contrary, the pleasantest, most sociable, genial and good natured little fellows one meets in all animated creation, when one understands them. Why, we can tear their beautiful comb all to bits right before their very eyes, and, without a particle of resentment, but with all the patience in the world, they will at once set to work to repair it, and that, too, without a word of remonstrance. If you pinch them, they will sting, and any body that has energy enough to take care of himself, would do as much had he the weapon.

9. From the text, what is the main idea of this passage?
   a. It's a misconception that bees are angry.
   b. People should not ruin beehives.
   c. Bees are always in a towering rage.
   d. People need to be patient with bees.

We as yet know very little of bees comparatively, and the more we learn, the easier we find it to be to get along without any clashing in regard to who shall be master. In fact, we take all their honey now, almost as fast as they gather it, and even if we are so thoughtless as to starve them to death, no word of complaint is made.

10. What is a detail that supports the main idea of this passage?
    a. We know very little about bees.
    b. If you pinch them, they will sting.
    c. Bees are the pleasantest, most sociable, genial, and good-natured little fellows.
    d. All of the above

Source: http://reader.library.cornell.edu/docviewer/digital?id=hivebees5017633#page/8/mode/2up
book page 8

EXERCISE 6.2

CHAPTER I

FIRST FLIGHT

THE elderly lady-bee who helped the baby-bee Maya when she awoke to life and slipped from her cell was called Cassandra and commanded great respect in the hive. Those were exciting days. A rebellion had broken out in the nation of bees, which the queen was unable to unable to suppress.

While the experienced Cassandra wiped Maya's large bright eyes and tried as best she could to arrange her delicate wings, the big hive hummed and buzzed like a threatening thunderstorm, and the baby-bee found it very warm and said so to her companion.

Cassandra looked about troubled, without replying. It astonished her that the child so soon found something to criticize. But really the child was right: the heat and the pushing and crowding were almost unbearable. Maya saw an endless succession of bees go by in such swarming haste that sometimes one climbed up and over another, or several rolled past together clotted in a ball.

Once the queen-bee approached. Cassandra and Maya were jostled aside. A drone, a friendly young fellow of immaculate appearance, came to their assistance. He nodded to Maya and stroked the shining hairs on his breast rather nervously with his foreleg. (The bees use their forelegs as arms and hands.)

"The crash will come," he said to Cassandra. "The revolutionists will leave the city. A new queen has already been proclaimed."

Cassandra scarcely noticed him. She did not even thank him for his help, and Maya felt keenly conscious that the old lady was not a bit nice to the young gentleman. The child was a little afraid to ask questions, the impressions were coming so thick and fast; they threatened to overwhelm her. The general excitement got into her blood, and she set up a fine, distinct buzzing.

"What do you mean by that?" said Cassandra. "Isn't there noise enough as it is?"

Maya subsided at once, and looked at Cassandra questioningly.

(From *The Adventures of Maya the Bee* by Waldemar Bonsels, 1922)

1. This passage is fiction because:

    a. It includes characters.

    b. It has a plot.

    c. Bees can't talk, so it is not based on real life.

    d. All of the above

2. The following illustration was most likely included in the nonfiction text *Constructive Beekeeping* by Ed H. Clark (1918) for the following purpose:

   a. To show readers how to tend to the bees with care.

   b. To help readers purchase a cross section for a new hive.

   c. To support the argument that bees are dependent on humans.

   d. To teach readers how to avoid being stung.

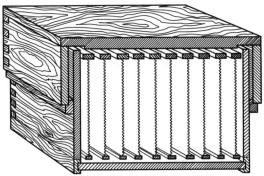

34   CONSTRUCTIVE BEEKEEPING

CROSS SECTION OF THE CONSTRUCTIVE HIVE

1. Good condenser.

2. Wind does not blow it off.

3. When once on a bump or jar from person or object does not misplace it.

4. Bees are more gentle to handle.

5. No bees are crushed when putting on the cover.

6. When the cover is removed in cold weather and put on again, the hive is just as comfortable as it was before the cover was taken off.

Source: https://biobees.com/library/general_beekeeping/beekeeping_books_articles/ConstructiveBeekeeping_EdClarke.pdf
book page 34

3. In this passage from *The Classic Beekeeper's Manual* by L. L. Langstroth, what might be the reason the word *Protector* is in italics?

   I attach very great importance to the way in which I give the bees effectual protection against extremes of heat and cold, and sudden changes of temperature, without removing them from their stands, or incurring the expense and disadvantages of a covered Bee-House. This I accomplish by means of what I shall call a *Protector* which is constructed substantially as follows.

Select a dry and suitable location for the bees, where they will not be disturbed, or prove an annoyance to others. If possible, let it be in full sight of the sitting room, so that they may be seen in case of swarming; and let it face the South-East, and be well protected from the force of strong winds. Dig a trench, about two feet deep; its length should depend upon the number of hives to be accommodated; and its breadth should be such that when it is properly walled up, it should measure from the outside top of one wall to another, just sufficient to receive the bottom of the hive. The walls, may be built of refuse brick or stones, and should be about four feet high from the foundation; the upper six inches being built of good brick, and the back wall about two inches higher than the front one, so as to give the bottom-board of the hives, the proper slant towards the entrance. At one end of this Protector, a wooden chimney should be built, and if the number of   [127]

   a. The author wants to let the reader know why the Protector is important.
   b. The author wants to stress that the reader should buy a Protector.
   c. The author would like readers to know he invented the Protector.
   d. The author is informing readers how to build an effective Protector.

4. Which of the following is the main idea of this passage?
   a. Beekeepers can learn to dig a trench.
   b. Bees are happier when they are warm.
   c. Protectors have many advantages.
   d. A well-built Protector is key to protect bees from the elements.

5. From looking at this book cover and title, what would a reader expect from the content?

Source:

How to Become a Magician, Containing a Grand Assortment of Magical Illusions as Performed by the Leading Magicians and Wizards of the Day; 1882; F. Tousey, New York.

Source: https://publicdomainreview.org/collection/how-to-become-a-magician-1882

   a. An account of a famous magician's life

   b. A fictional story based on a magician

   c. A manual with steps to perform tricks

   d. A history of magic

6. From the subtitles in this section, what information would the reader most likely learn?

and dipped in oil, may heat the inside of it. Before you light this paper, suspend the balloon in such a manner that it may, in a great measure, be exhausted of air, and as soon as it has been dilated, let it go, together with the wire basket, which will serve as ballast.

THE MAGIC BOTTLE.

Take a small bottle, the neck of which is not more than the sixth of an inch in diameter. With a funnel, fill the bottle quite full of red wine, and place it in a glass vessel, similar to a show-glass, whose height exceeds that of the bottle about two inches; fill this vessel with water. The wine will shortly come out of the bottle, and rise in the form of a small column to the surface of the water; while, at the same time, the water entering the bottle will supply the place of the wine. The reason of this is, that as water is specifically heavier than wine, it must hold the lower place, while the other rises to the top.

An effect equally pleasing will be produced if the bottle be filled with water and the vessel with wine.

THE WINE TRICK.

First, from the vessel which contains eight gallons, and is full of wine, let five gallons be poured in the empty vessel of five, and from this vessel so filled let three be poured into the empty vessel of three, so there will remain two gallons within the vessel of five. Then let three gallons, which are within the vessel of three be poured into the vessel of eight, which will now have six gallons within it; that done, let the two gallons which are in the vessel of five be put into an empty vessel of three; then of the six gallons of wine which are within the vessel of eight, fill again the five, and from those five pour one gallon into the vessel of three, which wanted only one gallon to fill it, so there will remain exactly four gallons within the vessel of five, and four gallons within the other two vessels. This question may be resolved in another way, but I leave that as an exercise to the wit of ingenious

two, and cause John to multiply that number which he shall have chosen by three; that done, bid them add the two products together, and let them make known the sum to you, or else demand of them whether the said sum be even or odd, or by any other way more secret endeavor to discover it, by bidding them to take the half of the said sum, for by knowing whether the said sum be even or odd, you do obtain the principal end to be aimed at; because if the said sum be an even number, then infallibly he that multiplied his number by your odd number (to wit: by three), did choose the even number (to wit: ten), but if the said number happen to be an odd number, then he whom you caused to multiply his number by your odd number (to wit: by three), did infallibly choose the odd number (to wit: nine).

THE GLOBULAR FOUNTAIN.

Make a hollow globe of copper or lead, and of a size adapted to the quantity of water that comes from a pipe (hereafter mentioned) to which it is to be fixed, and which may be fastened to any kind of pump, provided it be so constructed that the water shall have no other means of escape than through the pipe. Pierce a number of small holes through the globe, that all tend toward its center, and annex it to the pipe that communicates with the pump. The water that comes from the pump, rushing with violence into the globe, will be forced out at the holes, and form a very pleasing sphere of water.

THE WATER SUN.

Provide two portions of a hollow sphere that are very shallow; join them together in such a manner that the hollow between them be very narrow. Fix them vertically to a pipe from whence a jet proceeds. Bore a number of small holes all around that part where the two pieces are joined together. The water rushing through the holes will form a very pleasing water sun or star.

TO CAUSE A BRILLIANT EXPLOSION UNDER WATER.

Drop a piece of phosphorus, the size of a pea, into a tum-

Source: https://publicdomainreview.org/collection/how-to-become-a-magician-1882
book page 42–43

    a. Ways to purchase materials

    b. Directions on how to perform tricks

    c. Examples of the most popular tricks

    d. Places to perform tricks

7. Which is the function of the headings and subheadings on the following page?

This the day, and this the hour,
When it seems you have the power,
For to be a maiden's friend,
So, good ladies, condescend.

A tobacco-pipe full is enough. When the pewter is cold, take it out of the water, and drain it dry in a cloth, and you will find the emblems of your future husband's trade quite plain. If more than one you will marry twice; if confused and no emblems you will never marry; a coach shows a gentleman for you.

St. Agnes' Day.—Charm to know who your husband shall be.

Falls on the 21st of January; you must prepare yourself by a twenty-four hour' fast, touching nothing but pure spring water, beginning at midnight on the 20th, to the same again on the 21st; then go to bed, and mind you sleep by yourself, and do not mention what you are trying to any one, or it will break the spell; go to rest on your left side, and repeat these lines three times—

St. Agnes be a friend to me,
In the gift I ask of thee;
Let me this night my husband see—

and you will dream of your future spouse; if you see more than one in your dream, you will wed two or three times, but if you sleep and dream not, you will never marry.

Events Foretold by Planets.

JANUARY.—*Aquarius, or the Water-bearer.*

ABOUT the twentieth of the month the sun enters this sign: a man born at this period will be of an unruly, restless, fickle, and boisterous disposition; will be given to all whims and strange fancies; will undertake anything, however difficult, to accomplish any object he may have in view; not contented long in one place; soon affronted—slow to forgive; suspicious and always imagining danger, and, instead of endeavoring to subdue trouble, meeting it half way. In life he will be moderately successful, and enjoy a portion of happiness. In love he will display an amorous disposition, and be passionately attached to his mistress, until she yields to his wishes, or marries him; he will then grow indifferent, and rove until some other object fixes his attention.

A woman born at this time will be of a studious, indus-

and an affectionate wife.

FEBRUARY.—*Pisces, or the Fishes.*

About the twentieth of the month the sun enters this sign: a man born at this time will be designing, intriguing, selfish, unfaithful to his engagement; he will be mean, and subservient to those whom he thinks he can make useful to his schemes; but his end once obtained, he will take every opportunity to injure and betray them; in poverty he will be a sycophant, in prosperity a tyrant—haughty to equals and inferiors. In life he will generally be unsuccessful, although for a time he will often appear to have succeeded; in love he will be careless, indifferent, and unsteady—he will make a severe father and an unkind husband.

A woman born at the same period will be of obliging manners, delicate in her ideas, open and sincere in her friendships, an enemy to deceit—in love she will be faithful, and moderately inclined to the joys of Venus; she will be affectionate to her family; make a good and tender mother, and be a prosperous and excellent wife.

MARCH.—*Aries, or the Ram.*

About the twentieth of the month the sun enters this sign: a man born at this period will be of a bashful, meek, and irresolute disposition, hard to provoke to a quarrel, but difficult to be appeased when roused; in life he will be for the most part happy and contented—in love he will be faithful and constant, moderately addicted to its pleasures—he will be a kind, affectionate father, a good husband, a sincere friend, and of an industrious turn.

A woman born at the same time will be modest, chaste, good-tempered, cleanly in her habits, industrious, and charitable—in love she will be faithful, and in life she will be rather happy than otherwise, but be little concerned about worldly affairs—she will make an amiable mother, be decently fond of her husband, and moderately given to the joys of Hymen.

APRIL.—*Taurus, or the Bull.*

About the twentieth of the month the sun enters this sign: a man born at this time will be of a strong and robust constitution, faithful to his engagements, industrious, sober, and honest, but prone to anger—in life he will be ardent in his pursuits, but will meet with many vexations and disappoint-

Source: https://publicdomainreview.org/collection/how-to-become-a-magician-1882
book page 56–57

a. To tell the reader more information about planets

b. To warn the reader about dangerous events to come

c. To discuss how astrological signs affect the magician and his magic

d. To inform readers about upcoming magic shows on a calendar

8. What would be the benefit of including this chart?

THE PAIRS RE-PAIRED.

Tell out twenty cards in pairs, and ask ten people to take a pair each, and remember them.   Take up the pairs in their order, and lay them on the table in order, according to the accompanying table, which forms a memoria technica, and may be construed.   Mutus gave a name to the Coci (a people who have yet to be discovered).

M	U	T	U	S[1]
1	2	3	2	4
D	E	D	I	T
5	6	5	7	3
N	O	M	E	N
8	9	1	6	8
C	O	C	I	S
10	9	10	7	4

(1) The figures represent the pairs, *i.e.* the 1 under M signifies that M belongs to the *first* pair.

Source: https://publicdomainreview.org
/collection/how-to-become-a-magician-1882
book page 23

a.   To make directions more clear visually

b.   To define a term

c.   To provide an example of a game

d.   To add context to the game

9. What is most likely the purpose for including the following text feature?

Suppose the person who stands the third in order has put the ring upon the second joint of the thumb of his left hand, then:

The double of the rank of the third person is..............	6
To which add...	5
	11
Multiply the sum by...................................	5
	55
To which add...	10
And the number of the left hand.......................	2
	67
Which being multiplied by.............................	10
	670
To which add the number of the thumb..................	1
	671
And multiply again by.................................	10
	6710
Then add the number of the joint......................	2
And lastly, the number................................	35
	6747
From which deducting.................................	3535
The remainder is......................................	3212

Of which, as we have said, the 3 denotes the third person, the 2 the left hand, the 1 the thumb, and the last 2 the second joint.

Source: https://publicdomainreview.org
/collection/how-to-become-a-magician-1882
book page 41

a.   To outline steps for the magician to take to perform the trick

b.   To provide specific examples of magic strategies

c.   To list materials needed for the trick

d.   To define terms of the game

10. The purpose of including this text feature is:

> ### DICE.
>
> This is a certain and innocent way of finding out common occurrences about to take place. Take three dice, shake them well in the box with your left hand, and then cast them out on a board or table, on which you had previously drawn a circle with chalk. but never throw on Monday or Wednesday.
>
> *Three*—a pleasing surprise.
> *Four*—a disagreeable one.
> *Five*—a stranger who will prove a friend.
> *Six*—loss of property.
> *Seven*—undeserved scandal.
> *Eight*—merited reproach.
> *Nine*—a wedding.
> *Ten*—a christening, at which some important event will occur to you.
> *Eleven*—a death that concerns you.
> *Twelve*—a letter, speedily.
> *Thirteen*—tears and sighs.
> *Fourteen*—a new admirer.
> *Fifteen*—beware that you are not drawn into some trouble or plot.
> *Sixteen*—a pleasant journey.
> *Seventeen*—you will either be on the water, or have dealing with those belonging to it, to your advantage.

Source: https://publicdomainreview.org /collection/how-to-become-a-magician-1882 book page 51

   a. To define magical terms

   b. To describe different types of dice a magician can use

   c. To list the various interpretations of the dice

   d. To instruct a magician on how to throw dice

Analyzing Nonfiction

MUST KNOW

- It is important to analyze the rhetorical situation of a text: speaker, occasion, audience, purpose, subject, and tone.

- The ability to persuade depends on the strength of three appeals: ethos, logos, and pathos.

- Recognizing logical fallacies makes you a stronger reader, writer, and critical thinker.

arlier in this book, you learned about strategies and tools to help you navigate nonfiction. In this chapter, you will learn to identify and analyze the argument in the nonfiction you encounter. It is important for a nonfiction reader to examine the rhetorical situation, recognize persuasive appeals, and be aware of logical fallacies that manipulate.

Visual Arguments

One of the easiest ways to begin this chapter is analyzing visual arguments. Once you see examples of these arguments around you, the easier it will be to apply this understanding to lengthier texts.

In pop culture, you are exposed to arguments every day. Ads are everywhere you turn. You see them in magazines, on the sides of buses, inside the train and subway, on buildings, on social media, and in video games. When you lie on the beach, you may even see an ad in the sky!

You might not believe these ads affect you, but, in fact, teenagers are the target audience. Companies start early, trying to make you a lifelong consumer by spending billions of dollars to introduce you to their brand, influencing what you eat, drink, wear, and buy.

As an educated consumer, it is important to see advertisements for what they are: mini arguments that are extremely persuasive. Advertisements are an easy way to start thinking about the structure of an argument. All arguments have a claim.

 IRL Some teenagers think they are not swayed by advertising. Think again! Digital marketing experts estimate that most Americans are exposed to around 4,000 to 10,000 advertisements each day.

Claim

A claim is the position being taken in the argument. It is a statement that suggests what is true or good. A claim can also tell the audience what should be done or believed.

The following ad is a vintage ad for Del Monte, a company that has operated for over 130 years selling canned fruits, vegetables, and stock. The ad claims that its canned fruit is superior to others because a can of Del Monte "makes Summer last all year long."

Source: https://archive.org/details/DelMonte
CannedFoods1923A

If you happen to watch the Super Bowl each year, you probably look forward to the commercials as much as you do the game. In 2021, the Super Bowl attracted 96.4 million viewers, and, believe it or not, this number was lower than most years. Advertisers know that the Super Bowl generates a large audience, and many companies are willing to spend a great deal of money for commercials to be aired during the game.

IRL Advertisers are prepared to spend a great deal of money to persuade consumers! Just look at these two examples.

Did you know that a thirty-second commercial for Super Bowl LIV in 2020 cost about $5.6 million?

A Chanel perfume commercial that ran for three minutes was the most expensive commercial in history, costing $33 million for three minutes. It was released in 2004.

Commercials and Ads

Yes, commercials are arguments. Each thirty-second commercial sends viewers subtle messages that go beyond persuading the consumer to buy a product. Sometimes these messages appeal to a person's values, emotions, feelings, and logic.

For example, let's consider a commercial for a popular hair-care product. The celebrity smiles as she washes her hair in the shower. The suds that form are thick and soapy white. The faceless narrator's voice speaks softly from the background, insisting "ingredients are all natural," "with plant extract," and "its moisture from the root" "restores damaged hair" with "miracle formula." The celebrity is now fully dressed, emerging from her apartment with a few hair tosses for a night out with friends. There is a Christmas tree decked with lights, and the celebrity has perfectly wrapped gifts in her arms. Her hair is thick, luxurious, and perfectly set. "Celebrate your natural you," the voice reminds the audience. Sure, the advertiser wants to sell the shampoo, but the advertiser also appeals to vanity: If you use this hair product, your hair will look better, feel better, and everyone will notice, especially you!

Commercials are arguments: They attempt to persuade viewers to purchase items or buy services by appealing to their needs, wants, and desires. The commercial highlights the positive aspects of the product or service to be convincing.

What Is the Rhetorical Situation?

Anytime you want to communicate with others, in writing or in speech, you must think about the rhetorical situation: What do you want to say, who would you like to reach, and how will you meet your goal? Basically, the rhetorical situation is the reason why the text exists at all.

SOAPSTONE

In order to analyze a work or write one, students can use this acronym to get started: SOAPSTONE.

Subject	Ask yourself: What is the general topic, concept, or idea in the text?
Occasion	Ask yourself: Where or when did the text take place? It can be a large occasion, such as a major holiday or event, or a time period, such as the civil rights movement. The occasion can also be immediate, such as the cafeteria in your school has been renovated.
Audience	Ask yourself: To whom is the piece targeted or directed? Is it a person, group, specific gender, age, profession, or class?
Purpose	Ask yourself: What is the speaker's reason for writing? What is the speaker's message? What is the effect of the piece on the audience?
Speaker	Ask yourself: Who is the voice behind the text? What do you know about this voice? What is the speaker's background, experience, history, position, profession, race, age, class, gender, etc.?
Tone	Ask yourself: What is the author's attitude toward the subject? When you look for tone, consider the word choice, visuals, and sounds as clues. If it is a visual text, notice colors, images, fonts, and organization.

Let's use the commercial example to analyze through SOAPSTONE:

Subject	This commercial is about shampoo.
Occasion	From the gifts, holiday music, and tree in the commercial, the occasion seems to be Christmas.
Audience	Based on the details from the commercial, the audience seems to be young women who want to make an impression. It is targeted to a younger, financially set group. The celebrity is well known to a younger audience. She is wearing trendy clothes and high heels, and it looks like her apartment is high end. The party looks like an office party, so the ad could also be targeting young professional women.
Purpose	The commercial claims the shampoo can help women celebrate the holiday season in style.
Speaker	The shampoo company is the speaker, not the celebrity. The company is the one that is sending a message; the celebrity is only endorsing the product.
Tone	The tone is festive and celebratory. The commercial features a Christmas tree, lights, presents, and a formal dress. The celebrity is excited to see her friends. She is upbeat, smiling, and dancing in her apartment to music. The dress is bright red. Her lipstick is bold. Her hair is long, full, and silky. The narrator encourages us to "celebrate your natural you."

BTW

Here are a few tone words for you to know:

Ambivalent: having mixed feelings

Candid: honest, direct, straightforward

Cynical: distrustful

Laudatory: praising

Mocking: ridiculing

Solemn: serious, not funny

Witty: clever, entertaining

Let's analyze the rhetorical situation of an excerpt of a speech made by the former president, Barack Obama.

Back-to-School Speech at Wakefield High School
September 2009, Arlington, Virginia

EXAMPLE

Hello, everybody! Thank you. Thank you. Thank you, everybody. All right, everybody go ahead and have a seat. How is everybody doing today? How about Tim Spicer? I am here with students at Wakefield High School in Arlington, Virginia. And we've got students tuning in from all across America, from kindergarten through 12th grade. And I am just so glad that all could join us today. And I want to thank Wakefield for being such an outstanding host. Give yourselves a big round of applause.

I know that for many of you, today is the first day of school. And for those of you in kindergarten, or starting middle or high school, it's your first day in a new school, so it's understandable if you're a little nervous. I imagine there are some seniors out there who are feeling pretty good right now—with just one more year to go. And no matter what grade you're in, some of you are probably wishing it were still summer and you could've stayed in bed just a little bit longer this morning.

Who is the speaker?

Barack Obama is the speaker. He served as the forty-fourth president of the United States from 2009 through 2017.

Who is the audience?

The audience is schoolchildren in Arlington, Virginia, and also all of the school-aged children who are watching or listening from home.

What is the occasion?

The speech was given on the first day of school.

I know that feeling. When I was young, my family lived overseas. I lived in Indonesia for a few years. And my mother, she didn't have the money to send me where all the American kids went to school, but she thought it was important for me to keep up with an American education. So she decided to teach me extra lessons herself, Monday through Friday. But because she had to go to work, the only time she could do it was at 4:30 in the morning.

Now, as you might imagine, I wasn't too happy about getting up that early. And a lot of times, I'd fall asleep right there at the kitchen table. But whenever I'd complain, my mother would just give me one of those looks and she'd say, "This is no picnic for me either, buster."

So I know that some of you are still adjusting to being back at school. But I'm here today because I have something important to discuss with you. I'm here because I want to talk with you about your education and what's expected of all of you in this new school year.

Now, I've given a lot of speeches about education. And I've talked about responsibility a lot.

I've talked about teachers' responsibility for inspiring students and pushing you to learn.

What is the tone in this passage?

Barack Obama's tone here is sympathetic, understanding, and compassionate.

What is the subject?

The subject of this speech is the return to school.

I've talked about your parents' responsibility for making sure you stay on track, and you get your homework done, and don't spend every waking hour in front of the TV or with the Xbox.

I've talked a lot about your government's responsibility for setting high standards, and supporting teachers and principals, and turning around schools that aren't working, where students aren't getting the opportunities that they deserve.

But at the end of the day, we can have the most dedicated teachers, the most supportive parents, the best schools in the world – and none of it will make a difference, none of it will matter unless all of you fulfill your responsibilities, unless you show up to those schools, unless you pay attention to those teachers, unless you listen to your parents and grandparents and other adults and put in the hard work it takes to succeed. That's what I want to focus on today: the responsibility each of you has for your education.

I want to start with the responsibility you have to yourself. Every single one of you has something that you're good at. Every single one of you has something to offer.

What is the purpose of the speech?

Barack Obama wants students to know that they are responsible for the quality of their own education.

How does the tone shift here?

Barack Obama's tone is encouraging:

"Every single one of you has something that you're good at. Every single one of you has something to offer."

What Are Rhetorical Appeals?

Analyzing a nonfiction text also includes looking at a piece through the lens of three rhetorical appeals. The Greek scholar Aristotle identified three ways to persuade others: ethos, logos, and pathos. These three appeals are the foundations of any solid argument. Strong arguments include a balance of all three.

IRL	In Greek, the word *ethos* means *character.*
	In Greek, the word *pathos* means *suffering.*
	In Greek, the word *logos* means *reason.*

Ethos

As a teacher, I am often approached by students asking for extensions—more time to complete their work without penalty. Although I am firm to my rule "late is late," for certain students, I will make an exception based on their character. I do not play favorites, but there are students who have never been unprepared, students who find themselves in unusual circumstances, and students who deserve leniency. For example, when a student asks for more time, I ask myself: "Is this a student who is always responsible? Is this a student who has a good work ethic, who is attentive, who is cooperative, who shows good character, who is kind to me and to classmates?" The student's history, background, and character may influence my decision.

Ethos is the speaker's credibility. Is the speaker reliable, trustworthy, and sincere? Is the speaker an expert or well informed? If so, the audience will be more likely to be persuaded.

Here are some appeals to ethos:

As your doctor, I recommend that you get at least eight hours of sleep each night.

I have been running marathons for years, and I could give you some helpful tips.

Growing up in a dual-language household, I recognize the value of learning another language.

I received one hundred percent on my chemistry exam; I can help you if you are struggling.

I survived a car accident, and I hope my story convinces you that texting while driving is dangerous.

Pathos

When a student asks for an extension, sometimes they have been sick and couldn't complete the work. Sometimes the student has experienced a traumatic event, like a house fire or a death or illness in the family. Sometimes the student is depressed or having problems with friends. When a student confides in me, I feel sympathy and am easily persuaded, wanting to be an ally and help. I care about my students, and when they appeal to pathos, oftentimes I give in to their requests.

Pathos is the most common appeal used in an argument. At times, it can be used as manipulation. When people feel sorry for someone, they are more likely to say yes. When writers appeal to pathos, they often evoke anger, jealousy, grief, joy, passion, fear, loneliness, fellowship, awe, and guilt.

Here are some appeals to pathos:

If you were really my friend, you'd go with me.

I am failing two other classes, could you please give me extra credit?

Have I ever let you down before?

You'll be sorry if you don't listen to me.

If you vote for me, I promise you won't regret it.

Don't be the last one in school to get involved.

You're going against everything we've worked so hard to achieve.

Where would we be today without this tradition?

Logos

The strongest appeal in an argument is logos because it is rooted in fact. Sometimes when a student approaches me to change a grade, it is often because I made a mistake in the gradebook. Once a student politely asked me to check on his grade. When I did, I noticed that I put in a zero instead of one hundred. The grade was wrong, and, of course, I corrected the mistake immediately. He did not have to convince me at all. His argument was based on fact. I had incorrectly entered the wrong digits into the column.

Logos is an appeal to logic. The most effective arguments have support and evidence: facts, statistics, data, polls, graphs, charts, and expert testimony.

Here are some appeals to logos:

> The data is clear: Ninety-five percent of our students are college bound.

> The movie was an immediate hit; it won five top awards this year.

> Our restaurant has been a staple, serving this community for over fifty years.

> Research compiled from five top education companies in the country has shown students are behind in math.

> Veterinarians approved this dog kibble for younger puppies.

> One in every four students in American schools claim they have experienced bullying.

> A poll found that TikTok is the most popular app this year among adolescents.

> With over thirty years of teaching experience, Dr. Smith would be an asset to this school community.

Let's examine an email. Watch how the writer uses the three appeals—ethos, logos, and pathos—to support his request.

Good morning, Mrs. Scardina,

I hope you are as excited as I am for the upcoming vacation. I am writing to you because I will be leaving school a few days earlier because we are traveling to India to visit our family over the holiday break. The whole trip from New York to India is over thirteen hours, so we need a few travel days.

I know you are very busy this time of year, but I was hoping you could let me know what classwork or assignments I will be missing while I am away, so I can do them when I am there.

As you know, I care about your English class, and I don't want to fall behind. My grades are important to me! I am always prepared for class, and I wouldn't want my absences to put my studies at risk. Although I am looking forward to seeing my family in India, I am also extremely stressed about missing class time. Having the work with me will alleviate some of my anxiety about missing so many days.

We will be leaving on Tuesday. May I come see you before I go when it is convenient?

I appreciate any help you can provide!

Sincerely,

Amit

Appeals to ethos: Amit shows good character and respect by asking me if I am looking forward to the vacation. In addition, Amit acknowledges that I am busy, and this appeal to ethos shows consideration and understanding that I have much to do without wanting to add to my plate. Amit also shows that he is a good student who cares about his grades and my class, and that is why he would like to take work he will miss abroad. This appeal to ethos reinforces that he has good intentions. Finally, Amit shows goodwill when he says he will come at a time that is convenient for me.

Appeals to pathos: Amit appeals to my emotions when he reveals that he is anxious and stressed about missing so much school. As a teacher who cares for my students' well-being, I don't want him to go on this trip worried about grades and his work for my class. I realize that his family is more important than my assignments; therefore, I sympathize with him because he is torn between having fun and completing his responsibilities. I also am impressed with his maturity, that he has asked for work ahead of time so that he can be responsible, as he always is in my class.

Appeals to logos: Amit appeals to logic by reminding me that his travel to India is long; therefore, his family cannot wait for the break to start because the flight there will take almost a full day there and a full day back, thus cutting into the time they have off from school to be with family.

Let's continue our analysis of Barack Obama's Back-to-School Speech though the three appeals: ethos, logos, and pathos.

BTW

Keep in mind: Appeals can overlap in an argument. For example, consider this statement:

"As a teacher, I recognize that this current pandemic has been challenging for students, and through my twenty years of experience, I trust the research: Building strong relationships with them will help them succeed."

Ethos: *Here is an experienced teacher who cares about her students. She has been in the field for over twenty years and applies research to her practice. You can trust her.*

Pathos: *The current pandemic has been difficult for students. She is appealing to emotions.*

Logos: *Research shows that building relationships is key to teaching students.*

What Are Logical Fallacies?

Philosopher and author Julian Baggini once said, "Rhetoric is simply the use of language to persuade, and it can be used to persuade us of falsehoods as well as truths." Appeals can be used to build strong arguments, but if they are misused, they can also trick, manipulate, and mislead.

Consider this: It is to an advertiser's benefit to use appeals to manipulate us into buying products we don't really need or convince us that their product is superior. But as a consumer, we need to be careful of these messages and not be swayed easily or conned. Politicians may also benefit from using these appeals to win votes; however, as an educated citizen, it is helpful to recognize the difference between truth and dishonesty in order to select the best candidate for the people.

You will learn about a few logical fallacies to help you make wise choices in the future. Logical fallacies are flawed arguments. You should avoid them in your writing and challenge them when they appear.

Appeal to Fear

"Don't sit close to the TV, or you will strain your eyes." "Don't step on a crack, or you will hurt your mother's back." "Don't swallow gum, or it will stick on your stomach lining." "If you eat too much candy, your teeth will rot and fall out." People try to steer us by making us afraid. Parents, especially, use fear tactics to keep their children in line. Appeal to fear is when a claim is meant to make the audience afraid. However, appeals to fear are faulty because they are often not true or lack evidence to be taken seriously.

Appeal to Vanity

"You're my favorite teacher. Any chance I'll get an A this quarter?" When you try to flatter someone to get your own way, you are appealing to vanity. An appeal to vanity will play into the audience's pride or self-esteem to convince. Most people want to be liked; they want to feel appreciated; they want to be attractive; they want to be respected. When you dole out compliments for potential gain, you are appealing to vanity.

Appeal to Patriotism

As an American, you love your country, but sometimes you might have a different opinion about the best way to show your pride. An appeal to patriotism is when the speaker claims something specific is what makes one feel and look patriotic. Sometimes a jeep ad will sport an American flag: If you buy this jeep, you are a true American. Sometimes a politician will say if you support this bill, you value America. Pledging allegiance to the flag is viewed as being patriotic. However, these arguments are faulty. One's own beliefs about being a patriot are not the truth.

Appeal to Novelty

It seems each year a new model of the iPhone is released. My son begs for the latest edition of Xbox. My shampoo bottle changes with the new, improved formula. Appeal to novelty occurs when it is assumed that something is better or correct simply because it is new or modern. Recently, my kids received a new board game that was the modernized version of the classic, and we all hated the upgrades. A month ago, we went to our favorite restaurant only to be disappointed by the menu changes. Our favorite items were just not the same. My favorite mascara claims to lengthen lashes 2x the amount as before, but the new version just doesn't work as well. Just because something is new does not mean it is better.

Appeal to Popularity

Have you ever tried to win an argument with your parents by saying, "It's not fair. Everyone is doing it!" It's a faulty argument to believe that something is right just because many people support it, buy it, love it, or do it. Appeal to popularity or bandwagon appeal is a form of peer pressure. *Ad populum* is a Latin phrase meaning an appeal to the public or community. Widespread support does not make it right.

Appeal to Tradition

On Christmas Eve every year, I beg my mother to make small changes to the menu. We are Italian, and my mother has always prepared seven fish to celebrate. However, she puts out too much food, spends too much time on her feet cooking, and spends a fortune on groceries. Although each dish is delicious, there is a great deal of waste. We plead with her each year to cut back, but she refuses. "I've always done it this way," she argues. Appeal to tradition occurs when it is assumed something is better or correct because it is traditional.

EXERCISES

EXERCISE 7.1

Read the following short text and complete a SOAPSTONE, analyzing the rhetorical situation.

After assigning a task in class recently, one of my students asked me, "Will this be graded?" Whether given classwork or a formal response to complete, many of my students often consider how much energy, effort, and thought they should give to their work based on whether the work will be graded and how many points they will earn. As a veteran educator, I wish I didn't have to assign grades at all. I wish I could motivate my students to learn simply because of their need to be educated and informed citizens of the world. This need *should be enough.*

Samantha Yamashita, a young writer, argues that education is a privilege. For example, in many parts of the world, children are denied education because they cannot afford the school fees, are prohibited because of class or gender, or cannot safely attend due to war and other unfortunate factors. According to the World Bank, there are over 260 million children worldwide without access to education. In Syria alone, "over 1.8 million children were left without education in 2013" (World Bank). American students should understand that going to school is a luxury that many cannot attain. Learning should not be dependent on earning good grades but rather on having the desire to understand the world. Students should be engaged because they care.

Subject: What is the main idea of the piece? What is this piece about?	
Occasion: Is there an occasion for this piece? Is the speaker reacting to an event? Is this a current controversy? Is it a holiday?	
Audience: Who is the target audience? Men? Women? Adults? Teens? Parents? Teachers? Politicians? The general public?	
Purpose: What is the speaker's argument? What does the speaker claim? What is the speaker's position about the issue?	
Speaker: Who is the speaker? What do you know about them?	
Tone: How is the speaker feeling about the subject? Angry? Frustrated? Encouraged? Sympathetic? Sarcastic? Humorous? Serious?	
Three Examples of Tone: Find three sentences or words that show the speaker's tone.	1. 2. 3.

EXERCISE 7.2

Use the Coca-Cola ad to answer the following questions.

Source: https://www.wikiwand.com/en/Nixey
_Callahan

1. What does the ad claim about Coca-Cola?
   a. Drinking Coca-Cola will make you an athlete.
   b. Drinking Coca-Cola will make you well-liked.
   c. Drinking Coca-Cola will help you maintain your athletic performance.
   d. Drinking Coca-Cola will help your appearance.

2. Who is most likely the intended audience for this advertisement?
   a. Teenagers
   b. Athletes
   c. Managers of the Chicago White Sox
   d. J. J. Callahan and King George V

3. What is the subject of the ad?
   a. Baseball
   b. Coca-Cola
   c. J. J. Callahan
   d. The Chicago White Sox

4. Who is the speaker of the ad?

    a. Coca-Cola

    b. J. J. Callahan

    c. King George V

    d. The Chicago White Sox

5. What is the tone of this ad?

    a. Discouraging

    b. Humorous

    c. Admiring

    d. Comforting

6. This advertisement relies on which of the following appeals?

    a. Ethos

    b. Logos

    c. Pathos

    d. All of the above

7. The endorsement of a well-known athlete is an appeal to which of the following?

    a. Ethos

    b. Logos

    c. Pathos

    d. All of the above

8. Which of the following logical fallacies appear in this ad?

    a. Appeal to patriotism

    b. Appeal to novelty

    c. Appeal to fear

    d. Appeal to tradition

9. "The first ball used in the game recently played before King George V was tossed by the king to James Callahan." This line in the ad is an appeal to which of the following?

    a. Ethos

    b. Logos

    c. Pathos

    d. All of the above

10. What does Coca-Cola wish to persuade its audience of by featuring J. J. Callahan on this advertisement?

    a. If a well-respected athlete believes in Coca-Cola, it must be good.

    b. If others drink Coca-Cola, they too will be famous.

    c. If others drink Coca-Cola, they too will be able to sting the ball when they are 40.

    d. If you drink Coca-Cola, you will be fit to meet royalty.

EXERCISE 7.3

Identify the appeals: ethos, logos, or pathos (appeals can overlap).

1. Over one hundred dentists approve White Gel toothpaste.

   _____

2. I grew up in this town, so I know what's best. _____

3. According to Ethnologue, Chinese (and all of its varieties, such as Mandarin and Wu) is by far the most spoken language across the world, with 1.31 billion speakers. _____

4. You've known me my whole life, and you should trust me.

   _____

5. As a mother, I know what is best for my children.

   _____

6. If you climb that tree, you will fall and get seriously hurt!

   _____

7. Studies show that people who read fiction tend to be more empathetic.

   _____

8. Approximately 6.3 million companion animals enter U.S. animal shelters nationwide every year. _____

9. As your doctor, I recommend that you take daily vitamins.

   _____

10. Don't be the only person on the block with an untreated lawn.

    _____

EXERCISE 7.4

Identify the logical fallacy: fear, patriotism, popularity, vanity, novelty, or tradition.

1. You are so good at solving these equations! Can you help me with mine?

   _____

2. Don't be the only student at home! Come to the Halloween Howl!

   _____

3. If you love your country, wear red, white, and blue to support the troops!

   _____

4. The remake of *Spider-Man* is the best action movie yet.

   _____

5. Our school athletes have always worn their uniforms on Fridays. Let's keep the spirit alive! _____

6. Look how good you look in that car. You need to buy it.

   _____

7. Everyone in our family goes to Brown University, so you must too.

   _____

8. All your friends are voting for Sarah for class president, so you should too. _____

9. You're such a great friend. Any chance I catch a ride with you to the game? _____

10. My father is on the board of education. I think you can give me an A.

   _____

EXERCISE 7.5

Read the following excerpt from an argument essay, and respond to the following questions.

When I was in middle school, I begged my mother to take me to Glamour Shots, a well-known photography studio in our local mall. I was thirteen years old, and all of my friends were having their pictures taken there. The studio was known for making their subjects look like professional models. The portraits were too expensive for my parents to afford, but even still, they were very practical and probably had much better ways to spend their money than waste it on a sixty-minute photo shoot for their eighth-grader.

"Why do you even want these photos anyway?" my mother asked. Well, of course, all of the cool girls at school were posing for their shots there. At lunch, they'd pull out the glossy photos of themselves all made over, makeup and hair perfectly styled. They looked so gorgeous it took my breath away. So I guess it was the usual adolescent draw: I wanted to be trendy and popular too, but also, who wouldn't want to look perfect and flawless like a cover girl splashed across the front page of the latest teen magazine? Back in the '80s, I longed to look just like those thin, long-legged, Levi's-jeans-wearing goddesses that graced the covers of *Sassy* and *Seventeen*. Cindy Crawford, Elle Macpherson, and Brooke Shields were goddesses to me, and the attempt—at any cost—to transform into them for even an hour was tempting.

I never liked the photos my family took of me. I wasn't photogenic, and I cringed anytime I saw the prints after my mother developed them at the photo booth. I felt fat. I hated the angles in my permed hair. I hated my braces. In essence, I hated the natural me. Somehow I believed Glamour Shots could capture me in a way my parents couldn't. In their studio I would finally be beautiful under their magical lens.

Although I never got the chance to take those photos, I was recently reminded of Glamour Shots when I was on TikTok. A young woman was showing her image before and after with a filtering app called Beauty Filter. Filters are defined as "preset edits that can change and enhance your appearance." I was equally impressed and concerned. On one hand, this was the chance to have the Glamour Shots ability at one's fingertips; however, as an adult and mother, I was worried. What messages do these filters send young people today, and what will be some of the devastating effects to our children's self-esteem, body image, and confidence with their ability to change their appearance with a simple tap of a screen? Poutier lips? Tap. Higher cheekbones? Tap. Different eye shade or hair color? Tap. Instantly thin? Tap. Flawless skin? Tap. Symmetrical features? Tap.

As a young girl, I had the same desire to be anyone but myself, so I understand the urge to use the filters and, I am sure, would have done the same if I had the opportunity. Yet, to what extent will the availability of filters hurt today's youth? Will these apps affect how young people view their bodies? Filters on social media can negatively affect today's youth, leading to insecurity and body dysmorphia. In the article "Selfies, Filters, and Snapchat Dysmorphia: How Photo-Editing Harms Body Image," cosmetic surgeon Neelam Vashi explains, "People can take a photo of themselves and, in an instant, manipulate it. That makes a change feel more real and attainable" (Fagan, 2020).

1. In this excerpt, what does the writer argue?
   a. Teenagers should not use social media.
   b. Filters can negatively impact the way people view themselves.
   c. TikTok is responsible for body dysmorphia.
   d. Photo sessions at Glamour Shots are more popular today than ever.

2. Who might be the intended audience?
    a. Teenagers
    b. People who use filters
    c. Parents
    d. All of the above

3. What is the subject of the piece?
    a. TikTok
    b. Glamour Shots
    c. Filters
    d. Teenagers

4. What is the tone of the piece?
    a. Celebratory
    b. Critical
    c. Defensive
    d. Whimsical

5. Which statement would appeal to logos?
    a. In the article "Selfies, Filters, and Snapchat Dysmorphia: How Photo-Editing Harms Body Image," cosmetic surgeon Neelam Vashi explains, "People can take a photo of themselves and, in an instant, manipulate it. That makes a change feel more real and attainable" (Fagan, 2020).
    b. As a young girl, I had the same desire to be anyone but myself, so I understand the urge to use the filters and, I am sure, would have done the same if I had the opportunity.
    c. I never liked the photos my family took of me.
    d. "Why do you even want these photos anyway?" my mother asked.

6. Which statement would be an appeal to pathos?
   a. Although I never got the chance to take those photos, I was recently reminded of Glamour Shots when I was on TikTok.
   b. Filters are defined as "preset edits that can change and enhance your appearance."
   c. I wasn't photogenic, and I cringed anytime I saw the prints after my mother developed them at the photo booth.
   d. The studio was known for making their subjects look like professional models.

7. Which statement would be an appeal to ethos?
   a. As a young girl, I had the same desire to be anyone but myself, so I understand the urge to use the filters and, I am sure, would have done the same if I had the opportunity.
   b. So, I guess it was the usual adolescent draw: I wanted to be trendy and popular too, but also, who wouldn't want to look perfect and flawless like a cover girl splashed across the front page of the latest teen magazine?
   c. On one hand, this was the chance to have the Glamour Shots ability at one's fingertips; however, as an adult and mother, I was worried.
   d. All of the above

8. What is the occasion of the piece? What event prompted the author to write?
   a. The writer went to Glamour Shots and took pictures.
   b. The writer recently took a selfie and used a filter.
   c. The writer was recently on TikTok and noticed people using filters.
   d. The writer was diagnosed with body dysmorphia.

9. What would be the tone of this passage?

    When I was in middle school, I begged my mother to take me to Glamour Shots, a well-known photography studio in our local mall. I was thirteen years old, and all of my friends were having their pictures taken there. The studio was known for making their subjects look like professional models. The portraits were too expensive for my parents to afford, but even still, they were very practical and probably had much better ways to spend their money than waste it on a sixty-minute photo shoot for their eighth-grader.

    a. Reflective

    b. Angry

    c. Enthusiastic

    d. Formal

10. How would you describe the shift in tone?

    Although I never got the chance to take those photos, I was recently reminded of Glamour Shots when I was on TikTok. A young woman was showing her image before and after with a filtering app called Beauty Filter. Filters are defined as "preset edits that can change and enhance your appearance." I was equally impressed and concerned. On one hand, this was the chance for anyone to have the Glamour Shots ability at one's fingertips; however, as an adult and mother, I was worried. What messages do these filters send young people today, and what will be some of the devastating effects to our children's self-esteem, body image, and confidence with their ability to change their appearance with a simple tap of a screen? Poutier lips? Tap. Higher cheekbones? Tap. Different eye shade or hair color? Tap. Instantly thin? Tap. Flawless skin? Tap. Symmetrical features? Tap.

    a. Intrigued to concerned

    b. Angry to calm

    c. Defensive to aggressive

    d. Impartial to humorous

Flashcard App

NOTES

8 The Writing Process

MUST KNOW

⚡ Writing has many purposes.

⚡ Writing is a process.

⚡ The steps of the writing process include planning, drafting, sharing, revising, editing, and publishing.

The first part of this book explored what middle schoolers need to know about reading. Now it's time to shift our attention to writing, a big component of any English language arts (ELA) class.

In your earliest days of school, your elementary teachers taught you the foundations of good writing. In this chapter, we will review some of those concepts but also expand your understanding of what it means to write for a purpose and the authentic steps writers take in their craft.

What Are the Purposes of Writing?

Author's Purpose: When I was in middle school, I kept a diary. Each night before I went to bed, I would write about my experiences throughout the day, my encounters with my peers and teachers, and my reflections about myself and others. Why did I do this? you may ask. Tracking my daily thoughts and musing brought me comfort. The diary was a way to express myself and manage my feelings at an age when I felt the most change and insecurity. The diary writing made me feel safe and secure.

There are many reasons for us to write. It seems like in school you are writing all the time. Different classes expect you to write for different reasons. Maybe you are writing a letter to an author after you read a book in your ELA class. Maybe you are writing a report about a famous sculptor for your art teacher. Maybe you are writing an email to your teacher to ask questions about an upcoming assignment. Maybe you are comparing and contrasting two historical events in social studies. Outside of school, you might compose a text or write in your personal journal or diary. Writing has many different purposes. An author's purpose is the reason for writing.

It is important to know the purpose for writing because your purpose leads you to the form you will take, the organization pattern you will use, the style you will adopt, and the length you will write. Will you need supporting evidence? Will you need to add description? Well, that all depends on your purpose! Some purposes include evaluating, describing, comparing, analyzing, reflecting, and creating.

Although there are many purposes for writing, here are three main ones to know for ELA:

- Inform: to teach or enlighten the reader

- Entertain: to amuse the reader

- Persuade: to convince the reader to do, think, or believe something

Here are some formats writers can use to achieve their purposes:

Inform	Entertain	Persuade
Nonfiction	Comics	Letters
Essays	Short stories	Essays
Reports	Poems	Cartoons
News stories	Songs	Advertisements
Manuals	Fiction	Speeches
Letters	Plays	Reviews
Articles	Film scripts	Editorials
Blogs	Myths	Proposals
Newsletters	Fables	Brochures

What Is the Writing Process?

Writing Process: When I was your age, I dreamt of becoming a writer—the next Beverly Cleary or Judy Blume (two popular writers whom I adored). I would dream up new story ideas in my head, draft first chapters on an old word processor, and once I even gave my sixth-grade teacher a one-hundred-page manuscript to read!

For my thirteenth birthday, my aunt bought me a silver pen from Tiffany and Co. with faith that I would one day be a published author. However, over time I began to doubt my abilities. I would read classics such as *The Great Gatsby* by F. Scott Fitzgerald and *The Sun Also Rises* by Ernest Hemingway, and I would compare myself to these literary geniuses. How could I possibly write a book? *I am not talented like they are,* I thought. *I am not a writer.*

Instead, I became a teacher, and it wasn't until I started teaching writing that I learned about the writing process: the steps all writers take to generate a piece of writing. In my youth, I somehow believed a misconception: Writers sit down and write a book, and it's immediately great. They are so blessed with the gift of writing that writing is easy for them. I couldn't have been more wrong! Yes, many writers are born with a gift, but writing is challenging for even the best of writers. All writers struggle!

I wish I had learned this lesson much earlier, but I am glad to teach my students that writing is a series of steps. Writers go through multiple steps before they are satisfied.

> **BTW**
>
> *All writers have their own personal process of writing. The writing process is flexible. Writers often go back and forth between the various stages.*

What Are the Steps in the Writing Process?

Brainstorming: Coming up with a topic is always a struggle for my students. Brainstorming is the first step for any writing task. This initial stage helps you generate ideas. When you brainstorm, don't rule any idea out. It's okay to dismiss an idea later on, but at this point keep thinking! Ask yourself, "What do I want to achieve? Who is the intended audience? What structure do I want to use?"

There are various ways to brainstorm: Jot ideas on a piece of paper, share some ideas with a friend, look at models for inspiration. Sometimes it's helpful to make a chart or use a graphic organizer. Sometimes it's helpful to outline your ideas before you draft.

I always remind my students to choose a topic that is meaningful to them. When you write from the heart, with passion and enthusiasm, it makes the writing process easier. If you don't care about your topic, you will be less invested, and your indifference will come across in your writing.

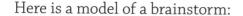

Here is a model of a brainstorm:

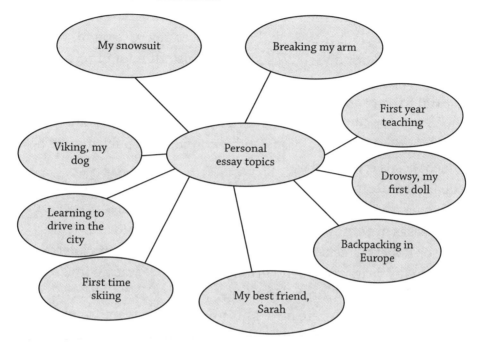

Drafting: Writer Anne Lamott once said, "All good writing begins with terrible first efforts. You need to start somewhere." Most writers consider drafting the messy phase. My students put too much pressure on themselves when they draft. They want their writing to be perfect immediately.

Drafting is a place to get your initial ideas down, take risks, and make mistakes! When my students draft, I tell them not to worry about grammar, punctuation, or word choice just now. It's more important to just write as much as you can.

When you draft, this is your first attempt. If you worry too much during the drafting stage, you may freeze up and not accomplish much. If you stop worrying about being perfect the first time around and get that pen moving or those fingers typing, you will have a lot of material to use versus a blank page. Remember, a draft is supposed to be imperfect. You will have grammar, spelling, and punctuation mistakes. There will be ideas that need more development. You will have to add more details or provide more support. That's why some refer to it as the rough draft.

Sharing: Throughout this book, I have shared my passion for cooking. It is rare that I cook for myself. When I cook it is often for others—my husband, my kids, my friends, and guests. With any art form, it seems only natural to want to share our creations with an audience. Writing is no different. Writers seek someone they trust to read their work and provide feedback. Whether this is a close friend, a confidant, a publisher, or a writer's group, feedback is critical to writing.

Feedback is information that can help someone improve. Feedback does not have to be negative and overly critical. It often includes praise for the successful areas of your writing and suggestions to improve.

Professor Robert Greene was a professor of journalism at Hofstra University many years ago when I attended there. He was an investigator for the New York City Anti-Crime Committee, and he was a successful reporter and editor for *Newsday*, where he led his investigative team to two Pulitzer Prizes in his career. To the journalism world, he was a celebrated writer who pioneered revolutionary journalistic techniques. To me, he was simply the journalism professor who delivered the first B+ of my academic career.

As an inspiring writer, I had always dreamt of seeing my byline in the *New York Times* or the *Washington Post*. With my pen from Tiffany and Co. in tow, I had written faithfully for my high school literary magazine and was an editor of the school newspaper, *The Phoenix.* I received praise from my peers and awards from my teachers. A grade of B+ left me riddled with self-doubt. As an immature eighteen-year-old in my first year of college, I didn't yet see the value of feedback and how it was essential to my growth as a writer.

Let's look at a first draft of an essay:

One reason Halloween should be moved to the weekend is because more parents would be able to supervise. When Halloween is on a weekday, families are in a rush. Kids must get home from school. Parents must get home from work. Sometimes parents might not get home until late. Everyone is rushing around and, oftentimes, kids are sent out to trick-or-treat on their own. When kids are on their own, their safety can be put at risk. Kids might be too trusting. They might go inside a stranger's home. They might even cause problems too. They might egg cars and homes. In addition, they might be reckless, crossing streets without watching carefully and not paying attention to passing cars. "Forty-three percent increased risk of a pedestrian death—about four extra children are killed trick-or-treating." They might even eat their Halloween stash without having parents check the candy over carefully. This is why moving Halloween to a weekend would keep children more safe.

Let's look at some feedback:

Revision: Have you ever looked at your work from when you were younger and HATED it? Maybe your parents saved an old piece of writing from your elementary school years. When you look at the work now with fresh eyes, do you cringe? I bet you can see how much you have grown as a writer and what you still needed to learn back then!

All great writers are dissatisfied with their first attempts at writing, and I wish I had realized this myself long ago! If I had, I might have not been so hard on myself as a student. *New York Times* writer Frank Bruni wrote, "smooth seas do not make skillful sailors."

Revision is my favorite stage, the one where the magic happens in writing. It's a common misconception that revision is merely correcting grammar and fixing spelling mistakes. Revision means to *re-see* or *look again*. In this stage, a writer goes through the draft, making changes. Part of revision is rewriting. Oftentimes, writers will rewrite many passages, tweak sentences, add details, and rearrange and reorder ideas. Even the best of writers revise!

Here are some ways to revise:

- Develop more: Add an anecdote, provide examples, use more evidence, add more research.

- Delete unnecessary or redundant parts.

- Change words: Make language stronger, more vivid.

- Revise sentences, combine sentences, add variety.

- Make a comparison.

- Show the causes or the effects.

- Add descriptive language.

- Show versus tell.

- Explain a process.

- Provide a definition.

- Add voice! *True, This clearly shows, I would say, I have to admit, Honestly, Why wouldn't we? Sure, Of course, Most of us would like to think, It is unlikely that, That's not to say, etc.*

John Green, the author of young adult (YA) hits *Looking for Alaska, The Fault in Our Stars*, and *Turtles All the Way Down*, shares that the most challenging part of the writing process for him is revision. He explains what happens when he writes:

Sometimes I will get to that point of realizing the story is terrible, and I'll think, "You know, I think I can plow through to an end here. And then I make it to the end of the draft a few months later. I'll still have to delete most of that draft in revision, and rewrite and rewrite and rewrite and rewrite before I have a book.

IRL Did you know Ernest Hemingway rewrote his last page of *A Farewell to Arms* thirty-nine times before he was truly satisfied with the wording?

Here is an example of revision from the previous essay:

One benefit for moving Halloween to a Saturday is the increased supervision this day would provide. On a weekday, many members of the community are at work and may not return until after dark. The Highway Data Loss Institute warns that the evening, "which ironically comes after so-called mischief night, can be very costly to homeowners" (Polanski). Unsupervised kids, especially teenagers, may use Halloween as an excuse to vandalize homes and cars. When I was in middle school, I remember seeing many teenagers roaming the streets, spraying colored shaving cream as they roamed quiet tree-lined streets and egged properties and vehicles, especially those in front of homes that were unattended. Gooey egg dripped from front porch doors and smeared across windowpanes. Although the teenagers may have thought their pranks were harmless, they did not realize the damage they left in their wake. According to AAA, "More vandalism claims are filed with insurance companies on Halloween than any other day of the year" (Polanski).

Besides causing havoc to our neighborhoods, kids who go trick-or-treating without their parents may also be put at risk. Unfortunately, when parents are at work during the week, they may have no other choice than to send their kids trick-or-treating on Halloween without them. Unattended kids could be reckless: talking to strangers; eating candy that is damaged, tampered with, or unsafe; or getting hurt when they cross streets carelessly without the help of an adult. Steven Reinberg, health day reporter for WebMD informs parents that "Trick-or-treating can quickly turn disastrous, with new research showing a more than 40 percent spike in pedestrian deaths on the spooky holiday." Reinberg further explains that the most dangerous time for kids to be crossing streets alone is around 6:00 pm. Evening is a dangerous time because drivers are rushing home from work, and kids are wearing dark costumes and walking between parked cars as they cross. They can't be easily seen. These factors contribute to the risk of death. Dr. Donald Redelmeier, a researcher at the

University of Toronto's Institute for Clinical Evaluative Sciences, estimates that there is a "Forty-three percent increased risk of a pedestrian death—about four extra children are killed trick-or-treating" (Reinberg). Clearly, if Halloween were moved to a Saturday permanently, supervision from community members and parents alike can make Halloween a much safer holiday for all involved. It just makes more sense!

Here are some examples of revision:

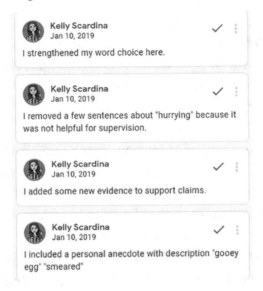

Editing: Writer and publisher Stephanie Roberts compares editing [fiction] to "using your fingers to untangle the hair of someone you love." When you edit any written work you are going through line by line to correct mistakes in spelling, fix punctuation, and adjust formatting and presentation. Teachers may call this step proofreading. This is the final step before publishing. It is a place to check that you have accomplished your purpose and that your work is clear and organized.

Here are some middle school blunders to correct:

- Capitalize the first word of each sentence.

- Capitalize proper nouns: names of specific people, places, things, products.

- Avoid text conventions in formal writing: i, u, btw, etc.

- Spell out a number if it is the first word in a sentence or a number is under nine. Use digits if the number is 10 or greater.

- Check to make sure you used the correct form of too, to, and two.

- Check to make sure you used the correct form of their, there, and they're.

- Don't forget to use spell check!

- Avoid run-on sentences, intentional fragments, and comma splices.

- Punctuate correctly: Use periods, commas, colons, and semicolons correctly.

- Avoid redundancy, ambiguity, and wordiness.

Publishing: Writer Ken Kesey noted, "When Shakespeare was writing, he wasn't writing for stuff to lie on the page; it was supposed to get up and move around." It's true: Shakespeare didn't write plays to be read. They were written to be performed. He wanted an audience. He wanted them to laugh, cry, question, wonder, react, and feel. Writers write for an audience in mind.

There are many ways to publish your work. Sometimes you will write for your teacher, sometimes you will write for a school newspaper or literary magazine, and sometimes you will write to share with your class. In my school, there is a writing celebration in which students share their writing in front of parents, teachers, and peers. Nothing is more rewarding than publishing your work.

BTW

Most teachers also provide rubrics that outline their expectations for your written work. When given a writing task, periodically check the rubric as you work through all the steps in the writing process to make sure you are meeting the guidelines provided and your work is aligned with these standards.

IRL There are many opportunities to share your writing outside of your classroom. A simple Internet search will yield dozens of places to submit your work for publication.

The *New York Times* Learning Network hosts many student writing contests each year for narrative writing, opinion writing, and cartoons.

Scholastic also offers essay contests.

The National PTA also offers a yearly Reflections writing contest.

Ask your teachers for more information.

EXERCISES

EXERCISE 8.1

1. Which of the following statements best defines the author's purpose?
    a. The author's reason for writing
    b. The initial brainstorm of ideas
    c. The topic of the piece
    d. The feedback an author hopes to receive

2. Why is it important for writers to know their purpose?
    a. A purpose gives the writing direction.
    b. A purpose influences the format and style of the writing.
    c. A purpose helps a writer shape the writing.
    d. All of the above

3. Why is the writing process useful?
    a. It can make the process manageable.
    b. You gain valuable feedback.
    c. You can grow as a writer.
    d. All of the above

4. Which is true about the writing process?
    a. A writer must follow each step in the correct order.
    b. A writer can go back and forth during the process.
    c. A writer must never deviate from the process.
    d. The process is valuable only to novice writers.

5. What are the purposes for writing?
   a. To inform
   b. To entertain
   c. To persuade
   d. All of the above

6. If you wrote a book review, your purpose for writing would most likely be which of the following?
   a. To inform
   b. To entertain
   c. To persuade
   d. To describe

7. If you wrote a poem, your purpose for writing would most likely be which of the following?
   a. To inform
   b. To entertain
   c. To persuade
   d. To analyze

8. In which stage would a writer correct the comma usage?
   a. Brainstorming
   b. Publishing
   c. Sharing
   d. Editing

9. In which stage would a writer most likely add repetition for emphasis?
   a. Brainstorming
   b. Publishing
   c. Revision
   d. Editing

10. What is one way a student can revise writing?
    a. Correcting spelling
    b. Fixing punctuation
    c. Adding descriptive words
    d. Capitalizing proper nouns

11. Revision includes which of the following?
    a. Substituting one word for another
    b. Adding voice
    c. Rearranging details in a paragraph
    d. All of the above

EXERCISE 8.2

1. In which of the following stages of the writing process would you most likely hear, "I like your character development, but your dialogue feels a bit unnatural for a teenager."
   a. Brainstorming
   b. Sharing
   c. Publishing
   d. Editing

2. This is an example of which stage of the writing process?

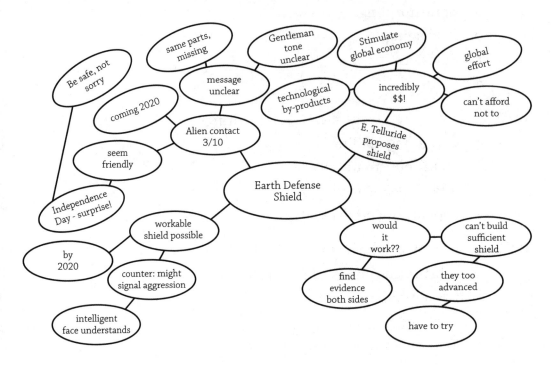

a. Editing
b. Sharing
c. Revising
d. Brainstorming

3. What would most likely be the purpose of this letter of recommendation?

   To Whom It May Concern:

   It is a pleasure to write a letter of recommendation for such a fine student as Krish Varghese. When he was a junior in my AP Language and Composition class last year, Krish was a fine student. He was responsible, reliable, and hardworking. Whether he had a reading assignment, homework, a project, or a presentation, Krish was always prepared for class. If he missed class, Krish always made sure that he contacted me by email or came to me on a free period to find out the work that he missed, to go over important information, or to pick up handouts. He made my class a priority, and he knew it was his responsibility to get the work.

   a. To entertain

   b. To instruct

   c. To inform

   d. To criticize

4. Which stage in the writing process is this writer?

   This fall, the United States experienced some of the consequences of global warming firsthand. California and bordering states experienced raging wildfires that were a direct result of our warming environment. The *New York Times* reported that "over 2 million acres" have been destroyed and Governor Gavin Newsome has called it a "state of emergency." ~~According to *BBC News*, the fires were the worst in eighteen years (McGrath).~~ Schools, buildings, and other infrastructure have been burnt and destroyed. According to *Junior Scholastic News*, "thousands have been hospitalized and 2,000 buildings have been destroyed."

   a. Publishing

   b. Revising

   c. Brainstorming

   d. Sharing

5. What is the intended purpose of this excerpt?

   This fall, the United States saw some of the consequences of global warming firsthand. California and bordering states experienced raging wildfires that were a direct result of our warming environment. The *New York Times* reported that "over 2 million acres" have been destroyed and Governor Gavin Newsome has called it a "state of emergency." According to *BBC News*, the fires were the worst in eighteen years (McGrath). Schools, buildings, and other infrastructure have been burnt and destroyed. According to *Junior Scholastic News*, "thousands have been hospitalized and 2,000 buildings have been destroyed." Scientists claim these fires are a direct result of the changing climate. They find climate change to play an "unequivocal and pervasive" part in the tragedy (McGrath). Thousands of people have been affected by "being driven from their homes" and there have been eighteen deaths (McGrath).

   a. To describe

   b. To entertain

   c. To inform

   d. To review

6. What is the author's purpose for the following writing?

   I began to plot and plan. *Maybe I would follow my sister's lead: forget to return the car one afternoon when she had to go to work. Maybe I would clean out the car and toss all her garbage and junk into the street. Maybe I would swipe $10 out of her dresser drawer where she kept her tips and use the money for gas.* Devious ideas began to fill my brain. I was determined to teach Stacy a lesson. During the year, she had stolen my license from my wallet and lost it, lent a favorite bathing suit to a friend and denied it, and *borrowed* an expensive outfit and ruined it. This incident was the last straw.

   a. To inform

   b. To persuade

   c. To entertain

   d. To review

7. What is the author's purpose for the following writing?

    If you were as enchanted as I by the life of Diana Spencer, a commoner who married into royalty and British scandal, capturing the heart of the world after her marriage to the future King of England, then Peter Morgan's *The Crown* is the next binge for you. The successful Netflix series portrays the harsh realities of living a life of privilege and exposes the truth to every girl who bought into the fantasy: Being a part of the royal family is not all that it's cracked up to be. In fact, it can be downright deadly.

    a.   To entertain the reader with a humorous story

    b.   To persuade the reader to watch *The Crown*

    c.   To inform the reader of the royal family's history

    d.   To describe Buckingham Palace to those who have never visited

8. After reading your friend's restaurant review in class, what revisions would you suggest?

    Everything on the menu is relatively reasonably priced, and if anything is more expensive, it's worth it. There is only a 20–30-minute wait for food unless the restaurant is packed. If there is a late delivery, the staff will usually contact you to mention that they are a little late. Everyone who works there is helpful.

    a.   Add some specific examples.

    b.   Rearrange the order of the details.

    c.   Take out the last line.

    d.   Add more details about the 20–30 minute wait.

9. Which stage of the writing process would a student benefit from by reviewing a rubric?

- Student writes a personal narrative which illustrates a theme.

- Student captures the reader's attention with a grabbing lead.

- Student develops the narrative with details and examples.

    a. During a brainstorm, the writer would make sure the topic is suitable for the purpose.

    b. During the drafting process, the writer would make sure to write an interesting introduction.

    c. During the revision process, the writer would make sure to support the theme with plenty of details.

    d. All of the above

Writing to Entertain

MUST KNOW

⚡ Use craft moves to reveal your purpose to your readers.

⚡ Show vs. tell when writing narratives.

⚡ Follow rules to write effective dialogue.

Writer Pat Conroy once said, "The most powerful words in English are, 'Tell me a story.'" People have always loved the power of stories. The history of the story goes back to early civilizations through oral storytelling and through drawings and images on cave walls. Stories were a way for people to keep a record of events, preserve culture, and pass along traditions. Although our methods of storytelling have evolved, one thing remains constant: Everyone has a story to tell. In this chapter, you will learn how to write for entertainment.

What Are Ways You Can Write to Entertain?

Writing to Entertain: If you want to entertain your audience, there are plenty of forms of writing to try. You can write a song. You can write a play or skit. You can write a poem. You can write a horror story. You can write a short story. The forms are endless. All you need is a bit of creativity and a wild imagination!

What Is Narrative Writing?

Narrative Writing is one of my students' favorite writing units. When you write a narrative, you get to use your imagination to create a character, establish a setting, and choose the conflict that the character faces. The character can be made up or you can be the character! Your setting can be a real place that you love or a fantastical place—a deserted planet, a kingdom of old, a futuristic planet. You can also write about yourself.

    Purpose: Sure, you're telling your story to entertain, but good personal narratives also have another intended purpose: Perhaps you want to share a lesson you learned, provide a moral to the reader, or express the way your views have changed. Your message will most likely be implied rather than stated. However, an effective writer uses craft moves to lead readers to the writer's intended purpose.

 **IRL** William Shakespeare wrote at least thirty-seven plays to entertain Elizabethan audiences. When he wrote, he made sure to please all the spectators who came to see his play—peasants, nobles, and even Queen Elizabeth herself! He had a talent for making sure he had a plot that was exciting, language that was witty, and characters who were moving so there was something for everyone to enjoy.

Craft Moves

Here are some craft moves narrative writers use to illuminate their purpose:

- Use description: Add sensory language.

- Shift time: Use a flashback or jump ahead in time.

- Create suspense: Keep your readers on their toes by withholding details until later.

- Add figurative language such as similes, metaphors, onomatopoeia, and personification.

- Choose a point of view: first person, second person, or third person.

- Establish a mood: Use words that produce a desired effect.

- Reveal character through actions, thoughts, appearance, and dialogue.

- Pick a setting that is meaningful to the story.

Personal Narrative: Most English language arts (ELA) teachers will ask you to write a personal essay about yourself. For this assignment, you will have to brainstorm a moment in your life that was meaningful to you. It will be impossible for you to write about everything you've experienced in two or three pages. Instead, you will focus on a small moment that was significant to you.

What Are Some Tips to Know for Writing a Personal Narrative?

Small Moments vs. Large Moments: When students brainstorm topics, they generally choose ones that are too large to cover in two or three pages. Because they try to squeeze a large topic down, the writing becomes too general, too rushed, and too superficial. Instead, try to find a small slice to zoom in on.

For example, one student wanted to write about her trip to India. She spent the first two pages writing about packing for the trip, the airplane ride, and arriving at her grandmother's home. She had already written half the paper, and she hadn't even begun writing about her trip to India. She only had a paragraph to squeeze in all the sites she visited, the wonderful food she ate, and the experiences she enjoyed. As a reader, I wasn't too interested in what she packed or what movie she watched on the plane. However, as I have never been to India myself, I would have loved to read more about her time there.

Here are some examples of ways to cut large moments down into smaller slices:

Large Topic	Small Slice
My trip to Disney World	Getting stuck on a ride
My summer at camp	The night of color war
My best friend in sixth grade	A funny sleepover
Getting a new dog	My dog's first haircut
Celebrating Christmas	One special gift

Avoid Cliché Topics: When I ask my students to write a personal essay, many of them tend to choose a cliché topic—an idea that is overused. After teaching over twenty years, I have read the same essay topic over and over: my summer at camp, my first time on a cruise, my trip to visit my grandparents, my dance recital. To be fair, I understand why students select these topics. After all, these events are big ones for most students. However, because most students have similar experiences, the essays are similar. I often tell my students a good personal essay is one that only *you* can write.

 IRL Even when we speak, we have the habit of using clichés—tired, stale phrases. You have probably heard these expressions too many times to count! Avoid them in your writing.

- You can't please everyone!
- Love is blind.
- There are other fish in the sea.
- Don't judge a book by its cover.
- The grass is always greener on the other side.

Here are some examples of good personal essay topics:

A special tradition that is unique to your family

An interesting experience that very few people experience

A game or activity that others would find unusual

A moment that changed you

An item you cherish

A personal achievement

A secret spot you enjoy

A collection you keep

Engaging Readers: Leads

Engaging Your Reader from the Start: The hook—the first few lines of your essay—should always grab your readers' attention and make them want to continue reading. The hook is often the most difficult part to write.

You want to give some essential details in the beginning without telling the whole story. The possibilities are endless, but there are a few types of leads to know.

Typical Lead: The word *typical* means ordinary, standard, common. Although a typical lead can help you get your ideas out, you should avoid this type of lead as it tells the reader the whole story up front, leaving little reason to read on. If you write a typical lead to start, be sure to revise it after.

Example: I was in sixth grade when my mother bought me a puffy, purple snowsuit for Christmas. It was hot and suffocating, and I begged and pleaded not to wear it. She made me feel guilty.

Action Lead: You do not have to start your story at the beginning. In fact, you should think of the most exciting event in your story and begin with an action. For example, you are running down the field, you are diving into the pond, you are skiing down the mountain, you are falling off your bike, or you are dropping to your knees.

Example: I lay on the cold concrete ground while the janitor hovered over me with his pliers. My peers in the classroom looked down at me with mild amusement as I stayed perfectly still like the teacher instructed. I wanted it off, and I wanted it off now.

Dialogue Lead: Instead of starting with action, many writers like to start their writing with dialogue, an interesting comment that you or person in the story says.

Example: "There's no way I am going to wear that!" I stubbornly insisted as I held the purple snowsuit up from the Christmas box from which it appeared. I was in sixth grade, and I knew from the moment I laid my eyes on the gift that my social life was over.

Reaction Lead: Another interesting approach is to show your inner thinking. Start your essay with the thoughts that were going through your mind at the time or the way you were feeling at the moment.

Example: No one can see me, I thought to myself as I hurried off the bus in search of a bathroom to hide in. I was going to take it off. I was going to leave it in the back of the stall for the day, and I was going to pretend I never had to wear it.

Mentor Texts: Everyone has a mentor, someone who has inspired you, helped you, or influenced you. Maybe it's a parent, or a teacher, or a coach, or an older cousin. An aspiring basketball player may look up to a professional player and try out some of their moves. A beginning cook might be influenced by a master chef and try some of their recipes. People learn from watching and imitating others. Writing is no different. Writers are inspired by other authors and texts they have read.

When looking for a way to start your own personal writing, looking at a mentor text can be helpful. Read other writers for writers' techniques.

Following are some examples of how I was influenced by popular young adult (YA) writers:

Mentor Text	My Writing
No parties, no shorts, no boys. These were my parents' cardinal rules. *Americanized: Rebel Without a Greencard?* by Sara Saedi	A puffy hat. A long scarf. A purple snowsuit. Could there be anything more embarrassing for a sixth-grader?
What I couldn't get out of my skull was the thought of their rough, grimy hands all over my clean sneaks. *The Stars Beneath Our Feet* by David Barclay Moore	What I couldn't stop seeing was my classmates' reactions, the way they jeered, the way they laughed, the way they pointed as I made my way down the hallway in my snowsuit.

 IRL Celebrities appreciate mentors too. The singer Eminem gives credit to Dr. Dre for mentoring him and inspiring his music. The classic artist Leonardo da Vinci was an apprentice to Andrea del Verrocchio, who passed along skills and techniques. Usher mentored Justin Bieber, and LeBron James makes it his mission to mentor young players.

Show vs. Tell: There's a popular saying, "Actions speak louder than words." When my boys act up at home, they are quick to say, "I'm sorry." Although I appreciate the apologies, after repeat occurrences their apologies start to lose their meaning. After a repeat occurrence, I'll finally give consequences. I tell them, "Don't tell me you are sorry. Show me by changing your behavior."

Good writing is similar: Don't tell your readers, show them. The Russian playwright Anton Chekhov makes this idea clear with this quote: "Don't tell me the moon is shining; show me the glint on the broken glass." Simply put: Telling is giving information; showing is bringing readers into the experience. Use sensory images and language so the readers can draw their own conclusions.

Here are some examples of telling vs. showing:

Telling Statements	Showing Statements
There was a terrible odor.	When I pulled out the garbage bag, I caught a whiff of the rancid tuna fish and moldy eggs left from their lunch last week.
My teacher was angry.	Red faced, my teacher stood glaring at us while she tapped her foot repeatedly.
It was a scary place.	The abandoned house was dark, and as we made our way into the foyer, the floorboards creaked and mice scampered before us.
My sister was nervous on stage.	From our seats in the audience, we could see my sister's lips tremble and her knees shake.

Here are some sensory adjectives to help you show vs. tell:

Taste	Touch	Sight	Sound	Smell
bitter	silky	fragile	banging	sweet
tart	satiny	bright	clashing	perfumed
delicious	shaggy	glowing	moaning	musty
savory	cuddly	luminescent	roaring	stale
gooey	prickly	polished	buzzing	rotten
creamy	bumpy	misty	wailing	stinky
juicy	gritty	curved	lulling	spicy
nutty	dusty	chunky	hoarse	salty
peppery	dirty	plaid	muted	medicinal
salty	filthy	sheer	popping	mild
rotting	throbbing	towering	snapping	rich
pickled	tight	crooked	deafening	bitter
tangy	firm	scrawny	howling	salty
smoked	greasy	slender	snarling	spicy

Dialogue: At this age, you have learned about dialogue, when a character speaks and has a conversation with another character in the story, but there are many ways to make your dialogue more effective.

- **Be brief:** Use dialogue sparingly. Many of my student writers overdo dialogue. They have characters speak back and forth frequently throughout their piece. This use of dialogue tends to be repetitive and boring for the reader. Consider what is the most important or interesting comment to include. Does it shed light on a conflict? If the dialogue does not have a purpose, then remove it.

- **Be purposeful:** Consider why you want to use dialogue at this point in the story. Ask yourself: What does the dialogue accomplish? Does it provide background information? Does it drive the plot forward? Does it add suspense? Does it reveal character?

- **Be authentic:** Consider the speaker's character. What would that character actually say, and how would that character say it? Often, little children may whine, speak incorrectly, or speak in one-word responses. Often a teenager will speak differently to friends than to parents. Often a teacher will speak more formally than a student. Often a foreigner might have an accent or speak a combination of two languages. It is okay to let a character speak in a natural voice.

Punctuating Dialogue: I am always amazed at how many students do not know how to punctuate dialogue by middle school. Let's review some rules to know:

- **Use quotation marks:** Quotation marks go around anything a character says.

  "Stop! You're going to get hurt!" the teacher screamed as she sprinted across the playground.

BTW

If you want to make a character sound more realistic, you can try to capture their dialects when they speak. A dialect is the language of a particular region. If your characters are from New York, they might speak differently than your characters from Texas or North Dakota.

- **Use a dialogue tag:** Be sure that you identify the speaker of the dialogue and show how the dialogue was spoken:

  "Stop! You're going to get hurt!" **the teacher screamed** as she sprinted across the playground.

- **Use a comma before and after a dialogue tag:**

  "Stop! You're going to get hurt," the teacher repeated.
  The teacher repeated, "Stop, you're going to get hurt."

- Use correct punctuation marks depending on the nature of your sentence:

  "Over there!" a student shouted as he pointed to Nick hanging from the bars.
  "I wonder," the student began to mutter, "if Nick is okay on the monkey bars?"

- **Indent each new speaker:** Each time a new character speaks in the same paragraph, you must indent and start a new line.

As Nick tried to master the monkey bars, he seemed shaky. He had a hard time moving from one bar to another, and it appeared as if he would fall. The teacher called to him from across the playground. Nick ignored her. "Did you hear me?" the teacher screamed as she approached.

"No," replied Nick as he continued to struggle.

"Stop! You're going to get hurt!" the teacher screamed.

BTW

Use vivid dialogue tags. Choose dialogue tags that help characterize the speaker or provide insight into their feelings, emotions, or mood. Try words besides said.

For example: hollered, fretted, sobbed, blubbered, whispered, lectured, scolded, ordered, accused, attacked, criticized, threatened, etc.

Let's look at a piece of a narrative essay:

While helping clean out my parents' attic the other day, my youngest sister asked my mother the same question she has been asking my mother all these years: "Hey, how come you made so many photo albums for Kelly and there are none of me?"	The writer grabs the audience's attention with an action lead.
It's the same question that *always* comes up each time we go into my mother's attic to rummage for old photos, find relics of our childhood, or locate items we hope she has saved for us for "when we had kids of our own."	The writer uses brief dialogue here to reveal the youngest sister's jealousy of her older sibling.
Each time, one my two fully grown sisters or my brother will irritably hold up the five glossy albums in bold reds and greens and laced in gold trim with labels clearly indicating *Kelly Age 1, Kelly Age 2, Kelly Age 3*, and so on, and then point to his or her own random photos thrown haphazardly together in one unorganized Ziploc bag.	The writer uses description— "glossy albums," "bold reds and greens," "laced in gold trim"—to show the time and attention an oldest child will often get compared to younger siblings.
Each time, my mother will patiently explain that as more children were born, her life became *just too hectic* to keep up with sorting and organizing photos to scrapbook their lives. This explanation rarely brings any comfort to my three younger siblings, who flip through the pages of my albums and see my mother's neat handwriting documenting every moment of my first few years of life.	The author's word choice in *flip* reveals the siblings' eagerness to find a photo of themselves. They are moving quickly and are clearly frustrated.
Each photo screams, "Look! There is Kelly getting her first haircut!" "Here is Kelly eating her first ice cream cone!" "Watch Kelly ride her first bike!" Meanwhile, my siblings can't even find a photo of the day they were born among those thrown together in the heap.	The writer uses specific examples to highlight the advantages her siblings believe she has because she is firstborn.
Yes, my mother always *meant* to shower my siblings with the same doting attention that she gave me, but with four kids running amok, undivided attention for four was just not possible. And although my brother and sisters have spent their years whining and complaining that the oldest child leads a charmed life, they have yet to see the drawbacks that being the eldest child brings!	The writer uses the word *amok* to show how challenging it is for parents of large families to accomplish much.
All my life, I have always felt the burden of being a role model. I always did what my parents told me. I never really rebelled, stepped out of line, or tested the waters. When my parents told me to be home at a certain time, I kept curfew. When my parents asked me to eat my vegetables, I downed the dreaded broccoli and spinach that was perfectly portioned on my plate. And when my parents demanded good grades, I delivered!	The author uses the repetition of the word *when* to emphasize how the oldest child tends to follow rules.

All through my school years, I aced tests, won academic awards, and graduated high school with honors. Earning lower than an A+ on an assignment meant one thing: disgrace. On the rare occasion I earned a ninety-three instead of a ninety-five, my mother and I would tediously review the problem and make sure I didn't slip up again. On the other hand, when my siblings went to school, little by little my parents let their expectations crumble. If Samantha got Bs, my parents gave her money; if Ben got Cs, my parents were thrilled and bought him video games; and if Ella would just graduate, they promised to buy her a car! I couldn't believe it! I was furious! "What did I get for all my hard work and effort?" I wondered bitterly out loud to my mother when my sister sped away in her new wheels the week after she completed summer school and earned her diploma. At the time, hearing that they were proud of me just didn't seem to compare to my sister's new Toyota Camry.

> The author uses varied sentence structure for pacing: The long list of expectations feels overwhelming.

There were other disadvantages too. Being the first child meant that I missed out on many opportunities that my siblings took for granted. Because I was the first, my parents were afraid to let me sleep over at a friend's house. Instead, friends only slept at ours. My parents were also afraid to let me go to the mall with my friends. Instead, my mother trailed behind us as she pretended to be a window shopper. In addition, my parents were afraid to let me go on class trips in school. Instead, my mother would volunteer to be class mom so she could go too.

> The author uses compare/contrast to show the ways her upbringing compared to her siblings.

Out of fear, my parents were overprotective of me. I was their first, and each first experience was scary. And yet, by the time my siblings were ready to claim their independence, my parents had loosened up a bit, and one by one my siblings were allowed to assert themselves. Samantha was able to go to sleep-away camp by the time she was in fourth grade. Ben was able to take the bus to the beach with his friends, and he was only twelve. Finally, Ella's curfew in high school was midnight—and when I was in high school, I was in bed by ten!

Oh yes, life was certainly unfair to the oldest child. I was an experiment. They tested the rules on me and made adjustments along the way. They made many mistakes as they parented me and learned the error of their ways while they raised the others. Contrary to my siblings' beliefs, being the oldest was not all it was cracked up to be.

> Here is the author's purpose: Being the first child has its perks and disadvantages.
>
> Each craft move the author makes is intended to reveal this message to the reader.

EXERCISES

EXERCISE 9.1

Read the following personal narrative and answer the questions that follow.

> It was 8:00 p.m., and the car was not there.
> It was 8:05 p.m., and the car was not there.
> It was 8:10 p.m., and still, the car was not there.

As the minutes ticked by, my anger began to build, and my resentment toward my sister continued to smolder. In five-minute increments, I repeatedly pulled the sheer, white bedroom curtain aside to see if the red Chrysler Neon that we shared had returned. As per our agreement, when my parents leased the car for us, I would use the car Monday through Friday, 8:00 a.m. to 1:00 p.m., to go back and forth to my college classes, and Samantha would take the car afterward to go to work. This agreement seemed fair at the time: The car would be waiting out front with a full tank of gas by 1:30 each afternoon for her, and she would return the car to me the same way Sunday night at 8:00.

Yet, slowly but surely, I would leave for school in the morning and the Neon was nowhere to be found. I would impatiently wait inside the house fuming, while my sister pulled up to the curb later and later, giving me inadequate time to get to school. Most of the time, the car floor was littered with empty soda bottles and old, crinkled fast-food containers, and a green light flashed "tank empty" on the dashboard.

At first I sped away, muttering under my breath and giving attitude, calling her "irresponsible," "rude," and "selfish," but more and more, the tension between us began to mount. I would constantly complain to my parents about her careless behavior, pleading with them to intervene and mediate; however, even with my parents' threats and warnings, they were idle: My sister could not bring herself to return the car promptly with a full tank of gas.

I began to plot and plan. *Maybe I would follow my sister's lead: forget to return the car one afternoon when she had to go to work. Maybe I would clean out the car and toss all her garbage and junk into the street. Maybe I would swipe ten dollars out of her dresser drawer where she kept her tips and use the money for gas.* Devious ideas began to fill my brain. I was determined to teach Samantha a lesson. During the year, she had stolen my license from my wallet and lost it, lent a favorite bathing suit to a friend and denied it, and "borrowed" an expensive outfit and ruined it. This incident was the last straw.

Sunday evening, I watched and waited for her to return the car. By 8:30, I was convinced that she would keep the car all evening and, once again, I'd be scurrying to class in the morning. I was fed up. It wasn't fair that she was so inconsiderate. *Once again*, she'd probably forgotten to fill the tank, and *once again*, I'd have to reach in my pocket and buy the gas. Suddenly, I had an idea!

My best friend honked out front. Jen would drive me to my sister's job where she was waitressing. I would use my set of keys to drive the car home, leaving my sister stranded at work. She would have to ask around for a ride home, and she would finally understand how insensitive she had been all along. Realizing the error of her ways, she would apologize and beg for my forgiveness.

Or so I thought.

Sneakily, we looped around the restaurant's parking lot, circling to find the car. Once we spotted it, Jen pulled the car alongside to let me out. I slithered out of the passenger seat, key in hand, ready to claim my prize. Safely inside and fastened securely in my seat, I turned on the ignition and slowly backed out of the parking spot. As I put the car into drive, I heard a sudden thump and a frenzied banging against my driver's-side door. My sister, who had been about to leave work early, caught me red-handed. Chasing me across the lot, she caught up to me as I was about to peel away. She pressed her face against the window, screaming, "Stop!"

Taken off guard, I panicked and automatically locked the doors, preventing her from getting inside. Despite her desperate pleas, I once again threw the car into drive, quickly slamming my foot on the gas pedal, thrusting the car violently into the rear of the black Honda Accord idling in front of me. With a sudden thud, I came to the realization that in my haste, I had knocked the fender loose from the car in front of me, and my first car accident became a harsh reality. Embarrassed and deeply ashamed, I fumbled in the compartment box and retrieved my insurance card for the furious, red-faced driver who was already making his way to my car. Thus, I came to realize, among other lessons, if you kick a stone in anger, you'll hurt your own foot.

1. What seems to be the author's purpose for writing this personal narrative?
    a. To prove that sisters fight
    b. To suggest that parents don't understand sibling rivalry
    c. To advise the reader not to share with siblings
    d. To illustrate how revenge can backfire

2. The writer attempts to hook the reader's attention with which of the following leads?
    a. Typical
    b. Action
    c. Reaction
    d. Dialogue

3. In which of the following sentences does the writer show vs. tell?
    a. My best friend honked out front.
    b. My sister, who had been about to leave work early, caught me red-handed.
    c. She pressed her face against the window, screaming, "Stop!"
    d. Devious ideas began to fill my brain.

4. Why does the author isolate this sentence from the paragraph?

    Or so I thought.

    a. This sentence helps create suspense.

    b. This sentence does not belong in the paragraph before or after.

    c. This sentence is dialogue so it must be indented.

    d. This sentence indicates a shift in time.

5. Which details help the author develop the conflict?

    a. It was 8:10 p.m., and still, the car was not there.

    b. Sunday evening, I watched and waited for her to return the car.

    c. Devious ideas began to fill my brain. I was determined to teach Samantha a lesson.

    d. All of the above

6. What is most likely the intention of the author's repetition in the opening lines of the essay?

    It was 8:00 p.m., and the car was not there.
    It was 8:05 p.m., and the car was not there.
    It was 8:10 p.m., and still, the car was not there.

    a. The repetition emphasizes the speaker's impatience.

    b. The repetition establishes the setting.

    c. The repetition reveals character.

    d. The repetition includes imagery.

7. What does this sentence show about Samantha without telling?

    During the year, she had stolen my license from my wallet and lost it, lent a favorite bathing suit to a friend and denied it, and "borrowed" an expensive outfit and ruined it.

    a. Samantha is responsible.

    b. Samantha is inconsiderate.

    c. Samantha is organized.

    d. Samantha is rude.

8. I *slithered* out of the passenger seat, key in hand, ready to claim my prize.

   What does the word *slithered* suggest about the speaker at this moment?

   a. The speaker is acting sneaky.
   b. The speaker is anxious.
   c. The speaker is forgetful.
   d. The speaker is flexible.

9. By 8:30, I was convinced that she would keep the car all evening and, once again, I'd be *scurrying* to class in the morning.

   What does the word *scurrying* reveal to the audience?

   a. The speaker is happy the car is there.
   b. The speaker is suspicious of her sister.
   c. The speaker will have to hurry to class.
   d. The speaker is frustrated that the car is messy.

10. Why does the author include the following description of the car's interior?

   Most of the time, the car floor was littered with empty soda bottles and old, crinkled fast-food containers, and a green light flashed "tank empty" on the dashboard.

   a. To reinforce Samantha's thoughtless actions
   b. To show one more example of Samantha's inconsideration
   c. To emphasize how much fast food Samantha ate
   d. To reveal how expensive gas can be

EXERCISE 9.2

Read the following narrative writing, and answer the questions that follow.

Two hundred dollars! It was the first time I made that much all on my own, and I could not wait to save it. It was my first month working at my first job at Rosie's restaurant. I never imagined that I would be able to get a job at my age. I am only fifteen and don't have my working papers yet, but I got lucky. My friend knew the owner, and before I knew it, I was dressed in the black cotton t-shirt and a pair of tight jeans that I got my mom to buy me from the mall.

Suddenly, instead of spending my summer days lounging in the pool or shooting baskets with my friends on a hot, humid day, I was busing tables of greasy plates, crumpled white cloth napkins, and half-empty plates of fries and soggy burger buns. Trembling, I would try to carry trays of water glasses to the tables without stumbling or dropping anything on the smooth, freshly mopped floor. Although being a busboy can be tough, working has been a positive experience.

Each day I entered the restaurant, I could hear the clatter of forks against plates and happy chatter of restaurant guests as they caught up with each other after their busy week. Even though the restaurant played dinner background music, the roar of a group laughing at a high-top echoed from the corner. The banging of pans clamored from the open kitchen that overlooked the restaurant. From tables, I could see chefs sweat as they prepared dishes quickly for their customers to enjoy. I could hear orders being shouted to the other cooks too. Paul yelled, "I need that Caesar salad on the fly!" I could see waitresses and waiters standing at the hot window waiting patiently for their orders of green salads, steaming rice bowls, and platters of dumplings to be ready.

Sometimes it could be hard to concentrate. I'd show up for my shift at 10:00 a.m. just as the chefs were prepping, and I'd work until 4:00 p.m. My stomach would be starving. It would start to growl from the delicious aroma that filled the air. My mouth would water at the aromas of french fries steaming as they were lifted from the deep fryer or the flatbread pizzas being baked to a crisp in the oven. I am normally a very picky eater at home, but now that I have worked around delicious food, I have gotten brave and tried some new dishes, like glazed duck and sticky rice and beans.

When I worked for many hours, I looked forward to the fried chicken sandwich the boss offered me on the house at the end of my shift. The chicken, crispy fried and golden, was layered between spicy mayo, thick-sliced red tomato, and slightly toasted baguette bread. The fries on the side were salty with flaky white grains of sea salt. Hungry, I would devour the sandwich in the car when my parents picked me up like a seagull at the beach gulping leftovers in the trash. It felt like I swallowed it whole in one big gulp! I was an animal pouncing on my prey.

Sometimes I'm so tired I want to just fall into my big, fluffy bed immediately, but my uniform is filthy. The black clothes show everything. There are red ketchup stains and drink spills from sticky soda and juice on my clothes and pants from all of the busing. However, when I see my stiff check in the glossy white envelope and the green cash from tips, the hard work is worth it. Hopefully, I'll have enough to buy a used car in a few years. Although on my weekends I could be relaxing, sleeping in, and gaming, trips to the bank have been even more rewarding.

1. What is the author's purpose for writing this personal narrative?
   a. To argue why eating out is a great experience
   b. To encourage readers to get a job at a restaurant
   c. To show how working can be a rewarding experience
   d. To explain why everyone should try new food

2. How does the writer hook the reader's attention in the lead?
   a. The author shares his reaction.
   b. The author poses a question to the reader.
   c. The author starts with action.
   d. The author begins with a description.

3. Which sentence is an example of show vs. tell?
   a. Sometimes it could be hard to concentrate.
   b. Hopefully, I'll have enough to buy a used car in a few years.
   c. Sometimes it could be hard to concentrate.
   d. There are red ketchup stains and drink spills from sticky soda and juice on my clothes and pants from all of the busing.

4. What is the writer's intention for the repetition used in these lines?

   I could see chefs sweat as they prepared dishes quickly for their customers to enjoy. I could hear orders being shouted to the other cooks too. I could see waitresses and waiters standing at the hot window, waiting patiently for their orders of green salads, steaming rice bowls, and platters of dumplings to be ready.

   a. The repetition shows how hard the staff works.

   b. The repetition reveals the bustling mood of the restaurant.

   c. The repetition indicates the speaker is anxious.

   d. The repetition emphasizes the dangerous conditions.

5. What is the purpose of the following description?

   My mouth would water at the aromas of french fries steaming as they were lifted from the deep fryer or the flatbread pizzas being baked to a crisp in the oven. I am normally a very picky eater at home, but now that I have worked around delicious food, I have gotten brave and tried some new dishes, like glazed duck and sticky rice and beans.

   a. Working at the restaurant was rewarding because it gave the writer the opportunity to expand his palate.

   b. Working at the restaurant was hard because there were too many menu items to remember.

   c. Working at the restaurant was a good experience because the food smelled delicious.

   d. All of the above

6. What is the purpose of this metaphor? I was an animal pouncing on my prey.

   a. The writer shows that he is happy his shift is finally over.

   b. The writer describes a challenge with a customer.

   c. The writer is famished after his shift.

   d. The writer is exhausted and wants to pounce on his bed.

7. How has the writer been changed by his experience?
    a. The writer has become more responsible.
    b. The writer has learned to try new food.
    c. The writer has realized the value of hard work.
    d. All of the above

8. Which of the following lines contain descriptive language?
    a. Although being a busboy can be tough, working has been a positive experience.
    b. The fries on the side are salty with flaky white grains of sea salt.
    c. I could see chefs sweat as they prepared dishes quickly for their customers to enjoy.
    d. I could hear orders being shouted to the other cooks too.

9. What is the writer's purpose for including the following dialogue?
    Paul yelled, "I need that Caesar salad on the fly!"
    a. The dialogue reveals that customers are unhappy.
    b. The dialogue contributes to the busy atmosphere.
    c. The dialogue shows that the chefs are angry.
    d. The dialogue creates suspense.

10. Which of the following words is an example of onomatopoeia?
    a. Clatter
    b. Trembling
    c. Laughing
    d. Echoed

Flashcard App

NOTES

Writing to Inform

MUST⚡KNOW

⚡ Informational writing is fact based and communicates information to the audience.

⚡ It is important to understand the difference between fact and opinion.

⚡ One important characteristic of informational writing is research from credible sources.

You may not realize it now, but in the future, you will be writing to inform more than you think. Eventually, you will have to write a resume and a cover letter telling a future employer about yourself and your skills. Most professions will also require you to write to inform: emails, reports, memos, letters, and proposals. In this chapter, you will learn essential skills for informative writing.

What Are Some Characteristics of Informative Writing?

Informative writing is a different type of writing than narrative writing and persuasive writing, which can include the author's opinions and beliefs. Informative writing, on the other hand, has identifiable characteristics:

- It is fact based.

- It is logical.

- It has a clear purpose: to provide information.

- It is unbiased, not opinion based.

- It is written in a linear structure.

Research: Whether you are writing a report about sea lions, an article for the school newspaper, or a feature story on the new principal at your school, you will need to research. Research is a process of finding out more information about a topic in an organized way. It is important that you establish your credibility as a journalist. You want your audience to believe you. You must research your topic. Find facts, statistics, and experts from reliable sources. Your audience will trust you more if your sources are reliable.

Types of sources:

- Newspaper

- Magazine

- Book

- Journal

- Documentary

- Report

Credible sources include your school databases, Google Scholar, government websites, educational institutions, and professional organizations. Always check the date of publication. If a source is more than ten years old, the information may not be current or accurate. You should also check to see if there is a respected, well-known author listed. A librarian is a great person to help you locate sources and verify their validity.

You should avoid Wikipedia, commercial websites, blogs, outdated articles, and sources with anonymous or no authors. Also avoid any source that is not grammatically correct or includes spelling errors.

BTW

When you conduct research, there are two types of sources: primary and secondary.

A **primary source** gives original information. The source was created during that time. It is a writer's original manuscript. It is a hieroglyphic on a cave wall. It is a photograph. It is a letter. It is an immediate, firsthand account. Other examples include diary entries, original recordings, and original newspaper articles.

A **secondary source** comments on a primary source. The commentary could include summary, criticism, analysis, or interpretation. Some secondary sources are books, journals, dictionaries, and encyclopedias.

 IRL | Here are a few examples of reliable sources:

- *BBC News*
- *Wall Street Journal*
- *Scientific American*
- *National Geographic*

What Is the Difference between Fact and Opinion?

Fact: Unlike creative writing, which relies on imagination, informative writing must be factual. Informative writing must be trustworthy. Writers must take time to present their readers with accurate information. According to the dictionary, a fact is "information that can be verified."

Opinion: An opinion is a person's feelings about something—a personal belief. Opinions are often based on facts, but opinions are not truth. An opinion is a viewpoint, judgment, or conclusion an expert might make after being informed.

Everyone is entitled to an opinion, but it is important to discern which opinions are credible from those that are not. For example, if you wanted advice on your writing, it would make sense to accept an opinion from your English teacher. However, if you feel sick in class it would be more beneficial to ask the school nurse. When it is an important issue, seek the opinions of experts in the field.

Here are some examples of each:

Fact	Opinion
It's estimated that McDonald's serves over 3.6 million little boxes a day. The first newspaper, *Acta Diurna*, was published in Rome.	I don't think fast food is healthy. All schools should promote a school newspaper.

What Are Some Types of Informative Writing?

News Story: We rely on news to get our information about the world around us. Journalists, those who write, report, and present the news, inform readers about politics, education, sports, healthcare, crime, weather, etc. Whether you have the newspaper delivered to your door, read news online, or listen to the evening broadcast, news educates us about events happening close by and abroad, and how we will be impacted.

Not all writing that appears in a newspaper is informative. Columns, editorials, op-eds, and cartoons are opinion based. They usually appear at the end of the paper in an opinion section. Look at headings to be clear if a piece is based on fact or opinion.

How Do I Write a News Story?

Newsworthy Reporting: When brainstorming a topic, you must make sure that your topic is newsworthy. Consider human interest, timeliness, proximity, controversy, and relevance.

Human Interest: Did a dog save its owner's life? Did a student get accepted to all of the Ivy League schools to which they applied? Did a teacher become a foster parent to their student? A human interest story would appeal to the reader on an emotional level.

Timeless: For the past few years, news about COVID-19 has dominated our news. News needs to be current. Your readers care about what is happening today or most recently. As time passes, a story can get old. People lose interest in old topics unless you provide a new angle or new information.

Proximity: It is human nature to care about the people, places, and events that are close by. It is human nature to care about the news that may affect or impact you. If a hurricane or blizzard is going to hit your area, you will follow the news more closely than you would if the same storm or dangerous weather were to hit an area 1,000 miles away. Of course, if you are planning to travel to this area or you have family in this area, you may feel more inclined to keep updated. The election in the United States

BTW

Bias is a leaning toward one side over another. The dictionary defines it as "a prejudice in favor of or against one thing, person, or group compared with another." Be careful when writing not to include bias. Sometimes our opinions can sway our writing even when we are trying to remain factual. Our news, especially, should remain unbiased.

Not all media is unbiased. There are some news sources that can be slanted. It is important to know which sources can be trusted. To stay well informed, be sure to get information through multiple sources so that you can have a well-balanced view.

impacts you more than an election in another country, although you certainly may care. But events that are happening close by tend to attract more reader attention.

Controversy: From gun rights to voting rights, it seems impossible to read the news and not see a story without controversy. Topics that include a conflict or have many sides to the issue attract readers.

Relevance: As a teacher, I tend to read stories about education. If you like a certain celebrity, you might be intrigued when a headline pops up about this individual. If you follow sports, you'd be interested in how a particular team performed. Readers choose to read topics that matter to them.

Inverted Pyramid: This is a structure to a news story that you should know. The first body paragraph of any news story consists of essential information—the most important details to know—and then the following body paragraphs contain less important information. Most people do not read the newspaper cover to cover. Journalists understand that readers will often skim, so an article will present the most newsworthy information first: who, what, when, where, why, and how.

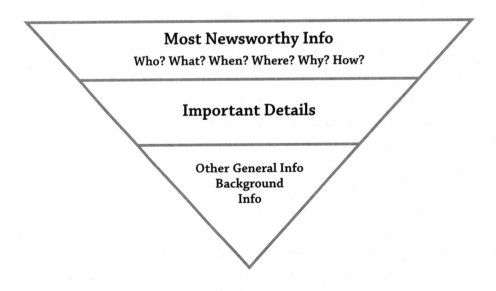

Let's look at a model of a news story lead:

National Junior Honor Society members held their annual bake sale in front of the Woodward Middle School on Valentine's Day to raise money for the American Heart Association. Over fifty students participated on Friday and raised over $500 for the organization.

Who: Members of the National Junior Honor Society

When: Valentine's Day, last Friday

What: $500 was raised in a bake sale

Where: In front of the Woodward Middle School

Why: To raise money for the American Heart Association

The Journalistic Style: As you develop your news story, keep in mind that the writing should be objective. That means you should not use *I, you, we,* or *us.* Use third-person point of view when you write: he, she, they, and them.

Incorrect: Yesterday, I saw students participating in the National Junior Honor Society's bake sale.

Correct: Yesterday, the members of the National Junior Honor Society held their annual bake sale.

In addition, news paragraphs are brief, often consisting of only a few lines, unlike traditional paragraphing in other informative writing assignments. The writing style is also simple and concise. Avoid flowery and overly descriptive language in a news story.

Let's look at a sample paragraph from a news story:

After several years of building student interest, school principal Brian Williams decided to put the gears in motion and approved the school newspaper. In a school-wide poll, Williams gave students the opportunity to name the paper. Through Google Classroom, students voted on their top choice of ten student-generated titles. The winner was selected: *WMS Press.*

 IRL The nation's first daily newspaper was the *Pennsylvania Packet and Daily Advertiser.* It was published on September 21, 1784.

Interviews: If you are assigned to write a news story for class, you will need to interview experts and witnesses for direct quotes. Experts can include anyone who was a witness, anyone who participated, or anyone who might be affected. For example, if you are writing a story about the new cafeteria menu at your school, you should interview the food services director, the cafeteria staff, and also students. If you are writing a story about remote learning, you should interview teachers, parents, and administrators. Who you interview depends on the story.

Direct Quotations: Quotes are an important feature of any news story. When you add someone else's words to your news story word-for-word, you are using a direct quotation. Direct quotes should always be accurate. You must add quotation marks around the actual words said. In addition, be sure to include *attribution:* identifying the source and why this person is an expert.

BTW

You can also paraphrase quotations, but you still must provide the source. This is known as an indirect quotation.

According to Mrs. Scardina, a veteran English teacher at Woodward Middle School, readers learn many skills while reading, including vocabulary.

Kevin Price, the quarterback of the Woodward Middle School football team, vowed to lead his team to a successful season.

For example:

Mrs. Scardina, *a veteran English teacher at Woodward Middle School*, said, "Readers learn vocabulary through context when they read."

Kevin Price, *the quarterback of the Woodward Middle School football team*, stated, "I intend to lead my team to victory this season."

Let's look at a model of an article for a school newspaper:

This fall, Woodward Middle School published its first newspaper. The first issue, with ten news stories, two editorials, two reviews, and one cartoon, was released November 5, 2020.

After several years of building student interest, school principal Brian Williams decided to put the gears in motion and approved the school newspaper.

According to Williams, the goal of the newspaper is to give students a voice and opportunities to write articles on current events going on in the school.

Most important information is given first.

The article is written from a third-person point of view.

An indirect quote is used here paraphrasing Williams.

Research about the value of school newspapers is important for readers to know.

Students can write about a new teacher, a sports event, building construction, etc. Students can also participate by writing a review for a movie or book or Netflix show.

According to Steven Wright, a journalism professor at Times University, a school newspaper is important. In his recently published article, "The Benefits of School Newspapers," Wright stated, "writing for a newspaper can teach students ethics."

Through a school-wide poll, Williams gave students the opportunity to name the paper. Through Google Classroom, students voted on their top choice of ten student-generated titles. The winner was selected: *WMS Press.*

The excitement and enthusiasm for the first newspaper grew at the annual club fair early this fall. At recess, middle school students, grades 6–8, received additional information from Mrs. Scardina and Ms. Breen, the newspaper advisers, about the newly formed club.

Students were given opportunities to become writers, photographers, editors, or layout staff. Over eighty students showed interest, showing up to the first meeting held on Wednesday, September 8. The response was so overwhelming that students were asked to go to other classrooms to join remotely, following COVID-19 guidelines.

Students were invited into the Google Classroom for the newspaper club so they could keep track of meetings, submit work, ask questions, and edit submissions. Going forward, students will still have options to attend the club virtually or in person.

According to Mrs. Scardina, "the virtual option gives more students the opportunity to be involved." The club meets weekly on Wednesday afternoons in room 214.

Direct quotations are included.

Mrs. Scardina and Ms. Breen understand that students have busy schedules. "We are a flexible club. If students can't join in the fall, they are welcome to come help in the spring. We want to work with them so that they can contribute in any way they can," explained Mrs. Scardina.

Attribution is given to sources.

The first newspaper staff aims to publish two issues per year. Ms. Breen added, "If we get the hang of it, next year there could be a possibility of publishing more."

What Is a Report?

Report: When I was your age, I remember having to write a report about Greek mythology. I remember my mother dropping me off at the town library because, unfortunately, the Internet was not available yet. I went to the card catalog—an antiquated tool—to look up my topic, and found books and periodicals that would help me write my paper. After finding my resources, I was able to start reading and taking notes.

Lucky for you, doing research is much easier today, but writing a report or research paper for class has not changed much. A report is writing in which you provide information about a topic. This academic assignment is a staple for many of your classes across the board. It is very likely you will have to write one for other disciplines ranging from science to art. In the future, you may also have to write a report for your job.

How Do You Write a Report?

Ask Questions: Sometimes, a teacher may give you a topic and assign what is to be covered. However, in many cases, you might not have specific guidelines. In this case, you can start by asking questions. When I was researching Greek mythology, I posed the following questions: What was the purpose of mythology? How was it recorded? What were common themes in the myths? What were some popular myths? Who were the myths written about?

Make an Outline: After you complete your research, plan each section. How will you best arrange your ideas? Writing an outline often helps you organize your ideas in a logical manner.

Let's look at an example of an outline:

I. What was the purpose of Greek mythology?	Question
a. To teach lessons	Supporting details
b. To explain events such as illness	
c. To justify customs	
II. How were the myths shared?	Question
a. Oral storytelling	Supporting details
b. Writing	
III. What were common themes in the myths?	Question
a. Fate	Supporting details
b. Power	
c. Love	
IV. Who were myths written about?	Question
a. Gods and goddesses	Supporting details
b. Creatures	
c. Heroes	

Use Modes of Discourse: I can't remember everything about my middle school report, but as a teacher who has assigned many reports, and as a writer myself, I know how to develop a research paper. I bet that as I wrote my mythology report, I defined mythology, compared and contrasted Greek mythology with Roman mythology, used many examples of different myths, and analyzed how myths provided comfort and reassurance to the people of the time. These are some of the modes of discourse. *Modes of discourse* can help you develop your writing: informative, persuasive, and argumentative.

Here are modes to know:

Mode	Purpose
Definition	To provide readers with a meaning of a term or concept
Compare/Contrast	To show readers similarities and differences between two things
Example	To provide readers with an instance
Cause and Effect	To show readers the reasons or results
Process Analysis	To show readers how to do something or to explain how something works
Classification	To show readers how the topic can be put into groups
Narration	To tell readers a story to illustrate a point
Description	To show readers what something smells like, looks like, tastes like, feels like, or sounds like

Let's look at an example of how the modes develop writing:

"Do you have the sequel to *The Hunger Games*, Mrs. Scardina?" asked Yogita.

My classroom library has over three hundred books for my students to browse when they are looking for their next read. I have all kinds of books on my shelves: graphic novels, realistic fiction, historical fiction, and fantasy, but the one genre that they all seem to reach for lately is dystopia.

If you've ever read *Divergent*, *The Maze Runner*, or *The Giver*, you have temporarily been thrust into a dystopian world: The land is burnt and smoking, the sun scorches the land, the dust rips across a settlement, and characters appear from their scanty shelters rubbing their eyes free from the dirt and grime. According to *Webster's Dictionary*, a dystopia is "an imagined world or society in which people lead wretched, dehumanized, fearful lives."

The author uses narration to show how popular the genre has become.

The author classifies her books into many groups.

The author describes a hypothetical dystopian landscape to show the harsh realities the characters may face in their future world.

The author defines *dystopia* so readers have an understanding of the term.

The author provides examples of dystopian characteristics.

The author compares and contrasts the two genres to clear up misconceptions.

The *New World Encyclopedia* provides some examples that characterize this genre: "human misery, poverty, oppression, violence, disease, and/or pollution."

Some readers confuse dystopia and fantasy. Although there are similar elements, they are two very different genres. Although they are both works of fiction and are imaginary, fantasy centers more on magic and superpowers, while dystopia focuses more on oppression and rebellion. For example, in the *Harry Potter* series, Harry Potter and his friends learn spells and charms to ward off evil. Katniss Everdeen, in *The Hunger Games*, must fight to survive an abusive Capital that has made the lives of those in the districts unbearable.

What makes dystopian literature so popular among my students? Many say they like when the teen characters stand up to authority when it is wrong and misguided. They like reading about powerful teenage characters who are brave and empowered. They also feel like they can relate; some see the dystopian characteristics in their world today.

> The author shows some of the possible reasons/causes that attract teens to dystopian literature.

Many students want to write their own dystopian stories after they read this genre. There are certain steps writers of this genre must follow. First, decide the fate of the future world. What has happened to make the setting dystopian? War? Global warming? A technological mishap? Next, create rules. How must the people live? What must survivors do to stay safe? Finally, consider who is in control. Who has the power? Who doesn't?

> The writer tells the reader steps to take if interested in writing a dystopian story.

BTW

An anecdote is a very brief story about a person or an incident used to illustrate a point to the reader.

EXERCISES

EXERCISE 10.1

Decide whether each of the following statements is fact or opinion.

1. Cell phones do not belong in the classroom. _____

2. The first iPhone was released in 2007. _____

3. Zhang Yiming is the originator of TikTok. _____

4. Middle school is more challenging than elementary school.

   _____

5. Everyone should own a dog. _____

6. The Harry Potter store opened in New York City on June 3, 2021.

   _____

7. The very first M&M was introduced on September 10, 1941.

   _____

8. Snapchat is a better app than Instagram. _____

   _____

9. Loki debuted in Marvel during the year 1949. _____

   _____

10. The best tourist attraction in New York City is Times Square.

    _____

EXERCISE 10.2

Read the following text, and answer the questions that follow.

Woodward District will open its doors to students again on September 3, after their five months of remote learning at the end of the previous school year. The district just released a ninety-nine page document outlining the safety procedures and protocols that students and teachers will follow upon return. Students will have a choice: to be part of a cohort and come to school every other day or to remain fully on remote learning until at least January.

According to *Education Week*, "As of September 2, 2021, 73% of the 100 largest school districts have chosen remote learning only as their back-to-school instructional model, affecting over 8 million students." Although some schools, such as Woodward Middle School, have offered live instruction this year, a majority of interviewed teachers agree: Teaching during a pandemic to two groups of students at once is not easy.

English teachers are especially struggling to find a way to deliver quality education to students who are learning from home remotely.

According to Dr. Philip Brown, English Supervisor K–12, teachers are struggling to work with two groups at once: fully remote students and live learners. Brown sympathizes with English teachers who are trying to "give equal attention to both groups as they would if they were in a normal setting."

English teachers have traditionally focused on group work, collaboration, and student-centered learning to support reading and writing instruction. "Figuring out how to substitute these best practices with ones that best serve remote learners is a real challenge," explained Dr. Brown. "We just don't have a model of what this new learning looks like."

1. This text is most likely:
   a. A research paper
   b. A memo
   c. A news article
   d. An editorial

2. What is the purpose of this text?
   a. To describe the school building
   b. To compare and contrast remote learning to in-person learning
   c. To inform the community that students will be returning to in-person learning
   d. To explain how the new procedures will be implemented

3. "Figuring out how to substitute these best practices with ones that best serve remote learners is a real challenge," explained Dr. Brown. "We just don't have a model of what this new learning looks like."

   This statement is an example of which of the following?

   a. Indirect quotation
   b. Direct quotation
   c. Inverted pyramid
   d. Fact

4. According to *Education Week*, "As of September 2, 2021, 73% of the 100 largest school districts have chosen remote learning only as their back-to-school instructional model, affecting over 8 million students."

   This statement is an example of which of the following?

   a. Direct quotation
   b. Indirect quotation
   c. Fact
   d. Opinion

5. Woodward District will open its doors to students again on September 3, after their five months of remote learning at the end of the previous school year. The district just released a ninety-nine page document outlining the safety procedures and protocols that students and teachers will follow upon return. Students will have a choice: to be part of a cohort and come to school every other day or to remain fully on remote learning until at least January.

   Which of the following details of the Inverted Pyramid is NOT provided in this lead?

   a. Who
   b. What
   c. When
   d. All of the above

6. Which of the following statements is an example of an indirect quotation?

    a. According to Dr. Philip Brown, English Supervisor K–12, teachers are struggling to work with two groups at once: fully remote students and live learners.

    b. Woodward District will open its doors to students again on September 3, after their five months of remote learning at the end of the previous school year.

    c. Brown sympathizes with English teachers who are trying to "give equal attention to both groups as they would if they were in a normal setting."

    d. English teachers are especially struggling to find a way to deliver quality education to students who are learning from home remotely.

7. Why are quotations from Dr. Brown included?

    a. Dr. Brown is an administrator and understands the struggles his staff faces.

    b. Dr. Brown is a parent of a student in the district who is happy that students will return.

    c. Dr. Brown is a teacher who does not know how to teach remotely.

    d. Dr. Brown is a pediatrician who can discuss the effectiveness of these protocols.

8. Why would this article be considered newsworthy to the Woodward community?

    a. Timeliness

    b. Relevance

    c. Proximity

    d. All of the above

9. Who would be another good person to interview for this article?

    a. Students

    b. Parents

    c. Teachers

    d. All of the above

10. What would be an opinion of this story?

    a. Schools need to offer a remote option during the pandemic.

    b. All schools in the county are opening schools this fall.

    c. Students have all received one-to-one Chromebooks.

    d. Students will begin school September 3.

EXERCISE 10.3

Match each of the following examples with the correlating mode of discourse. You may use a term more than once.

Compare/Contrast, Example, Narration, Description, Cause and Effect, Definition, Classification, Process Analysis

1. There are many majors for an English student to pursue in college: journalism, publishing, teaching, and communications. _____ _____

2. As a young adult, I wasn't sure which path to follow after I graduated with my BA in English, so I decided to get a master's degree in secondary education. _____

3. When it comes to lesson planning, effective teachers take several steps. First, they consider how to engage their students. Then, they compose essential questions that they want their students to be able to answer. Finally, they design activities that will help students master the concept. _____

4. Student-centered learning is a method of teaching which shifts the focus from the teacher to the student, making students more independent learners. _____

5. When teachers create lessons that are student centered, students become more independent, more engaged, and more motivated.

   _____

6. There are three styles of learning: visual, auditory, and kinesthetic.

   _____

7. One way student-centered learning differs from teacher-centered learning is that the teacher is a facilitator and students have a more active role in the learning process. _____

8. In a student-centered classroom, students are huddled, working closely together. Some students are standing at their tables while others are moving briskly to gather supplies. Colored markers, pencils, and large paper appear in the center as enthusiastic voices hover overhead. The energy is exhilarating as the teacher darts around the room to answer questions and assist. _____

9. "So for today, class, you will choose one of the following five activities to complete as a group," the teacher explains as she passes handouts to eager students. _____

10. There are several reasons why teachers are moving their lessons online: Students will have more accessibility, students will be more engaged, and students will use twenty-first-century skills. _____

    _____

EXERCISE 10.4

Read the following text, and answer the questions that follow.

Happy Meals have been a staple of the McDonald's menu for many generations. The McDonald's Happy Meal originated in 1973. Yolanda Fernández de Cofiño of Guatemala put together a "Ronald Menu" with kid choices. Although the catchy box and free trinket came years later, the purpose of the iconic red-boxed meal, now celebrating its forty-year anniversary (Heil), was to make dining out with children more manageable. Kids could order easily: They were given a box with a meal, a side, and a drink. The Happy Meal became an instant success. "Kids like to eat with their hands," noted Julie Hennessy, a marketing professor at Northwestern's Kellogg School of Management. "They tend to hate new tastes ... kids don't wish there were more options" (Weiner-Bronner).

Over time, since its original conception, McDonald's continued to focus on their little customers. Bob Bernstein, a founder of a communications and marketing agency, pushed the concept of the kid's meal further by adding the arches as handles on top of the box, fun illustrations and puzzles on the back, and free treats like a pencil and erasers inside (Sanchez). Eventually, the free gift became a toy, and then a series. In 1979, McDonald's revealed the characters from one of the popular shows of the day, *Star Trek*. The result was an instant hit, thus luring millions of returning customers for decades to come. The Happy Meal is still as successful as ever, and "it's estimated that McDonald's serves over 3.6 million little boxes a day" (Sanchez). Sam Oches, editorial director of Food News Media at *QSR Magazine*, argues that when it comes to eating out, "kids hold a veto vote—a family won't go to a restaurant where there's nothing for children to eat; therefore, McDonald's needs to care about the Happy Meals'" (Weiner-Bronner).

Although many kids enjoy the toy, there has been some backlash toward Happy Meals. Some cities, such as San Francisco in 2011, have gone as far at banning it. In 2010, the Center for Science in the Public Interest accused the company of an "insidious" use of Happy Meal toys to market to children (Weiner-Bronner). Others accuse the Happy Meal of being a lure, the hook that draws families into the chain restaurants. In her article, Karen Klein calls this marketing gimmick of including toys with meals "pernicious." Klein criticizes McDonald's for "teach[ing] kids to associate its less-than-ideal meals with fun, which is what matters to them more than the quality of the chicken or beef." For example, McDonald's includes a series of toys, releasing one new character per week, thus drawing kids to collect each one of them.

1. What is the purpose of the text?
   a. To provide readers with a definition of fast food
   b. To provide examples of toys in a Happy Meal box
   c. To show the effects of fast food on children's health
   d. To inform readers of the history of the Happy Meal

2. What type of writing is this text?
   a. A biography about the founders of McDonald's
   b. A newspaper article about the new, updated Happy Meal items
   c. A report about the history of the Happy Meal
   d. An editorial about the problems of fast food

3. What would an outline include for this text?
   a. The origins of the Happy Meal, the way it evolved over time, controversy behind the box
   b. The creators of the Happy Meal, the story of the toy, the popularity of the Happy Meal
   c. The history of fast food, the materials used to create the box, the success of the Happy Meal
   d. The differences between the original Happy Meal and that of today, the content of the Happy Meal box, the backlash against the box

4. What mode of discourse is used in the report?

    a. Narration

    b. Definition

    c. Classification

    d. Example

5. The McDonald's Happy Meal originated in 1973.
    This statement is which of the following?

    a. Fact

    b. Opinion

    c. Definition

    d. Example

6. When I ask my boys what they want for dinner, it is a guarantee that they will say "McDonald's" each and every time. Although I don't always give in, on the occasion that I do, my boys are mostly interested in getting a toy rather than eating the contents of their Happy Meal.
    This passage is an example of which mode?

    a. Definition

    b. Example

    c. Narration

    d. Process analysis

7. Over the years, the McDonald's Happy Meal has featured several popular characters, including Jessie and Woody from *Toy Story*, Mario and Luigi from *Mario Kart*, and Luke and Darth Vader from *Star Wars*.
    This passage is an example of which mode?

    a. Process analysis

    b. Classification

    c. Cause and effect

    d. Example

8. The original Happy Meal is iconic: Kids across generations recognize the bright-red box, the large golden arch handles, and the McDonald's smile logo across the front.

   This passage is an example of which mode?
   a. Narration
   b. Description
   c. Example
   d. Compare/contrast

9. On the other hand, Burger King tried to attract children by offering them paper hats that were fashioned into a king's crown.

   This passage is an example of which mode?
   a. Cause and effect
   b. Example
   c. Description
   d. Compare/contrast

10. There are three popular types of fast-food chains: burger chains, pizza chains, and chicken chains.

    This passage is an example of which mode?
    a. Cause and effect
    b. Example
    c. Classification
    d. Process analysis

NOTES

Writing to Analyze

MUST ⚡ KNOW

⚡ A literary analysis is the process of identifying the parts of a work of literature and understanding their relationships to one another.

⚡ A literary analysis about mood, imagery, symbolism, and allusions can help you understand a work of literature more deeply.

⚡ A literary analysis should have a hook, a clear thesis statement, topic sentences, supporting details, and text evidence.

n the beginning chapters of this book, you learned about fiction: how to identify it, how to read it, and the literary devices that fiction writers use to create beauty and make meaning. As a reader, it is also important to know how to analyze it.

Remember in chapter one, we reviewed ways to respond to a text through annotations, sticky notes, and journal responses. In most English language arts (ELA) classrooms, teachers will expect you to write a literary analysis to assess your understanding of a text. In this chapter, you will learn how to write an insightful literary analysis that includes deep thinking about imagery, mood, and symbolism.

What Is a Literary Analysis?

Unlike a summary, a literary analysis is an essay that asks you to evaluate a text formally. It requires you to interpret the way the parts of a text contribute to the text as a whole. For this task, you will interpret, evaluate, or provide your opinion about the text. Literary analysis is one of the most common forms of writing in an English course.

This genre of writing helps teachers determine the extent you understand the text. This essay can be assigned on any work you have discussed in class: a poem, an essay, a full-length novel, a short story, a film, or a combination of any two. Sometimes a teacher may ask you to write about how a theme is developed in a text or to compare and contrast two characters in a work. The analysis can vary. For many students, the first time writing a literary analysis can be a challenging task. This

BTW

Here are some possible prompts middle school ELA teachers might assign to students:

- What is an important theme in the text?

- How is a character in your reading complex?

- How does the author use a literary device in the text (symbol, setting, characterization, conflict, point of view, flashback, or irony) to support a purpose?

- How does the setting affect the story?

- What is one of the protagonist's weaknesses?

- What motivates the antagonist to act?

writing requires you to think critically, a skill that takes time, practice, and maturity. So, how do you start?

In order to begin a literary analysis, it is important to choose a good topic. Sometimes you may get an assigned topic, sometimes you may get a choice between a few topics, and sometimes you will have to come up with an idea on your own. You can analyze character, conflicts, settings, figurative language, and themes. There are also a few more literary devices that you can write about, devices that dig deep into the text's central meaning: imagery, mood, and symbolism.

What Are Some Insightful Ways to Analyze a Text?

Mood: Have you ever had a bad day at school? Chances are your family can sense that you are in a terrible mood. How? Your body language, your expressions, your tone of voice, and your actions all reveal your mood. Maybe you slammed your books on the counter. Maybe you collapsed on the couch with a big sigh.

Writers also give readers signals to help them determine the mood of the text. Mood is the feeling a piece of writing generates. It is the atmosphere of the text. When you are trying to analyze the mood, consider the words an author uses. Do you see a pattern? Are the words mostly positive or negative? The words authors choose are important and done intentionally. Did you have a bad day or a terrible day? Did you hate lunch or loathe it? Did you speed home or race home? A single word can change the meaning of a sentence.

BTW

A text can have more than one mood in different sections; however, there is usually one major, overarching mood to consider for the entire piece.

Here are some more mood words to know:

- Cheerful
- Reflective
- Gloomy
- Humorous
- Melancholy
- Whimsical
- Ominous
- Mysterious
- Tense
- Lighthearted
- Calm

Consider the stanza from "The Raven" that follows. How would the mood change if Poe substituted *cold* for *bleak*? What about replacing *ember* with *ash*? Or *presence* instead of *ghost*?

Once upon a midnight **dreary,** while I pondered, **weak** and **weary,**

Over many a quaint and curious volume of forgotten **lore**—

While I nodded, nearly napping, suddenly there came a **tapping,**

As of some one gently rapping, rapping at my chamber door.

"'Tis some visitor," I muttered, "tapping at my chamber door—

Only this and nothing more."

Ah, distinctly I remember it was in the **bleak December;**

And each separate **dying** ember wrought its **ghost** upon the floor.

Eagerly I wished the morrow;—vainly I had sought to borrow

From my books surcease of **sorrow**— sorrow for the lost Lenore—

For the rare and radiant maiden whom the angels name Lenore—

Nameless *here* for evermore.

In "The Raven," Poe uses certain words to create a mood that is dark, eerie, and haunting; for example, *midnight, dreary, forgotten,* and *terrors.*

Look at how the other bolded words in the poem contribute to the overall mood.

Imagery: We use our five senses to describe the world around us. Writers do too. Words can create pictures in readers' minds. Words can help a reader smell cinnamon buns rising in the oven. Words can help readers taste the salt of the ocean's waves. Words can help readers feel the intense heat of a car stuck in traffic. Words can help readers hear the leaky drip of a bathroom faucet. Imagery is a literary device that uses descriptive language to communicate through the readers' senses. These images evoke readers' emotions. Imagery can also contribute to the mood of the work.

Let's examine imagery in an excerpt from T. S. Eliot's poem "Preludes."

The winter evening settles down	
With smell of steaks in passageways.	Can you smell the steak?
Six o'clock.	
The burnt-out ends of smoky days.	Can you see the smoky days?
And now a gusty shower wraps	
The grimy scraps	
Of withered leaves about your feet	Can you see the grimy scraps of withered leaves?
And newspapers from vacant lots;	
The showers beat	
On broken blinds and chimney-pots,	
And at the corner of the street	
A lonely cab-horse steams and stamps.	Can you hear the horse stamp?
And then the lighting of the lamps.	

Symbolism: There are symbols all around us. When you see a dove, you may think of peace. When you see a heart, you may think of love. When you see an owl, you may think of wisdom. When you see a lamb, you may think of innocence. Symbols are things that represent something else. Often symbols can be physical objects or signs that stand for a concept or idea. Sometimes the symbol can even be a color! When you cross a street and you see a green light, you know this means to go. When you see a red light, you recognize this symbol means stop.

Just as in life, the literature you read may also contain symbols. An author may use an object or a repeating idea to symbolize a message or a theme. Sometimes authors use colors, weather, or nature as a symbol. For example, if the weather is rainy, dreary, or dark, the author may want to symbolize death, failure, or defeat. If the color white is mentioned frequently in the text, it may symbolize youth, innocence, or purity.

A symbol is an object, person, or event that stands for something else. In literature, authors and poets may use symbols to create meaning, reveal a theme, or expand a message. There are many symbols of death. Think about tombs, gravestones, the fall, leaves, time, hourglasses, and winter.

Let's look again at an excerpt from Edgar Allan Poe's "The Raven."

Open here I flung the shutter, when, with many a flirt and flutter,

In there stepped a stately Raven of the saintly days of yore;

Not the least obeisance made he; not a minute stopped or stayed he;

But, with mien of lord or lady, perched above my chamber door—

Perched upon a bust of Pallas just above my chamber door—

Perched, and sat, and nothing more.

Then this ebony bird beguiling my sad fancy into smiling,

By the grave and stern decorum of the countenance it wore,

"Though thy crest be shorn and shaven, thou," I said, "art sure no craven,

Ghastly grim and ancient Raven wandering from the Nightly shore—

Tell me what thy lordly name is on the Night's Plutonian shore!"

Quoth the Raven "Nevermore."

The black raven has also been associated with ill fortune and death.

In many works of literature, the sight of a raven implies bad times ahead.

It is no wonder that in Poe's poem, the raven reminds the narrator of the death of Lenore, who is believed to be Poe's deceased wife.

 IRL Unlike doves, which have positive symbolism, the raven has a history of negative associations. Ravens are known to feed on corpses. Even in the Bible, the raven is the messenger of bad news. In the book of Genesis, Noah sends a raven to find dry land. The Bible states, "At the end of forty days Noah opened the window of the ark that he had made and sent forth a raven. It went to and fro until the waters dried up from the earth." The raven never returns.

There are other popular symbols in literature to know. Writers tend to use these objects to represent certain ideas in their writing. Each culture has its own meaning for certain symbols. For example, in the United States, brides often wear white to represent innocence and purity. However, in China, brides dress in red as a symbol of joy and celebration.

snake = evil

eagle = freedom

light = knowledge

owl = wisdom

spring = rebirth

white = innocence

windows = opportunities

water = cleansing

darkness = danger

Allusion: If someone calls you Scrooge, chances are you understand that it is a negative reference. Scrooge is an unpopular character from *A Christmas Carol*. The person probably means you are being selfish. If you're having a horrible day at school, you might click your heels and wish you were home, a reference to Dorothy in *The Wizard of Oz*. An allusion is a reference in literature to a time, place, or person in history to make a point.

Let's examine the allusion to *Night's Plutonian shore* in "The Raven."

Then this ebony bird beguiling my sad fancy into smiling, By the grave and stern decorum of the countenance it wore, "Though thy crest be shorn and shaven, thou," I said, "art sure no craven, Ghastly grim and ancient Raven wandering from the Nightly shore— Tell me what thy lordly name is on the **Night's Plutonian shore!"** Quoth the Raven "Nevermore."	Night's Plutonian shore is a reference to the mythological Roman God Pluto of the underworld. Poe views the raven as a messenger of death.

 IRL

A *myth* is a traditional story that was used long ago to explain occurrences in nature and in the world that were misunderstood. Many constellations in our sky are named after mythological heroes from ancient civilizations, including the Middle East, Rome, and Greece.

Today it is common to hear *mythological allusions* in books, television shows, and movies. Next time you hear someone refer to some of the following allusions, you'll be in the know!

- *Achilles heel* alludes to a Greek warrior whose weak spot was the back of his heel. He died in combat because of this tragic flaw.

- *Pandora's box:* In Greek mythology, Pandora opened a box that her husband warned her not to open. Curiosity got the best of her, and when she opened the box, curses were unleashed onto mankind.

- *Herculean effort* refers to Hercules in Greek mythology. Hercules completed twelve tasks that took extreme strength and courage to complete.

Biblical allusions are references to the Bible or a certain scripture, story, or character. For example, in the play *Hamlet*, after Claudius confesses he murdered his brother, he makes a reference to Cain and Abel when he says, "Oh, my offence it is rank...it hath the primal eldest curse upon't" (Act III, iii).

Cain and Abel were the sons of Adam and Eve. Out of jealousy, Cain killed his brother Abel. When Claudius refers to this biblical story, readers understand Claudius's guilt.

What Should Be Included in a Literary Analysis?

Introduction: Whether it's a formal literary analysis or any other academic writing, start by hooking readers with an engaging first sentence to capture their attention. It doesn't matter whether your teacher assigned a prompt or not, you can still write a line or two that piques interest. You can start with a question, a famous quotation, a hypothetical scenario, or a clever rephrase of the prompt or assignment question, to name a few. Next, be sure to provide both the title and the author of the text, as well as a brief description of the work at hand. Finally, introduce what you intend to prove in your analysis, your thesis statement.

Thesis Statement: When you write an essay, you want to make sure that your readers know exactly the topic you are addressing and the direction your paper will take.

Topic Sentences: Consider topic sentences as your reasons to support your thesis. Topic sentences help writers organize their thinking. They use key words and phrases from the thesis to carry ideas throughout the paper.

> **Thesis:** Despite the systematic racism and sexism Grace experiences in the story, she becomes a symbol of resistance by challenging those notions.
>
> **Topic Sentence One:** Right from the beginning of the short story, Grace is taught that resistance is necessary for survival.
>
> **Topic Sentence Two:** The lessons of resistance she learns from her ancestors come in handy when Grace transfers to a new school and meets Brandon in the chess club.
>
> **Topic Sentence Three:** Grace also becomes a symbol of resistance to sexism as she resists Brandon's unwanted advances.

Transitions: As you write, you're going to need to move from one idea to another. How do you alert the reader that you have finished your discussion on one idea and are now moving to another? Transitions are words and phrases that help you move through your essay smoothly by joining ideas together.

Here are some transitions to use when you write:

- Along with

- Also

- Besides

- Another

- In addition

- Moreover

- However

- Furthermore

- Once

- Likewise

- For similar reasons

- Next, then, finally

Let's look at how transitions are used within the essay to maintain organization and flow:

Grace **also** becomes a symbol of resistance to sexism as she resists Brandon's unwanted advances. **After** Brandon deems himself the winner of their six-week chess match, he tries to kiss Grace and ignores her physical resistance by tightening his grip. **Once** Grace realizes her physical boundaries are not being acknowledged and respected, she verbalizes her protest, "Stop" (5). **Finally,** Grace asserts herself and does not care if it embarrasses or hurts him. She does not owe Brandon an explanation or apology, and she gives him none. Brandon **then** tries to portray himself as the victim and that the kiss was innocuous. Grace, **however,** calls out his problematic behavior and attempts to teach him the importance of consent. **In addition,** Grace asserts, "For future reference...none of that matters. Ask next time" (5). When she references the "ask next time," Grace is not hoping for another kiss by Brandon, but trying to teach him why he is in the wrong. **Moreover,** she wants him to learn to respect people's boundaries and their right to say no.

BTW

Underline or italicize the titles of full-length texts, and use quotation marks around shorter works of literature such as plays, poems, short stories, and essays.

Here is an example of a strong introduction for a literary analysis:

There are times in life when we are faced with injustice. In those times, we have a choice. *We can succumb to the powerful societal norms that perpetuate inequity, or we can choose to challenge them.* **In the story "Grace" by Darcie Little Badger,** *the character/protagonist chooses to stand up for herself and does not give in to the stereotypes [title and author].* **Despite the systemic racism and sexism Grace experiences in the story, she becomes a symbol of resistance by challenging those notions [thesis statement].**

Here are a few models of lead paragraphs of a literary analysis:

In his poem "Mending Wall," poet Robert Frost wrote, "Good fences make good neighbors." In other words, when it comes to others, respect boundaries, provide space, and don't meddle. A character who would benefit from this advice is Mrs. Rachel Lynde, a secondary character in Lucy Maud Montgomery's novel *Anne of Green Gables*. As a town gossip, Mrs. Lynde is always intruding into the lives and business of those in Avonlea, and her intrusive ways lead to many uncomfortable situations with Marilla Cuthbert.

In this lead, the writer uses a quote from another source to begin the lead.

The writer explains what the quote means and how it applies specifically to a character in the book.

The writer also includes the title and author of the book.

The writer includes brief context about who Mrs. Rachel Lynde is and the role she plays in the town and the book.

Finally, the writer ends with a claim, which the writer intends to prove throughout the essay.

How do two young men manage to get through life during the Great Depression, a period of a social and economic recession? How do these men cope with the loneliness of the California ranch life in the 1930s, while still gaining strength to be there for each other? In *Of Mice and Men* by John Steinbeck, the main characters, George and Lennie, struggle with difficulties such as unemployment and poverty as they make their way through the economic crisis. Throughout their journey to look for a job, the two realize that neither one of them will make it past this distress without each other. George and Lennie both learn that in order to survive they must support and care for each other and do whatever it takes to get past these rough times on the ranch.

In the book *Of Mice and Men,* John Steinbeck implies that friendship and compassion can be strengthened when people go through hardships in difficult times.

In this lead, the writer asks a question to engage the audience.

The writer includes context (background) about the book being analyzed.

The writer includes the title and author of the book.

Finally, the writer adds a claim, what the writer intends to prove in this essay.

Supporting Details: As you develop your analysis, it is always important to support your ideas with specifics from the text that clarify, explain, describe, illustrate, and expand the main idea of each paragraph. In addition, taking direct quotations from the text is also necessary.

After you have chosen a topic, it is important to go back into the text to gather evidence. As a teacher, I often ask my students to pick a topic *before* they read rather than afterwards because it makes the task of collecting supporting evidence easier. Students can easily keep track of useful quotations and details in the text on sticky notes or on a graphic organizer. Not only does this method save time (think of all the rereading it would require you to do), but it also helps you read more carefully when you have a specific purpose in mind.

It's like being a detective: As you read, you are constantly on the lookout for the small details that will help you accomplish your task. However, if your teacher assigns your topic afterwards, you will have to go back into the text to find the support that you need.

Context: As you write it will be important to include context, especially when you use cited material from any text. Context is background information about the situation. When you write about literature, art, movies, and films you cannot assume that your audience has had the same experience. How do you write about a short story that your reader hasn't read? How do you discuss a film that your audience hasn't watched? You must tell them what the text is about. Include details that explain who, what, when, where, how, and why. These will help the reader follow along and make sense of your ideas.

Writing without Context	Writing with Context
The sailor tells him that the island's name is "Ship-Trap Island" (1).	In the beginning of Richard Connell's short story "The Most Dangerous Game," two men on a yacht begin a conversation about a nearby island. The sailor tells his companion Rainsford the name of the island is "Ship-Trap Island" (1).

In the following body paragraph, you can see how the writer develops the main idea that *resistance is necessary for survival:*

Who? Grace, the main character in the story

When? She learned when she was younger.

What? She learned that resistance is necessary for survival.

How? Grace learned from her grandmother.

Why? Her ancestors, the Lipan Apache, were forced off their land.

Right from the beginning of the short story, Grace is taught that resistance is necessary for survival. From a young age, Grace hears the stories of how her ancestral grandmothers "resisted the men who tried to round them up and kill them or steal everything that mattered" (Badger 1) **[direct quotation from the text].** Her people, the Lipan Apache, "who trusted the [settlers'] promise of friendship," were forced from their land and were left without a homeland. Despite being stripped of their land and their identity, they survived **[supporting details].** Grace's Mama makes sure to remind her that regardless of the settlers' actions, they could not take their identity. They are always "Lipan Apache" (2). Grace's ancestral grandmothers serve as role models and foreshadow Grace's own type of resistance.

When writing about works of literature, it is common practice to write in the literary present tense. As you write, pretend that those events you are reading about are actually happening *now*.

Notice the bolded verbs in each sentence in the model are all in present tense.

The lessons of resistance she **learns** from her ancestors come in handy when Grace **transfers** to a new school and **meets** Brandon in the chess club. From their first encounter, Brandon **makes** Grace feel like an outsider. He **asks** her where she is from, and when she **responds,** "Vermont," Brandon **dismisses** her answer. This dismissal—meant to establish Brandon's power and privilege over Grace—**does** the opposite. She **recognizes** it and proudly **displays** who she **is** and where she **comes** from: "I am Lipan Apache from the Little Breech-clout band, Tcha shka-ozhaye, of the Kune Tse. My ancestral lands" (1). Grace not only **displays** her pride in her identity, she also **calls** Brandon's comment out by asking him the same question in return when he **shares** that he is from Florida. She **mocks** him when she **repeats,** "But where are you from?" (2). Sheepishly, Brandon **admits,** "OK, funny" (2). Grace **does** not let Brandon intimidate her. She **understands** his question **is** the kind of question that subtly **probes,** "Where are you from, brown-skinned girl?" (2). She not only resists the power he **tries** to wield over her here, but **challenges** his implicit racism.

Conclusions: After you write the introduction and body paragraphs, the last step is to wrap up your ideas in a well-written conclusion. Some teachers advise summing up your previous ideas. I like to tell my students the conclusion is a place to answer the following questions: So what? What now?

Why are your ideas important to consider? What should readers think? What should readers come to understand?

Here are some ways to conclude:

- Include a powerful quotation from another source about the book that seems to summarize your ideas.

- Use a transition such as: in other words, as you can see, without a doubt, certainly, it is clear, etc.

- Pose a question to the reader and, perhaps, answer it too.

- Use repetition.

Let's look at the ending to this literary analysis:

Although losing a friendship is hard, especially when it means being alone in a new school, Grace does not compromise herself nor her integrity to stay in the good graces of a boy who doesn't respect her. When he attempts to punish her by ignoring her and refusing to work with her on a group task, Grace does not negotiate. Instead, she stands up for herself and insists that the teacher let her work alone because Grace refuses to "work with anybody who disrespects [her] that way. Ever" (11). In the end, Grace knows that the only person she has to please is herself. She is her own ally.

> **BTW**
>
> *All sentences have at least one verb. A verb is a word that expresses action or a state of being.*
>
> *For example, action verbs include words like run, jump, think, hop, sing, dance, bring, fall, eat, bake, and hike.*
>
> *For example, linking verbs include words like is, was, were, be, been, and being.*

EXERCISES

EXERCISE 11.1

Read each of the following passages from F. Scott Fitzgerald's novel **The Great Gatsby,** *and respond to the questions that follow.*

Every Friday five crates of oranges and lemons arrived from a fruiterer in New York—every Monday these same oranges and lemons left his back door in a pyramid of pulpless halves. There was a machine in the kitchen which could extract the juice of two hundred oranges in half an hour if a little button was pressed two hundred times by a butler's thumb.

At least once a fortnight a corps of caterers came down with several hundred feet of canvas and enough coloured lights to make a Christmas tree of Gatsby's enormous garden. On buffet tables, garnished with glistening hors-d'oeuvres, spiced baked hams crowded against salads of harlequin designs and pastry pigs and turkeys bewitched to a dark gold.

1. What is the mood of this passage?
    a. Humorous
    b. Peaceful
    c. Enthralling
    d. Gloomy

2. Which of the following examples is an image?
    a. Pyramid of pulpless halves
    b. Spiced baked hams
    c. Garnished with glistening hors-d'oeuvres
    d. All of the above

There was so much to read, for one thing, and so much fine health to be pulled down out of the young breath-giving air. I bought a dozen volumes on banking and credit and investment securities, and they stood on my shelf in red and gold like new money from the mint, promising to unfold the shining secrets that only Midas and Morgan and Maecenas knew. And I had the high intention of reading many other books besides. I was rather literary in college—one year I wrote a series of very solemn and obvious editorials for the Yale News—and now I was going to bring back all such things into my life and become again that most limited of all specialists, the "well-rounded man." This isn't just an epigram—life is much more successfully looked at from a single window, after all.

3. Midas and Morgan and Maecenas are examples of which literary device?
   a. Simile
   b. Personification
   c. Allusions
   d. Imagery

4. King Midas turned everything he touched to Gold. J. P. Morgan was a financier, and Maecenas was a wealthy patron of Rome. Why might F. Scott Fitzgerald make reference to these men in the previous paragraph?
   a. The narrator is comparing himself to these men.
   b. The narrator is inspired by these men.
   c. The narrator is critical of these men.
   d. The narrator does not want to be like them.

A pause; it endured horribly. I had nothing to do in the hall, so I went into the room. Gatsby, his hands still in his pockets, was reclining against the mantelpiece in a strained counterfeit of perfect ease, even of boredom. His head leaned back so far that it rested against the face of a defunct mantelpiece clock, and from this position his distraught eyes stared down at Daisy, who was sitting, frightened but graceful, on the edge of a stiff chair.

5. What is the mood of this passage?

  a. Tense

  b. Casual

  c. Frantic

  d. Serene

6. Which line does not include imagery?

  a. Line 1

  b. Line 2

  c. Line 4

  d. Line 5

"We've met before," muttered Gatsby. His eyes glanced momentarily at me, and his lips parted with an abortive attempt at a laugh. Luckily the clock took this moment to tilt dangerously at the pressure of his head, whereupon he turned and caught it with trembling fingers, and set it back in place. Then he sat down, rigidly, his elbow on the arm of the sofa and his chin in his hand.

"I'm sorry about the clock," he said.

My own face had now assumed a deep tropical burn. I couldn't muster up a single commonplace out of the thousand in my head.

"It's an old clock," I told them idiotically.

I think we all believed for a moment that it had smashed in pieces on the floor.

"We haven't met for many years," said Daisy, her voice as matter-of-fact as it could ever be.

"Five years next November."

7. What might the clock symbolize in this passage?

  a. Regret

  b. The passage of time

  c. Friendship

  d. Knowledge

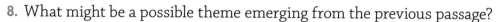

8. What might be a possible theme emerging from the previous passage?
   a. Good friends stick together through thick and thin.
   b. You can't relive the past.
   c. Honesty is the best policy.
   d. Practice makes perfect.

About halfway between West Egg and New York the motor road hastily joins the railroad and runs beside it for a quarter of a mile, so as to shrink away from a certain desolate area of land. This is a valley of ashes—a fantastic farm where ashes grow like wheat into ridges and hills and grotesque gardens; where ashes take the forms of houses and chimneys and rising smoke and, finally, with a transcendent effort, of ash-grey men, who move dimly and already crumbling through the powdery air. Occasionally a line of grey cars crawls along an invisible track, gives out a ghastly creak, and comes to rest, and immediately the ash-grey men swarm up with leaden spades and stir up an impenetrable cloud, which screens their obscure operations from your sight.

9. Which mood best describes this passage?
   a. Hopelessness
   b. Optimism
   c. Idyllic
   d. Lighthearted

10. What might the setting of this passage symbolize?
   a. Freedom
   b. Enlightenment
   c. Life
   d. Decay

EXERCISE 11.2

Read the following model of literary analysis, and answer the questions that follow.
Model Literary Analysis on the Young Adult book Orbiting Jupiter *by Gary D. Schmidt*

How does an eighth-grader who "almost killed a teacher," and who already has a child of his own, sleep with himself at night? Does he wake from nightmares? Does he look out the window in search of Jupiter? Does he read the pages of *Octavian Lost,* hoping to fall back into a deep slumber without waking up his foster brother beside him? Although Joseph has just left a juvenile detention center with a history of a violent past and appears troubled and withdrawn to most, his new family soon learns just how loyal and determined he is at heart. In the novel *Orbiting Jupiter* by Gary D. Schmidt, Joseph isn't the "psycho" everyone believes him to be.

When Joseph first shows up in the fall to live with Jack and his foster family on their farm in Maine, he is initially quiet and standoffish, keeping to himself and talking very little to his new family. Although they try to be kind to him when the social worker delivers him to their home, Joseph is untrusting. When Jack tries to teach Joseph how to milk the cows on the farm, Joseph leaves the barn insisting, "I don't care" (6). He refuses to talk to Jack or his family about his past, and when they try to initiate conversation with him, he seems uncomfortable. He won't shake his new father's hand and won't let his new mother hug him. When Jack's father stands behind Joseph just to get a pail, the closeness triggers a bad reaction in Joseph. He jumps up as if "something exploded" beneath him" (9). The family can tell that something traumatic has happened to Joseph in the juvie hall that makes him stand on edge. Even when the bus driver curiously asks Joseph, "Are you that kid that has a kid?" Joseph backs down the steps, refusing to ride the bus and instead chooses to walk to school in "twenty-one degrees" (12). Jack defends Joseph by getting off the bus as well and is warned by the principal to "be careful of Joseph Brook...you don't know anything about him" (22). Despite the principal's advice, Jack continues to support his foster brother and keeps trying to chip away at Joseph's tough exterior.

Although Joseph makes it hard for Jack to get to know him better, eventually, he drops his guard enough for Jack to see that Joseph is also loyal and determined. When Jack leaves the comfort of the warm bus to walk to school in the cold with Joseph, Jack is surprised when Joseph opens his backpack and tells Jack, "Give me some of your stuff" (13). Joseph's simple gesture tells Jack that Joseph appreciates Jack's "having his back," and Joseph starts to trust Jack a little more. When the boys fall into the ice when they stand on a lake, Joseph takes the blame, telling Jack's father, "He came onto the ice for me" (44). Joseph stands by Jack, proving he is loyal in return.

Despite the fact that several teachers, students, and the principal give Joseph a hard time at school, believing he is violent and "not like us" (21), Joseph proves himself to be dedicated to his family. Even though his real father has beaten him, neglected him, and put him in harm's way, Joseph is determined to find his baby daughter who has been taken from him by a system who thinks he's too young to raise a daughter. Joseph may be too young to be a father, but he's not too young to love.

Finally, Joseph wasn't born violent. He wasn't born troubled. External factors made him that way. Being beaten, being ignored, being neglected made a young boy like Joseph harden, pull away, and close himself off to the world; however, once his foster family took the time to get to know him, they were able to see that below the surface was a boy just waiting to be loved. And once he was shown love, there was no one more loyal.

1. Which of the following statements is the thesis statement?
   a. In the novel *Orbiting Jupiter* by Gary D. Schmidt, Joseph isn't the "psycho" everyone believes him to be.
   b. How does an eighth-grader who "almost killed a teacher," and who already has a child of his own, sleep with himself at night?
   c. Does he wake from nightmares?
   d. When Joseph first shows up in the fall to live with Jack and his foster family on their farm in Maine, he is initially quiet and standoffish.

2. How does the writer capture the reader's attention in the lead paragraph?
   a. The writer poses a question for the reader to consider.
   b. The writer uses a startling detail from the book.
   c. The writer makes the reader sympathize with Joseph.
   d. All of the above

3. When Joseph first shows up in the fall to live with Jack and his foster family on their farm in Maine, he is initially quiet and standoffish, keeping to himself and talking very little to his new family. What is the purpose of this line from paragraph two?
   a. It serves as a hook to draw the reader's attention.
   b. It serves as a topic sentence, giving the essay direction.
   c. It serves as a supporting detail, providing evidence.
   d. It serves as an example, developing the essay.

4. Which of the following statements from paragraph two is a direct quotation from the text?

    a. Although they try to be kind to him when the social worker delivers him to their home, Joseph is untrusting.

    b. He refuses to talk to Jack or his family about his past, and when they try to initiate conversation with him, he seems uncomfortable.

    c. When Jack tries to teach Joseph how to milk the cows on the farm, Joseph leaves the barn insisting, "I don't care."

    d. Despite the principal's advice, Jack continues to support his foster brother and keeps trying to chip away at Joseph's tough exterior.

5. Which of the following is a specific detail in paragraph three?

    a. When Jack leaves the comfort of the warm bus to walk to school in the cold with Joseph, Jack is surprised when Joseph opens his backpack and tells Jack, "Give me some of your stuff."

    b. Joseph's simple gesture tells Jack that Joseph appreciates Jack's "having his back," and Joseph starts to trust Jack a little more.

    c. When the boys fall into the ice when they stand on a lake, Joseph takes the blame, telling Jack's father, "He came onto the ice for me."

    d. All of the above

6. Which word from paragraph four is considered a transition?

    a. Despite

    b. Determined

    c. Young

    d. Students

7. Despite the principal's advice, Jack continues to support his foster brother.

   Which word is a verb in this sentence?

   a. Despite

   b. Advice

   c. Continues

   d. Brother

8. The writer's intent in this essay is to prove which of the following?

   a. Joseph is a difficult kid.

   b. Joseph is not likable.

   c. Joseph is a complex character.

   d. Joseph is living in foster care.

9. Which line from the essay helps the writer provide context for the audience?

   a. How does an eighth-grader who "almost killed a teacher," and who already has a child of his own, sleep with himself at night?

   b. Although Joseph has just left a juvenile detention center with a history of a violent past and appears troubled and withdrawn to most, his new family soon learns just how loyal and determined he is at heart.

   c. Although they try to be kind to him when the social worker delivers him to their home, Joseph is untrusting.

   d. All of the above

10. The purpose of this literary analysis is to prove which of the following?

   a. To argue that Joseph is a complex character

   b. To prove that Joseph has conflicts

   c. To claim that foster kids can find support

   d. To show that a farm setting can be ideal for a child in need

EXERCISE 11.3

1. What is the difference between a reader's response and a literary analysis?
    a. A response is informal; an essay is formal.
    b. The response is less structured than a literary essay.
    c. A response has fewer guidelines than a literary essay.
    d. All of the above

2. What is true regarding responding to literature?
    a. Writing should be in the present tense.
    b. Writing should focus only on your personal experiences.
    c. Writing should be brief.
    d. Writing should consist of a plot summary only.

3. Why should students consult the teacher's rubric before they submit their writing?
    a. Rubrics state the assignment directions.
    b. Rubrics remind students of the due date.
    c. Rubrics provide clear expectations to students.
    d. Rubrics offer helpful suggestions.

4. What is the purpose of a transition?
    a. To organize your ideas
    b. To emphasize your ideas
    c. To support your ideas
    d. To develop your ideas

5. Which transition would not be effective between paragraphs?
   a. Besides
   b. Another
   c. In addition
   d. For example

6. Which of the following is the correct format for titles?
   a. "Anne of Green Gables" is a novel by Lucy Maud Montgomery.
   b. The Most Dangerous Game is a short story by Richard Connell.
   c. *Anne of Green Gables* is a novel that takes place on Prince Edward Island.
   d. *The Most Dangerous Game* is a classic short story about survival.

7. What does *context* mean?
   a. Background information
   b. Chapters in a work of fiction
   c. The introduction of an essay
   d. Textual evidence

8. What is the purpose of providing textual evidence in a response to literature?
   a. To repeat important ideas
   b. To summarize important ideas
   c. To support important ideas
   d. To introduce important ideas

9. What is the function of a lead paragraph?
   a. To capture the interest of the reader
   b. To establish a purpose for writing
   c. To provide important background information
   d. All of the above

10. One way Rainsford uses his wit on the island is relying on his hunting experience.

This line in the essay is most likely an example of:

   a. Lead paragraph

   b. Thesis statement

   c. Textual evidence

   d. Topic sentence

EXERCISE 11.4

Identify the verbs in each of the following sentences, and change them from past tense to present tense.

1. Rainsford did not believe the sailor's superstitions about Ship-Trap Island.

   _____

2. Rainsford argued that jaguars do not feel fear.

   _____

3. In the beginning of the story, the men were talking about hunting.

   _____

4. The men thought hunting was the best sport in the world.

   _____

5. Whitney believed jaguars felt fear of pain and dying.

   _____

6. Rainsford heard a noise that startled him.

   _____

7. Rainsford lost his footing on the yacht and fell into the water below.

   _____

8. Rainsford swam to the nearest island.

   _____

9. Rainsford thought the noise sounded like gunshots.

———————————————————————————————————————

10. Rainsford did not recognize the sound of the animal on the island.

———————————————————————————————————————

EXERCISE 11.5

Read the following analysis of* The Odyssey, *and respond to the questions that follow.

With the inauguration of Kamala Harris as America's first female vice president, the United States has made a lot of progress when it comes to gender roles. In this country, and in others around the world, having a position in politics and holding a place of power has been mostly one limited to men. It has taken hundreds of years for women to be seen as equals. In our world today, women's voices are finally being heard and represented. Women have come a long way from those illustrated in Ancient Greece, where the roles of men and women were traditional. Homer's *The Odyssey* shows readers just how much gender roles have changed since then. In *The Odyssey*, men and women had their rightful place in society. Men were seen as brave warriors who traveled the world and experienced adventures, while women held more conventional roles as the loyal wife, dutiful mother, and good homemaker. In addition, women were seen as valuable prizes to be won.

In the beginning of *The Odyssey*, the male characters are seen as courageous. They are portrayed as adventurous travelers who fight wars, defeat monsters, and face hard trials and conflicts. In *The Odyssey*, Odysseus has been away from home for twenty years. He is known for fighting bravely in the Trojan War. The muse introduces him in the beginning of the text as "a man skilled in all ways contending" (Homer 9. 2). The muse continues to give him praise when she says, "he plundered the stronghold on the proud height of Troy" (9. 4). Other male characters in the text are seen as travelers too. They are out in the world. For example, Hermes flies to find Odysseus in Calypso's cave. "His shoes carry him over water or over endless land in a swish" (9. 35–36). Odysseus's son Telemachus also leaves Ithaca to find his lost father. In addition to travel, the idea that men should be warriors is also seen when Odysseus introduces himself to the King of the Phaeacians when he is a guest. Odysseus talks about his home in Ithaca. Although it is "rocky" it was "good for a boy's training" (5. 136).

Besides being good fighters, men are also viewed as clever and bright. Odysseus not only has a tough body, he also has a strong mind. He uses his brain to resist the lotus eaters and outwit his enemies and trick them, such as when he defeats the one-eyed Cyclops. When asked his name, Odysseus tells the Cyclops his name is "nobody." After Odysseus stabs the Cyclops in his eye, the monster cannot even get help because "nobody tricked" (9. 404) him. Even though the monster is a giant compared to Odysseus and is stronger, Odysseus says, "I drew on all my wits and ran through tactics" (9. 418). Man is viewed in the Greek world as someone who is strong physically and mentally.

Unlike the men who roam, explore, and fight, women in *The Odyssey* tend to be viewed as excellent homemakers. From goddesses to humans like Penelope, the women are always described living in comfortable dwellings, doing arts and crafts such as knitting, singing, or gardening. In the beginning, Odysseus is the goddess Calypso's captive, but the experience is not that terrible because she treats him well, makes him comfortable, and brings him good things to eat and drink. Her home is kept beautiful. She grows "violets" and "parsley" (5. 49–50). Her cave has a "hearthstone, a great fire blazing," and she is singing "in a sweet voice before her loom" (5. 49–50). When the god Hermes arrives to demand Odysseus's release, Hermes is also impressed by her home and says, "Even a god who found his place would gaze and feel his heartbeat with delight" (5. 64–65). Later in his journey, Odysseus describes the goddess Circe in a similar way when he says she grows "violets" and "parsley" (5. 553–554). Her home is also described as "quiet," and he notices that "low she sung" (5. 551–553). He says, "here's a young weaver singing a pretty song to set the air atingle on these lawns and paven courts" (5. 557–559). Circe also is shown to be a good hostess and homemaker as she invites Odysseus and his men into her home. She seats them and treats them to a meal of "cheese and barley and amber honey mixed with Pramnian wine" (10. 565–567).

Although both of these goddesses want to keep Odysseus for their own, he wants to return to his "quiet Penelope" (5. 114). He knows she is not immortal or as beautiful as the goddess Calypso, but his wife is obedient. She has waited for his return home for twenty years. Her loyalty and duty to her husband are shown in many places in the text, such as "her nights and days are wearied out with grieving" (15. 974), and when she sees Odysseus's bow, she "sank down, holding the weapon on her knees and drew her husband's great bow out and sobbed and bit her lip and let the salt tears flow" (15. 1098–1099). Women in this text cater to men.

Finally, men are the ones in power and control while women are powerless. Men need to save and protect women. Odysseus returns and plans to compete in a bow and arrow contest with the suitors who want to marry his wife. Penelope tells the men she is the "prize" for the contest (15. 1115). Odysseus orders that the women in the house "lock their own doors and not show her face but keep seen at her weaving" (21. 1171). Then after Odysseus defeats all the suitors, he is unhappy with his wife because she does not instantly accept him. After twenty years being away, he is mad that his wife is a "strange woman" and her "heart is an iron in her breast" (21. 1350). Even her son tells her she is a "cruel mother" because she is being cold to his father. They expect her to act normal right away and adjust back to normal instantly. In this time, women must always be good wives.

So much has changed since Homer wrote *The Odyssey*. It is good to see that today women and men can both be strong, intelligent, and powerful. Men and women today are more equal than ever before.

1. What does the author analyze in this essay?
   a. The role of government in the United States compared to other countries
   b. The history of women in United States politics
   c. The traditional gender roles in *The Odyssey*
   d. The themes present in the *Odyssey*

2. How does the writer hook the reader's attention in the lead paragraph?
   a. The writer uses a current event.
   b. The writer shares an anecdote.
   c. The writer poses a question.
   d. The writer uses description.

3. What is the purpose for providing the example of Kamala Harris's inauguration?
   a. The writer wants to celebrate the first woman to be vice president of the United States.
   b. The writer wants to argue that more women need to run for political positions.
   c. The writer wants to illustrate the progress women have made since *The Odyssey* was written.
   d. The writer wants to compare and contrast women in politics to women in other professions.

4. According to the essay, what is one difference between men's and women's roles in *The Odyssey*?
   a. Men are expected to be courageous while women are expected to be intelligent.
   b. Men are expected to fight battles while women are expected to be homemakers.
   c. Men are expected to travel while women are expected to hold political positions.
   d. All of the above

5. Which of the following statements would be considered a topic sentence?
    a. Finally, men are the ones in power and control while women are powerless.
    b. She has waited for his return home for twenty years.
    c. Men and women today are more equal than ever before.
    d. Odysseus not only has a tough body, he also has a strong mind.

6. Which of the following words would be considered a transition?
    a. Unlike
    b. Finally
    c. For example
    d. All of the above

7. Which sentence helps the writer provide context to the reader?
    a. In *The Odyssey*, Odysseus has been away from home for twenty years.
    b. Men and women today are more equal than ever before.
    c. Finally, men are the ones in power and control while women are powerless.
    d. It is good to see that today women and men can both be strong, intelligent, and powerful.

8. Which of the following lines would be considered a specific example?
    a. It is good to see that today women and men can both be strong, intelligent, and powerful.
    b. Unlike the men who roam, explore, and fight, women in *The Odyssey* tend to be viewed as excellent homemakers.
    c. Circe also is shown to be a good hostess and homemaker as she invites Odysseus and his men into her home.
    d. In the beginning of *The Odyssey*, the male characters are seen as courageous.

9. She grows "violets" and "parsley" (5. 49–50).

    This sentence is an example of which essential literary analysis requirement?

    a. Topic sentence

    b. Thesis statement

    c. Transitional sentence

    d. Textual evidence

10. What do the numbers in the parentheses indicate?

    a. The number of times the quote appears in the text

    b. The number of pages read

    c. The book number and line numbers

    d. The chapter and the pages

EXERCISE 11.6

Mother to Son
Langston Hughes

> Well, son, I'll tell you:
> Life for me ain't been no crystal stair.
> It's had tacks in it,
> And splinters,
> 5 And boards torn up,
> And places with no carpet on the floor—
> Bare.
> But all the time
> I'se been a-climbin' on,
> 10 And reachin' landin's,
> And turnin' corners,
> And sometimes goin' in the dark
> Where there ain't been no light.
> So, boy, don't you turn back.

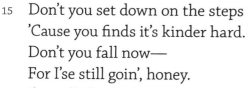

15 Don't you set down on the steps
    'Cause you finds it's kinder hard.
    Don't you fall now—
    For I'se still goin', honey.
    I'se still climbin',
20 And life for me ain't been no crystal stair.
https://poets.org/poem/mother-son

1. Looking at the language in the poem, the words *tacks, splinters,* and *no carpet* symbolize which idea?
   a. Hardships
   b. Relationships
   c. Inconvenience
   d. Consequences

2. Which lines indicate a shift in tone?
   a. Lines 1 and 2
   b. Lines 2 and 3
   c. Lines 7 and 8
   d. Lines 8 and 9

3. How does the tone shift in these lines?
   a. Hopelessness to encouraging
   b. Anger to joyful
   c. Despairing to cynical
   d. Defensive to humorous

4. Where there ain't been no light.
   So, boy, don't you turn back.
   Don't you step down on the steps.
   'Cause you finds it's kinder hard.

What is the message the mother gives her son in these lines?

a. Be aware of the dark.

b. Look before you leap.

c. Keep going.

d. Watch your back.

5. What is meant by the lines "And reachin' landin's/And turnin' corners"? (10–11)

a. The mother was a failure.

b. The mother was organized.

c. The mother was resilient.

d. The mother was observant.

6. What does the mother mean when she refers to the "crystal stair" in line 1?

a. The mother didn't have a comfortable life.

b. The mother was born wealthy.

c. The mother wasn't able to make good choices.

d. The mother wasn't able to see clearly.

7. What might the image "boards torn up" symbolize?

a. The destruction of the stairs

b. The lack of support in life

c. The opportunity to start again

d. The fear of advancing

8. Which line contains imagery?

a. Boards torn up

b. Don't you fall now

c. I'se still climbin'

d. So, boy, don't you turn back.

9. What might the following lines symbolize?
   And sometimes going in the dark/Where there ain't been no light
   a. Death
   b. Love
   c. Hopelessness
   d. Wisdom

10. What might be the poem's theme?
    a. With perseverance, one can overcome.
    b. When faced with problems, run away.
    c. When stressed, exercise.
    d. Parents can help children succeed.

NOTES

Writing to Persuade/Argue

MUST KNOW

 Both persuasive and argument writing attempt to convince others.

 Argument writing presents the audience with both sides of an issue.

 Rhetorical strategies can help writers craft their arguments.

Earlier, you learned how to analyze some of the nonfiction texts you encounter. You learned how to read nonfiction texts through the lens of the rhetorical situation and the three appeals. You also learned to beware of logical fallacies, mistakes in reasoning. In the English language arts (ELA) classroom and in many of your other courses, you will be asked to write persuasively and build strong arguments. In this chapter, you will learn some **must know** tips to compose these types of writing.

Persuasion vs. Argument

What Is Rhetoric?

Plato once said, "Rhetoric is the art of ruling the minds of men." Convincing others is a skill. Whether you want to persuade your parents to extend your curfew or you want to rally students to recycle in the cafeteria, you will need to consider the best way to achieve your goal.

Persuasion and argument have similar goals, but persuasion is based on opinion and feeling, while argument is rooted in logic and reason. Persuasive writers want the audience to agree with them. They want the audience to believe they are right. Argument writers will present both sides, acknowledging that multiple views exist. The audience is expected to weigh all the information and evidence presented and determine what they believe.

 IRL The word *rhetorical* originated in English in the mid-fifteenth century. It means *eloquent.*

What Are Some Types of Persuasive Writing?

Persuasion: Persuasion is trying to influence someone. This skill should be very familiar to you. In fact, you probably use this skill regularly. Maybe you want to convince your friend that the new *Spider-Man* sequel was the best yet. Maybe you want to convince your parents to let you take a day off from school. Maybe you want to convince your teacher to give you more time on an assignment. Commercials, print ads, essays, poems, songs, and speeches are some types of persuasive writing.

How Do You Write a Persuasive Essay?

Choose an issue. My son is in third grade. He is writing a persuasive essay claiming that his dog Viking is the best dog ever. This is a very simple topic; however, he chose this topic because he cares about it. Viking is important to him. What is important to you? What is a topic that compels you to write?

As a middle-schooler, there are many possible ideas around you: Could the cafeteria food be improved? Should your school offer new electives? Should your school have a debate team?

As a teenager, there are many possibilities to draw upon: Do teens spend too much time on their phones? Are teens today more stressed than past generations? Is it better to go to the movies or stream them from home?

As a citizen, there are many important topics to consider: Are teens today more involved in politics than in previous times? Should voting rights be protected? Should vaccines be mandatory?

Focus on one side. My son thinks Viking is the best dog ever. His cousin, however, disagrees. She thinks Viking is too small to have fun. She thinks Viking isn't trained well, and she thinks Viking is boring. Taking a side means choosing your position on an issue. For example, you can agree that vaccines should be mandated or you can disagree.

Identify convincing reasons. My son believes Viking is the best dog ever because he is smart, loyal, and obedient. These are simple reasons. After all, he is only eight, but you must come up with reasons why you hold the opinion that you do.

If you believe the cafeteria food needs to be improved, your reasons could include:

1. The food is unhealthy.

2. The choices are limited.

3. There are no vegetarian options.

If you believe teens are more politically active than previous generations, your reasons could include:

1. Social media gives teenagers a platform.

2. More teenagers believe they can affect change.

3. Teenagers today have experienced many tumultuous events in their lives.

Persuade through emotion, logic, and character. In the "Analyzing Nonfiction" chapter, you learned about ethos, logos, and pathos. Persuasive writing relies on these three appeals to convince your audience.

Here's how my son uses the three appeals:

Ethos: I have had a dog for two years now, and my experience with Viking shows that he is the best dog ever. I have had experiences with other dogs and, in my opinion, Viking is much better behaved.

Pathos: When I get off the school bus, Viking is already at the window waiting for me. His tail is wagging, and he is barking with excitement. I can hear his barks through the door.

Logos: Viking is a goldendoodle and stands at fifteen inches in height and weighs twenty-five pounds. His medium build allows him to play in ways that a more petite dog couldn't.

Let's try this topic: Teens are more politically active than past generations.

Ethos: As a teenager, I am concerned about global warming. In my lifetime, I have read about icebergs melting and lakes disappearing, and I am concerned about my future. It is important for me to get involved.

Logos: According to an article in the *New York Times*, "Research shows that a voting generation is typically shaped for life by what happens politically in their teen years and early 20s."

Pathos: Today's teenagers have experienced a pandemic, protests, and school shootings that have left them feeling frustrated with the status quo.

Let's look at the persuasive essay on filters:

When I was in middle school, I begged my mother to take me to Glamour Shots, a well-known photography studio in our local mall. I was thirteen years old, and all of my friends were having their pictures taken there. The studio was known for making their subjects look like professional models. The portraits were too expensive for my parents to afford, but even still, they were very practical and probably had much better ways to spend their money than waste it on a sixty-minute photo shoot for their eighth-grader.

> Appeals to ethos: The author had a similar experience with appearance and beauty.

"Why do you even want these photos anyway?" my mother asked. Well, of course, all of the cool girls at school were posing for their shots there. At lunch, they'd pull the glossy photos of themselves all made over, makeup and hair perfectly styled. They looked so gorgeous it took my breath away. So, I guess it was the usual adolescent draw: I wanted to be trendy and popular too, but also, who wouldn't want to look perfect and flawless like a cover girl splashed across the front page of the latest teen magazine? Back in the '80s, I longed to look just like those thin, long-legged Levi's-jeans-wearing goddesses that graced the covers of *Sassy* and *Seventeen*. Cindy Crawford, Elle Macpherson, and Brooke Shields were goddesses to me, and the attempt—at any cost—to transform into them *even for an hour* was tempting.

> Appeals to pathos: The author uses examples and language to make the audience sympathetic, feeling bad for her.

I never liked the photos my family took of me. I wasn't photogenic, and I cringed anytime I saw the prints after my mother developed them at the photo booth. I felt fat. I hated the angles in my permed hair. I hated my braces. In essence, I hated the natural me. Somehow, I believed Glamour Shots could capture me in a way my parents couldn't. In their studio, I would finally be beautiful under their magical lens.

Although I never got the chance to take those photos, I was recently reminded of Glamour Shots when I was on TikTok. A young woman was showing her image before and after with a filtering app called Beauty Filter. Filters are defined as "preset edits that can change and enhance your appearance." I was equally impressed and concerned. On one hand, this was the chance to have the Glamour Shots ability at one's fingertips; however, as an adult and mother, I was worried. What messages do these filters send young people today and what will be some of the devastating effects to our children's self-esteem, body image, and confidence with their access to change their appearance with a simple tap of a screen? Poutier lips? Tap. Higher cheekbones? Tap. Different eye shade or hair color? Tap. Instantly thin? Tap. Flawless skin? Tap. Symmetrical features? Tap. With these concerns in mind, I think teenagers should not use filters.

Appeals to logos: The author provides a definition of filters for those in the audience who may be unfamiliar.

First, filters can affect self-esteem. Teenagers already feel anxious about their appearance. When they see this new version of themselves, they are bound to find even more fault in their natural self. Studies show that social media already causes teenagers to experience anxiety and depression. Filters will only exacerbate these debilitating emotions. In an article published on the Child Mind Institute website, Caroline Miller includes a quote from clinical psychologist Dr. Hamlet: "If that's their model for what is normal, it can be very hard on their self-confidence."

The author provides her first reason: Filters affect self-esteem.

Second, filters also feed into the notion that there is a perfect appearance. What is the definition of beautiful? Who establishes these unrealistic expectations? A one-size-fits-all definition of beauty does not exist. Filters create an unrealistic standard of beauty. When teenagers see these edited pictures online, they tend to feel ugly in comparison.

The author appeals to logos by quoting a reputable source with a direct quotation from an expert.

The author includes a second convincing reason: The filters create unrealistic standards of beauty.

Argument

When you hear the word *argument*, you probably think of a big, noisy fight. At this age, you tend to argue with your siblings, your parents, and your friends. So, it's natural to think of an argument in a negative light. However, arguments don't have to be loud or heated. In fact, most arguments are so quiet you might not even realize they are there. Arguments are everywhere: in books, essays, editorials, movies, speeches, plays, ads, and commercials. Even a saying on a t-shirt can be an argument!

An argument is a line of reasoning given to prove a point. An argument isn't always used for criticism. Arguments reveal someone's viewpoint. It is an exchange of views. It is a set of reasons to persuade others. Arguments can be short or long, but they all follow a similar pattern. An argument makes a claim, presents supporting evidence, and boils down to a conclusion. The more credible the support, the stronger the argument.

 IRL Here are some popular arguments you may have heard:

- If you work hard, you can accomplish your dreams.
- Eat healthy if you want to live a longer life.
- Happiness is a state of mind.
- Too much screen time is not good for children.

How Do You Build an Argument?

Consider format. There are many ways to structure an effective argument, but here is a basic model for beginners. As you become better at writing, you can experiment with more sophisticated structures.

- Hook and thesis

- First claim with supporting evidence

- Second claim with supporting evidence

- Third claim with supporting evidence

- Conclusion

BTW

Writing should never be formulaic. It's important to take risks, be creative, and understand why writers make the decisions they do. It's like any skill—learn the foundations and then break free from the form. As a baker, I started by following recipes exactly. As I've become more experienced, confident, and knowledgeable, I've altered recipes, improved recipes, and even created recipes. It's the same with writing. Don't be afraid to deviate.

Choose a position. What side of the issue are you on? Where do you stand? Your position must be arguable, open for dispute. When you write an argument, it's important to research your topic fully. Sometimes students choose a topic and take a side because they have already established a stance on the issue. However, after learning more, they begin to feel differently. They begin to realize there are multiple perspectives to consider and many factors that make the issue complex.

When you argue you can fully defend, challenge, or qualify.

I fully agree with the school's new cell phone policy.	The writer defends the policy.
I fully disagree with the school's new cell phone policy.	The writer challenges the policy.
Although there are good intentions behind the school's new cell phone policy, the new cell phone policy has not been effective.	The writer qualifies.

Here are some more sentence starters to help you express your position:

Defending

- I believe...

- It is right that...

- It is true that...

- It is correct...

- I support...

- It is right that...

Challenging

- I disagree with...

- I don't support...

- I don't believe...

- It is not fair...

- It is not right...

- It is wrong to...

Qualifying

- I have mixed feelings...

- I am of two minds...

- I recognize _____ but...

- Although it seems _____, however...

- Of course, _____, but still...

- True, _____, but...

- Sure, _____, and yet, _____

BTW

Do not oversimplify issues. The best way to argue is to qualify. Qualifying does not mean changing your position or switching sides. When you qualify, you show the audience that you recognize that the issue is not black or white, all or nothing. Through your research, you acknowledge that there are multiple factors and perspectives. By qualifying you will seem more credible and trustworthy.

Establish claims. Why do you think the new cell phone policy is unfair? Why are you against book censorship? Why do you believe the traditional grading system is ineffective? When you write an argument, you must establish claims, the reasons to support your position.

Here is an outline of claims for an argument essay:

Too much screen time can negatively impact teenagers.	Thesis
Too much screen time can affect the mental health of a teenager.	Claim #1
Too much screen time can affect the physical health of a teenager.	Claim #2
Too much screen time can also affect learning.	Claim #3

Support the claim. It's important to research and gather evidence to support your claim. Look for information that is current, credible, and reliable. The best evidence includes statistics, facts, case studies, expert testimony, and polls.

Here is the same outline with supporting evidence:

Too much screen time can negatively impact teenagers.	Thesis
Too much screen time can affect the mental health of a teenager.	Claim #1
a. Adolescent psychologist Evie Callahan reports that screen time has caused "more anxiety, depression, and other mental health struggles than previous generations."	Evidence
Too much screen time can affect the physical health of a teenager.	Claim #2
a. A Stanford Children's Health study reported "only 5% of U.S. teens are meeting their exercise goals."	Evidence
Too much screen time can also affect learning.	Claim #3
a. A National Institutes of Health study found that children who spent more than two hours a day on electronic devices scored lower on thinking and language tests.	Evidence

Reasoning

Connect evidence with reasoning. Once you have added your evidence and support, don't leave the reader hanging. It's not the reader's job to make the connection between your evidence and the claim. This is the writer's responsibility. Explain why the evidence is important. How does the fact or statistic support your claim? Be clear.

Here is the same outline with reasoning:

Too much screen time can negatively impact teenagers.	Thesis
Too much screen time can affect the mental health of a teenager.	Claim #1
a. Adolescent psychologist Evie Callahan reports that screen time has caused "more anxiety, depression, and other mental health struggles than previous generations."	Evidence
When teenagers engage with social media, they often feel bad about themselves. They see pictures and posts from friends and peers that make their own lives seem dull in comparison. Sometimes they may experience rejection for not being included in an event. Or they feel jealousy that others are traveling and doing fun activities that they are not experiencing themselves. These examples contribute to higher rates of depression and anxiety.	Reasoning

Too much screen time can affect the physical health of a teenager.	Claim #2
a. A Stanford Children's Health study reported "only 5% of U.S. teens are meeting their exercise goals."	Evidence
With an increase in screen time, teens are staying indoors more and not moving. They are not as active as they should be. Leading a sedentary life can bring about many health issues, such as obesity and diabetes.	Reasoning
Too much screen time can also affect learning.	Claim #3
a. A National Institutes of Health study found that children who spent more than two hours a day on electronic devices scored lower on thinking and language tests.	Evidence
Teens who spend too much time on the screen can develop issues with focus and concentration. It also may make learning feel boring, thus reducing motivation in the classroom.	Reasoning

Distinguish between counterclaims. Argument writing differs from persuasive writing because it takes into account other sides and perspectives. An effective argument provides the pros and cons so the audience can arrive at their own conclusions. Addressing counterclaims also helps the writer appear more credible, trustworthy, and knowledgeable.

Counterargument: When you argue with a friend in a conversation, there will be opposition. After listening to what your friend has to say, you can offer a counterargument, which attempts to discredit or prove the viewpoint wrong. When you write an argument, your audience cannot argue with you directly, but you can anticipate some of their objections and respond to them in the body of your essay.

> **BTW**
>
> A writer can also build credibility by conceding. A writer can admit that there is some truth or merit to the opposition's viewpoint. However, the writer should also follow up with a rebuttal, explaining why the opposition is misguided, incorrect, or confused.
>
> **It is true:** Screen time can offer invaluable opportunities to socialize with peers and build relationships. **However,** online social interactions cannot replace the benefits of face-to-face interactions.

Refutation: A strong argument will address a counterclaim, but it will also include a refutation to prove the opposition wrong. If you don't provide a refutation, the reader will be confused, thinking you switched sides.

Let's look at an example of counterargument and refutation:

Although teenagers claim that screen time offers invaluable opportunities to socialize with peers and build relationships, online social interactions cannot replace the benefits of face-to-face interactions.	Counterargument acknowledges the other side.
In fact, studies have shown that too much screen time can affect the way teenagers relate to others. Research published in *Computers in Human Behavior* concluded that "preteens who spent time away from screens became better at reading human emotions compared to their peers who were not restricted from screens."	Refutation offers evidence to offset the opposition's position.

Conclusions: Strong conclusions are just as important as effective beginnings. There are many ways to conclude an argument essay, but the best one is a call to action. What do you hope your readers will do with this information? What do you hope happens next? What do you want your readers to change, do differently, or believe instead?

Here are some other effective conclusion suggestions:

- Provide a suggestion.

- Offer a compromise.

- Give readers something new to consider.

- Include an *imagine this* or a hypothetical situation.

- Ask a rhetorical question that leaves the audience thinking.

How Can You Craft Your Argument?

Rhetorical Question: "What in the world?" Did you ever ask a question out loud without really expecting an answer? This is a rhetorical question, and writers often post questions to their audience expecting a reply. A rhetorical question asks the audience to think. It is also a great way to establish a voice in your writing and appear conversational. It also creates a dramatic effect.

 Here are some famous examples of a rhetorical question:

In Shakespeare's tragedy *The Merchant of Venice*, Shylock asks rhetorical questions:

> If you prick us, do we not bleed?
>
> If you tickle us, do we not laugh?
>
> If you poison us, do we not die? and if you wrong us, shall we not revenge?

Sojourner Truth delivered a speech in 1851 called "Ain't I a Woman?"

That man over there says that women need to be helped into carriages, and lifted over ditches, and to have the best place everywhere. Nobody ever helps me into carriages, or over mud-puddles, or gives me any best place! And ain't I a woman? Look at me! Look at my arm! I have ploughed and planted, and gathered into barns, and no man could head me! And ain't I a woman?

Rhetorical Strategies

Hypophora: Sometimes writers go a step forward and answer the question posed themselves. This strategy is known as hypophora, and it can capture your audience's attention as they listen to hear if their inner thinking is correct. This is an effective strategy in argument writing as it shows the writer is knowledgeable and knows the answer, establishing trust and credibility.

Here is an example of hypophora from John F. Kennedy's 1962 moon speech:

But why, some say, the moon? Why choose this as our goal? And they may well ask why climb the highest mountain? Why, 35 years ago, fly the Atlantic? Why does Rice play Texas?

We choose to go to the moon. We choose to go to the moon in this decade and do the other things, not because they are easy, but because they are hard, because that goal will serve to organize and measure the best of our energies and skills, because that challenge is one that we are willing to accept, one we are unwilling to postpone, and one which we intend to win, and the others, too.

Anaphora: "We choose to go to the moon. We choose to go to the moon." This is a rhetorical device known as anaphora. It is a type of repetition where the first word of each phrase or clause repeats to emphasize ideas or to create an effect or anticipation. The audience expects the words to repeat.

IRL The Gettysburg Address is considered one of the best American speeches of all time.

Abraham Lincoln uses anaphora in the Gettysburg Address:

But, in a larger sense, we cannot dedicate—we cannot consecrate—we cannot hallow—this ground. The brave men, living and dead, who struggled here, have consecrated it, far above our poor power to add or detract.

EXERCISES

EXERCISE 12.1

Read the following text, and answer the questions that follow.

I was in Nice, August 31, the day Princess Diana died.

Standing in the lobby of our hostel, my two friends and I—who had just spent the past six weeks backpacking through a myriad of European cities—were shocked. As little girls, we had watched her televised wedding to Prince Charles in 1981. We were awed by her designer gown of ivory taffeta, intricately embroidered with sequins, frilled lace, and 10,000 pearls. We were stunned by the 3,500-person crowd that stood for hours to catch a quick glimpse of the people's princess. At seven years old, we watched with envy as a real princess wed her Prince Charming, the epitome of our wildest dreams. Now, sixteen years later, the Princess of Wales was pronounced dead, killed in a car crash in a Paris tunnel after being chased by paparazzi. The fairy tale did not have a happy ending after all.

If you were as enchanted as I by the life of Diana Spencer, a commoner who married into royalty and British scandal, capturing the heart of the world after her marriage to the future King of England, then Peter Morgan's *The Crown* is the next binge for you. The successful Netflix series portrays the harsh realities of living a life of privilege and exposes the truth to every girl who bought into the fantasy: Being a part of the royal family is not all that it's cracked up to be. In fact, it can be downright deadly.

Currently in its fourth season, *The Crown* begins with the sudden coronation of a young Queen Elizabeth II (played by Claire Foy) after her father, King George, dies. Only twenty-five years old, inexperienced, and insecure, Queen Elizabeth is thrust into the position of power and struggles to adapt to her new role as leader of the modern world. This task of navigating the old world of rules, protocol, and procedure is not an easy task to maneuver for the queen or any other member of her inner circle. The family works tirelessly to promote an image of perfection and purity to the public, to hide flaw, fault, and scandal, and to portray themselves as incapable of mistake or folly. In the name of tradition, children are separated from their families, sent to boarding schools, foreign universities, and military life against their dreams and wishes. Forbidden from divorce and undesirable love matches, the queen, her sister, Princess Margaret, and several members of different generations of royalty all become victims of broken hearts and loveless marriages. It seems as if living life in Buckingham Palace spares no one from the miseries and sorrows of everyday life. In fact, it seems that the members of the monarchy actually suffer and perish more.

If anything, *The Crown* illuminates just how unhappy life as a new princess can be in the portrayal of Princess Diana's (played by Emma Corrin) lonely months after her marriage to Prince Charles in season four. Angry and jealous of Charles's ongoing relationship with Camilla Shand, Princess Diana spends days under the covers in her bedroom refusing to come out, roller-skates alone in the corridors of the palace, and waits eagerly for a phone call from her prince when he is away for months—a call that never comes. Why would anyone want to be a princess? *The Crown* shows just how isolating and depressing the life of a princess can be.

1. This piece is most likely which of the following?
    a. A news story about the latest royal scandal
    b. A biography of Princess Diana
    c. A letter to the show's producer
    d. A review of a popular show

2. The purpose of this piece is:
    a. To argue that the life of a princess is downright awful
    b. To persuade the reader to watch the show
    c. To convince the reader to boycott Netflix
    d. To urge the audience to learn more about Princess Diana

3. The writer hooks the audience's attention by:
    a. Sharing a startling fact about Princess Diana
    b. Comparing her life to that of Princess Diana
    c. Sharing an anecdote
    d. Defining royalty

4. Why does the writer choose to share her childhood memories of Princess Diana?
    a. She was always fascinated with her but never realized how hard being royalty could be.
    b. She was sad to hear about the tragedy.
    c. She hoped to meet Princess Diana in person during her travels.
    d. She hopes others will learn more about her.

5. Which of the following examples from *The Crown* show that Princess Diana may have struggled as a princess?
    a. We were awed by her designer gown of ivory taffeta, intricately embroidered with sequins, frilled lace, and 10,000 pearls.
    b. Princess Diana spends days under the covers in her bedroom refusing to come out.
    c. It seems as if living life in Buckingham Palace spares no one from the miseries and sorrows of everyday life.
    d. In fact, it can be downright deadly.

6. Which rhetorical strategy does the writer use to craft the following passage?
    We were awed by her designer gown of ivory taffeta, intricately embroidered with sequins, frilled lace, and 10,000 pearls. We were stunned by the 3,500-person crowd that stood for hours to catch a quick glimpse of the people's princess.
    a. Rhetorical question
    b. Hypophora
    c. Anaphora
    d. All of the above

7. Why does the writer include the specific details about Princess Diana's wedding?

    a. To make the reader jealous

    b. To show why little girls would admire a princess

    c. To argue that the wedding dress was too elaborate

    d. To convince readers to watch the next royal wedding

8. "Why would anyone want to be a princess?" Which rhetorical strategy does the writer use here?

    a. Rhetorical question

    b. Hypophora

    c. Anaphora

    d. Example

9. What is the intended effect of the anaphora in these lines?

    We were awed by her designer gown of ivory taffeta, intricately embroidered with sequins, frilled lace, and 10,000 pearls. We were stunned by the 3,500-person crowd that stood for hours to catch a quick glimpse of the people's princess.

    a. Readers want to see the dress for themselves.

    b. Readers understand why the girls were impressed.

    c. Readers are saddened by the tragedy.

    d. Readers become envious of the display of wealth.

10. What is the intended effect of this rhetorical question: "Why would anyone want to be a princess?"

    a. Readers will want to become royalty.

    b. Readers will challenge their misconceptions about royalty.

    c. Readers will never watch the show now.

    d. Readers will be compelled to learn more about the British royalty.

EXERCISE 12.2

Read the following text, and answer the questions that follow.

Anywhere you go, you will see people staring at their phones. You may see people on their phones in the movie theater, on the train, or in line at the supermarket. Sometimes you might even see someone looking at a phone while driving! Teens might be the biggest group of users nowadays. They come home from school and they might want to create a TikTok video, watch videos on YouTube, or check out a celebrity's newest Instagram post. This "digital connectedness" all sounds fun, but it has come to my attention that there are some negative problems caused when teens spend too much time online. Besides feeling more anxiety and depression, teens can also be cyberbullied.

One reason for concern is that teens who spend too much time on social media may experience anxiety and depression because of what they see online. When teenagers go online they can view the lives of celebrities and the lives of their friends. Teens often compare themselves to the images they see. For example, they may see fancy homes or luxurious vacations and feel sad and depressed because their lives are not as exciting. In the article "Teens Are More Anxious Than Ever: Is Social Media to Blame?," the author, Denise Ambre, explains that teens develop a distorted view of life. What this means is that teens cannot tell the difference between reality and the fantasy they see online. The author says some of them might not realize that the posts they see are the "messiness of life scrubbed out." Caitlin Hearty is a seventeen-year-old who admits that when she goes online she "feels left out" (Ambre 2021). Teens can see pictures of what their friends are doing. Maybe their friends are hanging out or attending a party, and the viewer who wasn't invited can see it. Before social media, the teen may not have known. Now teens have a "front seat to all of this" (Ambre 2021). Teens are going to feel anxiety and depression as they continue "to measure their worth by likes and followers" (Ambre 2021). Basically, what this means is that the online world has become a big popularity contest.

In addition, being connected on social media has caused an increase in suicide because of cyberbullying. When teens used to be able to escape bullying after the school day, now social media brings the teasing and bullying home to them in their own space. Over the past few years there have been so many sad stories of teens who were bullied so badly online that they took their own lives. Parents and educators were not aware of the online teasing that led these kids to take their own lives. According to the article "Teen Suicide Rates Rising, Study Says Social Media Could Be a Factor," the Associated Press warns us that due to social media "suicides have risen from 2010–2015." One seventeen-year-old who was interviewed, Chloe Schilling, explained that "no one posts the bad things they are going through." When the average teen is spending more than "five hours online," it is going to impact how they feel about themselves. According to the article, "Thirty-six percent of all teens reported feeling desperately sad or hopeless, or thinking about, planning or attempting suicide" (Teen 2017). What this means is that social media may be harming teens more than helping them.

Although there are many downsides to social connectedness for teens, there are benefits to screen time if it is limited. In the article "Video Games Can Be Harmless and Even Helpful," the student writer discusses some ways that being online can help teens. Playing an online game such as *Fortnite* can give teens a way to play with friends and the community online. A common hobby can also give teens something to talk about at school. In addition, playing games can "soothe your brain and help you calm down" (Student). However, even Cheney Wu, the author, warns that teens should play fewer than "three hours" a week. What this means is that small amounts of time are okay, but long times spent can bring on big consequences.

In conclusion, phones now can monitor the amount of time teens spend on their phones. They can see how much time they are on social media and how much time they spend watching videos and playing games. Teens should be encouraged to monitor their time and track it each day so they know how to balance on-screen time with off-screen time. When off screen, teenagers need to make sure they are going outside, getting exercise, and spending time with family and friends—staying connected face to face in order to reduce depression, anxiety, and other downsides of using devices too much.

1. What type of writing is the text?
   a. A review praising an Apple product
   b. An editorial criticizing TikTok
   c. A report informing readers about the dangers of too much screen time
   d. An essay arguing that teens can be harmed by social media

2. Who might be the intended audience?
   a. Parents
   b. Teenagers
   c. Guidance counselors
   d. All of the above

3. Which sentence is a claim?
   a. However, even Cheney Wu, the author, warns that teens should play fewer than "three hours" a week.
   b. One seventeen-year-old who was interviewed, Chloe Schilling, explained that "no one posts the bad things they are going through."
   c. In addition, being connected on social media has caused an increase in suicide because of cyberbullying.
   d. Playing an online game such as *Fortnite* can give teens a way to play with friends and the community online.

4. Basically, what this means is that the online world has become a big popularity contest.
   This sentence serves as:
   a. A grabbing hook
   b. Supporting evidence
   c. The thesis statement
   d. A tie between the evidence and the claim

5. According to the article, "Thirty-six percent of all teens reported feeling desperately sad or hopeless, or thinking about, planning or attempting suicide" (Teen 2017).

   This line serves which purpose in the essay?

   a. It states the argument.

   b. It provides evidence for a claim.

   c. It opposes the opposing viewpoint.

   d. It unpacks the evidence.

6. Although there are many downsides to social connectedness for teens, it is not all bad if the time spent online is limited.

   What is the purpose of this sentence?

   a. It provides evidence.

   b. It concedes to an opposing view.

   c. It explains the significance of provided evidence.

   d. It states a claim.

7. However, even Cheney Wu, the author, warns that teens should play fewer than "three hours" a week.

   This sentence is important because:

   a. It is evidence that too much screen time can cause depression.

   b. It is the writer's summary of the evidence.

   c. It is one reason why unlimited screen time can be harmful.

   d. It is a rebuttal to the benefits that screen time brings.

8. Playing an online game such as *Fortnite* can give teens a way to play with friends and the community online.

   What is the purpose of this sentence?

   a. It is an example of the benefits screen time provides teens.

   b. It is a comparison of other online games.

   c. It is a fact that supports the benefits of online gaming.

   d. It is an opinion about the dangers of online gaming.

9. What type of evidence did the writer use to support the claims?
   a. Interviews with experts
   b. Results from polls
   c. Statistics
   d. All of the above

10. How does this essay conclude?
    a. The reader is given a question to consider.
    b. The reader is asked to imagine a world without phones.
    c. The reader is called to action.
    d. The reader is provided with solutions.

NOTES

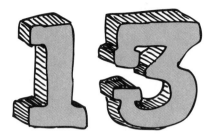

13 Conventions to Know

MUST ⚡ KNOW

⚡ Avoid plagiarism: using another work without permission.

⚡ When you use a direct quotation, be sure to ICE: incorporate, cite, explain.

⚡ When you use evidence from the text, be sure to follow citation rules.

I n the English language arts (ELA) classroom and in many of your other classes, you will be assigned various writing tasks that will require you to use information from outside sources. This is a skill that you will learn in middle school and will continue to use throughout high school and well beyond. In the previous chapters, you have seen models of literary analysis and argument writing, which both include source materials. In this chapter, you will learn some rules for working with sources: how to avoid plagiarism, how to use source materials with ease, and how to cite these materials correctly.

What Is Plagiarism? How Can You Avoid It?

Plagiarism: When you take someone's ideas and claim them to be your own, you have plagiarized. Plagiarism is, in essence, cheating. If you were to lie and tell everyone that you wrote the lyrics to a popular song, or that you created one of the TikTok dances, or that you invented a well-known product, you would be accused of plagiarism. Believe it or not, there are actually lawyers who fight to protect the legal rights of writers, inventors, and artists so their ideas cannot be used without permission. Theft of property can result in jail time or fines. Plagiarism is a serious offense in school as well. You could end up in detention, be suspended, receive a zero for an assignment, or fail a class.

There are many forms of plagiarism or academic dishonesty. When I was younger, I was taught that copying information from a textbook or article without citing it was considered plagiarism. Now, technology has expanded ways in which cheating can occur. Taking information from the Internet without citing the source is also considered plagiarism.

BTW

Here are some other forms of plagiarism that students overlook: Copying a friend's work and submitting it as your own is one way you can plagiarize. Turning in old work for a new class is another form of dishonesty. Yes, using your own work in a different class is also cheating! Many high school teachers and university professors frown on recycling work. They expect you to do original work for the purpose of their class.

Even *mosaic plagiarism* is problematic. This is when students think taking a few words from a source is okay. They think they can change a few words from the original source and pass the ideas off as their own. It's not okay. Anytime you take any words or ideas that are not your own, you are cheating.

Avoiding Plagiarism

How Do You Use Source Materials without Plagiarizing?

Citation is the conscious borrowing of someone else's writing or ideas for your writing. As long as you give credit or refer to the source of your information, it is okay to use words or ideas that are not your own. If the information you are taking is common knowledge, then you do not have to cite. For example, George Washington was the first president of the United States of America. This fact is considered public knowledge.

Paraphrasing vs. Direct Quoting: There are two types of ways to borrow someone else's ideas. You can *paraphrase* or you can copy *word-for-word* by using quotation marks. Either way, you must provide attribution to the original source. You must let the reader know the source of the information.

Paraphrasing: When you use outside sources for your work, you can either cite the words exactly as stated in a text, or you can paraphrase, reword, and rewrite the ideas or concepts using your own words. However, even if you paraphrase, those words and ideas belong to someone else. You must provide the original source inside your sentence or at the end of a sentence.

Here are two examples using our mentor text *Anne of Green Gables:*

Original Text: Mrs. Rachel Lynde lived just where the Avonlea main road dipped down into a little hollow, fringed with alders and ladies' eardrops and traversed by a brook that had its source away back in the woods of the old Cuthbert place; it was reputed to be an intricate, headlong brook in its earlier course through those woods, with dark secrets of pool and cascade; but by the time it reached Lynde's Hollow it was a quiet, well-conducted little stream, for not even a brook could run past Mrs. Rachel Lynde's door without due regard for decency and decorum; it probably was conscious that

Mrs. Rachel was sitting at her window, keeping a sharp eye on everything that passed, from brooks and children up, and that if she noticed anything odd or out of place she would never rest until she had ferreted out the whys and wherefores thereof.

Plagiarism: Mrs. Rachel Lynde lives on a road in Avonlea. It is fringed with alders and ladies' eardrops and traversed by a brook that had its source away back in the woods of the old Cuthbert place.

Word-for-Word Citation: The main road where Mrs. Rachel Lynde lives is described as a "little hollow fringed with alders and ladies' eardrops" (1).

Paraphrase: In the book *Anne of Green Gables* by Lucy Maud Montgomery, Mrs. Rachel Lynde lives very close to the Cuthbert place. Her home is on the main road, and the author situates this character there so that she can be privy to all of the secrets in Avonlea. No one can hide from her gaze.

Here is another example from a passage from *The Woman and the Car* by Dorothy Levitt, published in 1901.

Now, as to ordinary garments, dress for the season of the year exactly as you would if you were not going motoring. I would advise shoes rather than boots as they give greater freedom to the ankles and do not tend to impede the circulation, as a fairly tightly laced or buttoned boot would do, but this is a matter of individual taste. In winter time it is advisable to wear high gaiters, have them specially made, almost up to the knee.

Word-for-Word Citation: In her book *The Woman and the Car*, Dorothy Levitt urges women to wear "shoes rather than boots as they give greater freedom to the ankles" (15).

Paraphrase: In the book *The Woman and the Car*, women are advised to consider the shoes on their feet when driving. Shoes can give women better access to the pedals and brakes, whereas boots can be challenging as they interfere with circulation (Levitt 15).

How Do You Cite the Work from Other Sources?

When you were in elementary school, teachers may have asked you to support your thinking with text evidence, but they may not have asked you to use Modern Language Association (MLA) guidelines and cite correctly.

Now that you are in middle school, following the rules of citation will be more important. There are several systems of citation; however, the most common for students in the ELA classroom is MLA.

IRL There are three major citation styles used in academic writing. Your teacher will determine which one to use.
- Modern Language Association (MLA)
- American Psychological Association (APA)
- Chicago Manual of Style (CMOS)

In-Text Citation: As you insert citation into the body of your writing, you will need to cite internally, inside the paper. The highlighted lines in the following sample literary analysis show examples of in-text citation.

Right from the beginning of the short story, Grace is taught that resistance is necessary for survival. From a young age, Grace hears the stories of how her ancestral grandmothers **"resisted the men who tried to round them up and kill them or steal everything that mattered" (Badger 1)**. Her people, the Lipan Apache, **"who trusted the [settlers'] promise of friendship,"** were forced from their land and were left without a homeland. Despite being stripped of their land and their identity, they survived. Grace's Mama makes sure to remind her that regardless of the settlers' actions, they could not take their identity. **They are always "Lipan Apache" (2)**. Grace's ancestral grandmothers serve as role models and foreshadow Grace's own type of resistance.

For literature, when you want to cite the text word-for word, you must follow the following rules:

1. Use quotation marks around the words you borrowed from the text.

2. Add the author's last name and the page numbers from the source: (Montgomery 2);

BTW

If you are using only one source, you only have to refer to the author's last name in the first citation you use. After that, you can use the page number only.

If you are using more than one source in your writing, continue to use the authors' last names in each and every citation so your reader knows exactly which work you are discussing.

if the quotation comes from more than one page, use a dash: (Montgomery 2–3).

3. Place a period at the end of the sentence, after the parentheses: (Montgomery 9).

For poetry, cite the line numbers instead: In Robert Frost's poem "Mending Wall," we are reminded, "Good fences make good neighbors" (43–44).

In the poem "Mending Wall," we are reminded, "Good fences make good neighbors" (Frost 43–44).

For nonfiction texts, include the author's last name and page number: (Scardina 186). If the source does not use page numbers, then do not include a page number: (Scardina).

BTW

If you are citing a work from William Shakespeare, internal citation would look like this:

(3.1.21–23)
Act/scene/page numbers

or

(III.i.21–23)
You can also use Roman numerals.

Citation Rules

What Are the Best Ways to Work Cited Material into Your Writing?

ICE: Many English teachers use the acronym ICE to help students remember how to work with in-text citations. ICE stands for introduce, cite, and explain. I, personally, also like to use the *I* for incorporate. (I'll explain more momentarily.)

Here are some more helpful tips for in-text citation that you need to know.

Introduce: What does it mean to introduce a quote, you may ask? I like to explain this concept in this way: If you went to a party or event and you didn't know everyone, a thoughtful host would most likely make introductions. The host would bring you around and introduce you to the others. "Hello, Mike, I'd like you to meet Priya," the host might say politely. In addition, the host might go so far as to tell you some other pertinent information that you should know. For example, a host might say, "Mike, this is Priya, my old friend from middle school." The host might also remind you, "Mike, you know Priya...remember, you met her last year at my party?" Or the host might jar your memory like this: "Mike, remember that time I told you about my friend who helped me with the fundraiser? Well, this is Priya!"

In any case, when it comes to adding sources to your writing, you have to be the host to your own work. Help readers out by introducing the source materials to your readers so they can follow your writing more clearly. Introducing a source helps your reader recognize that the words or ideas that follow are not yours. This introduction helps alleviate confusion.

Here are some effective examples of introducing sources:

- The author writes,

- The poet explains,

- Kelly Scardina, an English teacher, suggests,

- Aristotle, a famous Greek philosopher, once argued,

Use strong verbs to introduce a quote. There are hundreds of ways to replace the word *said*. Said is a boring word. Said does not reveal much about the tone of the speaker. There are stronger verbs that can.

When Mrs. Rachel Lynde inquires after Marilla's health, Marilla **says**, "Oh, no, I'm quite well although I had a bad headache yesterday" (2).	When Mrs. Rachel Lynde inquires after Marilla's health, Marilla **assures** Rachel, "I'm quite well although I had a bad headache yesterday" (2).

Incorporate the quotation smoothly into your own writing. What does this mean? I like to use the analogy of sewing. Think of the way a needle and thread move in and out of a piece of fabric. Writers do the same with their words. They weave quoted material in and out of their own writing.

BTW

Use strong verbs to replace the word said:

praised, gushed, thought, muttered, remarked, sighed, bellowed, insisted, confirmed, mentioned, admitted, repeated, soothed, reassured, professed, complained, yelled, echoed

Notice how much more the author writes in the second model in comparison to the first. You never want your citation to be larger than your own work. Your teacher wants to see what you think and not what the text says.

Poor Citing	Effective Citing
When Mrs. Rachel Lynde arrives at the Cuthbert home to inquire about Matthew Cuthbert's trip, Marilla is not surprised. **"Marilla's lips twitched understandingly. She had expected Mrs. Rachel up; she had known that the sight of Matthew jaunting off so unaccountably would be too much for her neighbor's curiosity"** (2).	When Mrs. Rachel Lynde arrives at the Cuthbert home to inquire about Matthew Cuthbert's trip, Marilla is not surprised. Being neighbors for so long, Marilla knows Rachel must satisfy her **"curiosity,"** and had expected Rachel to arrive at **"the sight of Matthew jaunting off."** As soon as Rachel begins to speak, Marilla's **"lips twitch understandingly"** (2).

Notice how the writer weaves the text in and out of the writing like a needle goes in and out of fabric. The writer's quoted material is brief and situated INSIDE the writer's sentences, not after, as in the first model.

Poor Citing	Effective Citing
When Mrs. Rachel Lynde arrives at the Cuthbert home to inquire about Matthew Cuthbert's trip, Marilla is not surprised. **"Marilla's lips twitched understandingly. She had expected Mrs. Rachel up; she had known that the sight of Matthew jaunting off so unaccountably would be too much for her neighbor's curiosity"** (2). Marilla knows exactly why Rachel is visiting: to get gossip.	When Mrs. Rachel Lynde arrives at the Cuthbert home to inquire about Matthew Cuthbert's trip, Marilla is not surprised. Being neighbors for so long, Marilla knows Rachel must satisfy her **"curiosity,"** and had expected Rachel to arrive at **"the sight of Matthew jaunting off."** As soon as Rachel begins to speak, Marilla's **"lips twitch understandingly"** (2). Marilla knows exactly why Rachel is visiting: to get gossip.

BTW

Keep quotations short. Some students take too many lines from the text. Teachers frown on quotations that are too long. Why? For one, taking too much from the text takes the attention away from your own writing. In many cases, a long quotation will overshadow your own writing. The reader will spend more time rereading passages from the text instead of reading your ideas and interpretations. Some professors call this padding.

Rule of thumb: Your own writing should be longer than any words you cite.

When you are writing a paper that requires you to use outside sources, those that provide you with essential research, data, statistics, expert testimony, and quotes from the text, you need to provide readers with the following information: What is the original source? That might include the name of a writer, a poet, a researcher, a comic, a photographer, an illustrator, a scientist, etc. You might also have to provide additional information for the source: when it was published, where it was published, and who published it.

What Are Some Tips to Know When Citing?

When students cite, they sometimes do it sloppily or in a way that causes much confusion to the reader. Their quotation material may be added in a way that makes the writing awkward and hard to comprehend.

Here are some don'ts when it comes to citing:

- Don't say, "The text says" or "In the text, it says."

- Don't put the page number at the beginning. Page numbers go at the end of a sentence.

- Don't say, "Page five states" or "On page five the writer says."

- Don't include anything other than the author's last name and the page number in the parentheses: (page 8), (Montgomery, 8), (Montgomery page 8), or (Montgomery, #8).

Here are some do's when it comes to citing:

- Before you cite, include the context (background): Who? What? When? Where? Why? How?

> **BTW**
>
> *Citation may also occur at the bottom pages of your work in footnotes or at the end of your paper in endnotes.*
>
> *A footnote makes citation easier for the writer because the information does not interfere with the flow of the writing. The reader can simply read the pertinent information at the bottom of the page. A number or a symbol appears at the end of the sentence indicating that the notes are at the bottom for the reader to access.*
>
> ***Example:*** *For years, scholars have disagreed with this interpretation.[8]*

When Mrs. Rachel Lynde arrives at the Cuthbert home to inquire about Matthew Cuthbert's trip, Marilla is not surprised. Being neighbors for so long, Marilla knows Rachel must satisfy her **"curiosity,"** and had expected Rachel to arrive at **"the sight of Matthew jaunting off."** As soon as Rachel begins to speak, Marilla's **"lips twitch understandingly"** (2). Marilla knows exactly why Rachel is visiting: to get gossip.	**Who?** Mrs. Rachel Lynde **Where?** The Cuthbert home **When?** She goes to visit Marilla because she saw Matthew Cuthbert leave. **Why?** She wants to find out where Matthew is off to. **How?** She goes to visit her neighbor, Marilla.

- When you take text evidence to cite, use the quoted material to support your ideas. Don't use quoted material to repeat your ideas.

In this example, the cited material is used to repeat the writer's ideas.	**In this example, the quoted material supports the idea that Mrs. Rachel Lynde is manipulative.**
When Mrs. Rachel Lynde arrives at the Cuthbert home, she asks how they are feeling. She tells Marilla that she was concerned about their health. She saw Matthew driving, and she thought they were sick. "I was kind of afraid *you* weren't, though, when I saw Matthew starting off today. I thought maybe he was going to the doctor's" (2).	When Mrs. Rachel Lynde arrives at the Cuthbert home, she cannot hide her curiosity from Marilla. Rachel tries to pry information from her neighbor by being manipulative. She pretends she came by because she is worried about Marilla's health. She feigns concern when she admits, "I was kind of afraid *you* weren't, though, when I saw Matthew starting off today. I thought maybe he was going to the doctor's" (2).

Explanation: This is the part of the citing that many students forget. It is also the most important part of ICE. After you cite the text, be sure to explain: Make clear connections between the quoted material and your purpose. Why did you want to include these words, these lines, or these passages? Do not leave the heavy lifting for the reader. You need to discuss how this cited material directly supports your thinking.

Grace hears the stories of how her ancestral grandmothers "resisted the men who tried to round them up and kill them or steal everything that mattered" (Badger 1). Her people, the Lipan Apache, "who trusted the [settlers'] promise of friendship," were forced from their land and were left without a homeland. Despite being stripped of their land and their identity, they survived. Grace's Mama makes sure to remind her that regardless of the settlers' actions, they could not take their identity.	After the quoted material is incorporated into the writing, the writer explains why this quotation from the text is important.

What Are Some Tools That Can Make It Easier for Writers to Add Source Materials?

Sometimes when you are trying to incorporate a quote, it can get tricky. The words don't fit easily into your own writing. Practicing often helps. The more you learn to adjust the size of quoted material and take the more meaningful parts, the easier it will get. However, brackets and ellipses can also help.

Brackets: Use square brackets [ ] when you have to alter or adjust a quotation to work in your writing. These brackets tell the reader that you had to change the original text for citation purposes.

Excerpt from "The Most Dangerous Game": "Don't talk rot, Whitney," said Rainsford.

"You're a big-game hunter, not a philosopher. Who cares how a jaguar feels?"

"Perhaps the jaguar does," observed Whitney.

"Bah! They've no understanding."

"Even so, I rather think they understand one thing—fear. The fear of pain and the fear of death."

Use of Brackets
During a conversation about hunting, Rainsford dismisses Whitney's opinion regarding the pain of the hunted, claiming, "Bah! [jaguars] [have] no understanding" (2).
Notice that the original text says "they've." The change to *jaguars* makes the citation clearer to the reader.

Ellipsis: Another helpful tool is the *ellipsis*, three evenly spaced dots that allow you to omit parts of a quotation, especially a long one. The ellipsis can only be used in the *middle* of a sentence and never at the beginning or the end, as some students mistakenly do. An ellipsis can simplify a quote to help a writer get to the point more quickly.

Use of the Ellipsis
"Even so, I rather think they understand one thing—fear. The fear of pain and the fear of death."
Whitney insists, Perhaps the jaguar does...understand one thing—fear" (2).
Notice how the ellipsis joins two quotes together from different lines in the passage.

Here's another example:

Original Quote	Use of the Ellipsis
"I was kind of afraid *you* weren't, though, when I saw Matthew starting off today. I thought maybe he was going to the doctor's" (2). Don't do this: Mrs. Rachel Lynde says "... I was kind of afraid you weren't, though" (2). Or this: Mrs. Rachel Lynde says, "I was kind of afraid you weren't, though..." (2).	Mrs. Rachel Lynde tries to pry information from Marilla during her visit when she expresses concern for Marilla's health: "I was kind of afraid you weren't, though ... I thought maybe he was going to the doctor's" (2). Notice how the ellipsis can shorten this quote if you don't want to use the whole thing.

Works Cited Page: Once you are done with your paper, you will create a Works Cited page, a page that includes a list of all of the sources you have used in your paper.

Here are some quick guidelines. (Note: This is for MLA; other formats may vary.)

- A Works Cited page appears at the end of your paper.

- A Works Cited page is its own page.

- The sources you include should be alphabetized by the first term in each entry. (Use the first word of the author's last name or the title if there is no author.)

- The title should say Works Cited. It is centered on the top of the page.

- Use left alignment and double space the entire list with one-inch margins.

- Use a hanging indent after the first line of each entry.

Here is an example:

Works Cited

Barber, William. "The Racist History of Tipping." *POLITICO Magazine,* 17 July 2019, www.politico.com/magazine/story/2019/07/17/william-barber-tipping-racist-past-227361.

Ford Foundation. "Forked: Celebrating a New Standard for American Dining." *Ford Foundation,* 26 Jan. 2016. www.fordfoundation.org/just-matters/just-matters/posts /american-tipping-is-rooted-in-slavery-and-it-still-hurts-workers-today.

Greenspan, Rachel. "'It's the Legacy of Slavery': Here's the Troubling History Behind Tipping Practices in the U.S." *Time,* 20 Aug. 2019. time.com/5404475/history-tipping-american -restaurants-civil-war.

"Blndsundoll4mj." *YouTube,* uploaded by Trisha Paytas, 1 Jan. 2010, www.youtube.com /user/blndsundoll4m.

"Minimum Wages for Tipped Employees | U.S. Department of Labor." *Minimum Wages for Tipped Employees,* 2021, www.dol.gov/agencies/whd/state/minimum-wage/tipped.

 IRL Students today are lucky! There are several online programs that can assist you with a Works Cited page. Gone are the days of memorizing the rules or looking them up.

Noodle Tools and EasyBib help students generate Works Cited pages easily. Both programs import the Works Cited page to Google Docs, making the process less challenging for today's students.

EXERCISES

EXERCISE 13.1

Use your knowledge of citation rules to answer the following questions.

1. Which citation is correct?
   a. (Dickens page 11)
   b. (Dickens, page 11)
   c. (Dickens 11)
   d. (Dickens #11)

2. When would you use brackets in an in-text citation?
   a. To omit a part of a quotation
   b. To make a quotation longer
   c. To make a quotation shorter
   d. To alter a quotation

3. Which of the following quotations is incorporated and cited correctly?
   a. The text says, "Mrs. Rachel was sitting at her window, keeping a sharp eye on everything that passed" (1).
   b. On page 1 it states, "Mrs. Rachel was sitting at her window, keeping a sharp eye on everything that passed..." (1).
   c. Mrs. Rachel is nosy. "Mrs. Rachel was sitting at her window, keeping a sharp eye on everything that passed" (1).
   d. "Keeping a sharp eye on everything that passed," (1) Mrs. Rachel is the first to know of anything that happens in Avonlea.

4. In the following sentences, which is the best use of the ellipsis?
    a. According to Whitney, hunting is the best sport "for the hunter …
       not for the jaguar" (2).
    b. Whitney believes hunting is the best sport … "for the hunter" (2).
    c. Whitney believes hunting is the best sport "for the hunter …" (2).
    d. Whitney believes hunting is the best sport … "for the hunter" and
       "not for the jaguar" … (2).

5. Brackets can be used to:
    a. Change the tense of a quotation
    b. Change a pronoun in a quotation
    c. Change a word in a quotation
    d. All of the above

6. Which of the following statements about using quoted material is true?
    a. It should be brief.
    b. It should be introduced first.
    c. It should be explained after.
    d. All of the above

7. What is the correct definition of plagiarism?
    a. Borrowing ideas without permission
    b. Citing incorrectly
    c. Failing to provide evidence
    d. Giving too many details from a text

8. An example of academic dishonesty would be:
    a. Copying a few lines without proper citation
    b. Submitting a friend's paper as your own
    c. Using a past assignment for a different class
    d. All of the above

9. When you cite the text, you need to include:
    a. Exact words from the source
    b. The source in which it appears
    c. The page number
    d. All of the above

10. What is true about paraphrasing?
    a. When writers paraphrase, they take words from a source exactly as they are.
    b. When writers paraphrase, they do not need to provide the original source.
    c. When writers paraphrase, they use their own words to explain an idea or concept but also give attribution to a source.
    d. When writers paraphrase an original source, they are never plagiarizing.

EXERCISE 13.2

Read the following model essay. Using your knowledge from this chapter, answer the multiple-choice questions.

It's June 22nd, and the last period of the day has rung. You breathe a sigh of relief and race out the door into the warm sunshine. Another year is done, and you can finally relax and put books, homework, tests, and assessments out of your mind for a few weeks and enjoy the academic freedom summer brings—for now. Just as you go to toss your three-ring binder into the trash, you remember the summer reading handout your English teacher assigned you as you reluctantly fish the double-sided and stapled paper out. Skimming the list of book suggestions, you question irritably, "Ugh, more work? Why can't I just enjoy my vacation without reading?"

As an English teacher and avid lifelong reader, I must admit that I have never considered reading a book as work or a chore, and personally can think of no better way to spend my summer than with a *New York Times* best seller in my hands as I lounge lazily on the beach; however, I can understand why some students may perceive reading as another task to be completed. Although very few students are thrilled to receive an assignment over the summer break, there are many valuable benefits to continue reading.

First, making reading a consistent habit and part of one's routine can have tremendous benefits on reading abilities. Reading should not just be a school activity picked up in September and dropped in June. Just like athletes preparing for their games by keeping fit and training regularly, students can keep their minds mentally agile for the fall by reading throughout the summer. Richard Steele, Irish writer and playwright, once said, "reading to the mind is what exercise is to the body."

There is no doubt that practicing any skill will lead to tremendous progress for the learner. For example, we see proof with musicians. "It's like if you play an instrument but put it down for three months," said Laurie Calvert, a teacher who is working as the Director of Teacher Outreach at ED. She wrote an academic thesis on improving summer reading programs at her North Carolina high school: "You're not going to be as good as a person who continues to play the instrument over those three months." What Calvert suggests is obvious: We all know that practice makes perfect, and reading is no different than any other skill a learner wants to master.

Even if you don't enjoy reading for pleasure, one reason you might want to delve into a few books this summer is to prevent summer slide. As students return to school this fall after an eight-week vacation, many of them—perhaps especially those from disadvantaged student groups—will be starting the academic year with achievement levels lower than where they were at the beginning of summer break. This phenomenon, "sometimes referred to as summer learning loss, summer setback, or summer slide—has been of interest to education researchers going back as far as 1906" (Cooper). David M. Quinn, Assistant Professor of Education at the University of Southern California, and Morgan Polikoff, Associate Professor of Education at USC Rossier, summarized several findings regarding summer slide and noted ways to combat the problem. In their report "Summer Learning Loss: What Is It and What Can Be Done About It?," they found that "on average, students' achievement scores declined over summer vacation by one month's worth of school-year learning and ... the extent of loss was larger at higher grade levels."

What this report suggests is that without continued practice, valuable reading skills that were gained throughout the year will be lost. Skills that took a whole year to cultivate may fade from memory, and valuable progress may be wasted. One study using data from over half a million students in grades two through nine from a southern state (from 2008 to 2012) found that "students, on average, lost between 25–30 percent of their school-year learning over the summer; additionally, black and Latino students tended to gain less over the school year and lose more over the summer compared to white students" (Atteberry).

Regardless of ethnicity, socioeconomic level, or previous achievement, "children who read four or more books over the summer fare better on reading comprehension tests in the fall than their peers who read one or no books over the summer" (Allington). From the study, it is clear to see that for college-bound students and those who want to keep their edge in the classroom, reading over the summer provides many benefits academically.

With academics in mind, reading can benefit college-bound students in more ways than one might think. First, studies show that continued reading improves performance on standardized tests such as the ACT and SAT. If you have taken these tests or are preparing to, you'll recall that both tests have sections that test reading speed and comprehension. It has been proven that students who struggle in these areas are not reading enough outside of school.

The test preparation company Galen Education's website advises students who want to be college ready to read widely outside of the classroom if they want to be prepared for college-level work: "No matter the major, in college, students will be doing a lot of reading for their courses. Strong reading skills are essential for excelling in high-level academics. The more practice students have with reading difficult texts, the more prepared they will be." In fact, colleges and universities highly endorse summer reading for incoming freshmen.

In the NPR article "Summer Reading for the College Bound," Julie Depenbrock includes an interview with senior Madison Catrett, an eighteen-year-old from south Georgia. Her high school was mostly white, Christian, and conservative—a place "where education is not as important as football," said Catrett. She's bound for Duke University in the fall, and "she's a little nervous to go somewhere new, somewhere so different from her hometown." Luckily, she and other Duke freshmen have a built-in conversation starter: the reading they've all been assigned—Richard Blanco's *The Prince of Los Cocuyos* (Depenbrock). "I'm excited about it. It gives us something extra to talk about—common ground we might not otherwise have," said Catrett.

In what they call a *common reading program*, colleges and universities are encouraging their incoming students in their freshman classes to read a common text together. And these programs make sense. Educated people read. At this level of education, students should not be learning to read, but rather reading to learn. What university would not want to draw lifelong readers to their campuses? Reading gives students access to new knowledge and points of view. One of the overarching benefits of reading is what people can learn from the content they read. They can be exposed to other cultures, new places, unique ideas, and so much more.

Despite all the benefits reading may bring, many students are not convinced; they do not see summer reading as pleasure but rather as another task they must complete. Simply put, they are not invested. To some extent, I agree with their views. For most students, their summer reading experience has mostly consisted of stale reading title suggestions created by teachers in a last-ditch effort to make reading fun and exciting. However, current research and best practices have indicated that the only way students will truly embrace reading over the summer is if they are presented with choice. Similar studies show that when students are given the opportunity to choose their own reading titles, they will become more engaged.

In an article published in *The English Leadership Quarterly* titled "The Top Five Reasons We Love Giving Students Choice in Reading," five benefits of providing our students with choice are presented: "choice empowers the student, valuing the choice values the student, choice leads to real and meaningful conversations, choice leads to independence, and choice establishes and deepens relationships." What this article suggests is that if teachers want students to buy into reading over break, they must be afforded the same respect we give to real readers: Students must have control over what they read, how they read, and when they read. Students should read because they value the intrinsic joys and pleasures reading can bring and not because a grade is attached. I am willing to admit that when teachers expect students to think and act as real readers, students will rise to the occasion.

In conclusion, English writer, poet, and philosopher Gilbert K. Chesterton once said, "there is a great deal of difference between an eager man who wants to read a book and the tired man who wants a book to read." It is the last day of school, the last period of the day. Most of you will breathe a sigh of relief as you make your way into the warm sunshine and the first hours of freedom. I hope as you embark on your journey of renewal, you will take time to "sharpen the saw" (Covey). Take time to balance your life with spiritual relaxation and mental stimulation. With a choice of millions of titles that await you, I hope you can bring yourself to choose one.

1. How would you describe the following example?

   "It's like if you play an instrument but put it down for three months," said Laurie Calvert, a teacher who is working as the Director of Teacher Outreach at ED. She wrote an academic thesis on improving summer reading programs at her North Carolina high school: "You're not going to be as good as a person who continues to play the instrument over those three months."

   a. A word-for-word quotation
   b. A paraphrase
   c. An example of plagiarism
   d. A footnote

2. Which of the following statements from the passage is the author's own ideas, not an outside source?

  a. I hope as you embark on your journey of renewal, you will take time to "sharpen the saw" (Covey).

  b. In conclusion, English writer, poet, and philosopher Gilbert K. Chesterton once said, "there is a great deal of difference between an eager man who wants to read a book and a tired man who wants a book to read."

  c. "I'm excited about it. It gives us something extra to talk about—common ground we might not otherwise have," says Catrett.

  d. As an English teacher and an avid lifelong reader, I must admit that I have never considered reading a book as work or a chore, and personally can think of no better way to spend my summer than with a *New York Times* best seller in my hands as I lounge lazily on the beach.

3. What would be the best verb to use to introduce Calvert's analogy?
    "It's like if you play an instrument but put it down for three months," said Laurie Calvert, a teacher who is working as the Director of Teacher Outreach at ED.

  a. Explains Laurie Calvert

  b. Describes Laurie Calvert

  c. Warns Laurie Calvert

  d. Suggests Laurie Calvert

4. Why is this example of citing effective?

   David M. Quinn, Assistant Professor of Education at the University of Southern California, and Morgan Polikoff, Associate Professor of Education at USC Rossier, summarized several findings regarding summer slide and noted ways to combat the problem. In their report "Summer Learning Loss: What Is It and What Can Be Done About It?," they found that "on average, students' achievement scores declined over summer vacation by one month's worth of school-year learning and … the extent of loss was larger at higher grade levels."

   a. It provides the reader with the origin of the cited material.

   b. It uses quotation marks around the original words from the source.

   c. It introduces the quoted material appropriately.

   d. All of the above

5. The bolded lines in this passage best illustrate which of the following steps of ICE?

   In an article published in *The English Leadership Quarterly* titled "The Top Five Reasons We Love Giving Students Choice in Reading," five benefits of providing our students with choice are presented: "choice empowers the student, valuing the choice values the student, choice leads to real and meaningful conversations, choice leads to independence, and choice establishes and deepens relationships." **What this article suggests is that if teachers want students to buy into reading over break, they must be afforded the same respect we give to real readers: Students must have control over what they read, how they read, and when they read. Students should read because they value the intrinsic joys and pleasures reading can bring and not because a grade is attached.**

   a. The writer is incorporating quoted material.

   b. The writer is introducing quoted material.

   c. The writer is citing the source currently.

   d. The writer is explaining the cited material.

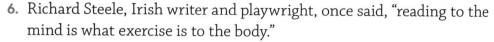

6. Richard Steele, Irish writer and playwright, once said, "reading to the mind is what exercise is to the body."

   Which component of ICE is this example demonstrating?

   a. The writer is introducing the quoted material.

   b. The writer is explaining the quoted material.

   c. The writer is paraphrasing the quoted material.

   d. All of the above

7. First, studies show that continued reading improves performance on standardized tests such as the ACT and SAT.

   What feedback would you give this student?

   a. Include the citation for this source.

   b. Add quotation marks.

   c. Add the page number from the source at the end.

   d. Change the verb *improves* to *enhances*.

8. This phenomenon—sometimes referred to as summer learning loss, summer setback, or summer slide—has been of interest to education researchers going back as far as 1906. [1]

   This example demonstrates which of the following?

   a. Brackets

   b. Footnote

   c. Paraphrase

   d. Plagiarism

9. "Minimum Wages for Tipped Employees | U.S. Department of Labor." *Minimum Wages for Tipped Employees*, 2021, www.dol.gov/agencies/whd /state/minimum-wage/tipped.

   This example demonstrates which of the following?

   a. An in-text citation in an essay

   b. An example of a paraphrased sentence

   c. An example of plagiarism

   d. A source from a Works Cited page

10. Regardless of ethnicity, socioeconomic level, or previous achievement, "children who read four or more books over the summer fare better on reading comprehension tests in the fall than their peers who read one or no books over the summer" (Allington).

    Why does the writer most likely use this cited information in the essay?

    a. The cited material supports the argument that summer reading is valuable.

    b. The cited material suggests that students can take a break over the summer.

    c. The cited material proves that reading is the most important subject in school.

    d. The cited material explains why reading comprehension tests are important for students to take.

Flashcard App

Answer Key

1

Close-Reading Skills

EXERCISE 1.1

1. C. Meek means quiet, gentle, submissive.

2. B. The people in the town joke around that Rachel Lynde is the boss in the marriage.

3. A. These details show that Mrs. Rachel involves herself too much in the lives of others.

4. B. Matthew Cuthbert is a private person. He doesn't talk much, and he does not tell people about himself.

5. D. All of the examples make Mrs. Lynde suspicious and bring attention to Matthew Cuthbert.

6. C. A sorrel is a chestnut-colored horse.

7. A. Matthew Cuthbert is shy and reserved. He does not like leaving home much or socializing.

8. D. Mrs. Rachel Lynde cannot concentrate until she finds out where Matthew Cuthbert is going. All of her energy is devoted to following the lives of her neighbors.

9. A. *Betokened* means indicated.

10. B. *Pressing* means urgent, critical, a problem that needs immediate attention.

EXERCISE 1.2

1. D. Comparing the text to your own life is a connection.

2. A. Prediction occurs when you make a guess about what will happen next.

3. C. When you share your opinion, you are reacting to the text.

4. B. Comparing two characters from two works is a text-to-text connection.

5. A. Using text evidence to support an idea is an example of an inference.

6. C. Sharing your feelings about the text is a reaction.

7. D. Strong readers ask questions about the text.

8. D. Strong readers use the context of the sentence to figure out the definitions of words they don't know.

9. D. Active readers make insightful observations about the meaning of the text.

10. A. An inference is an educated guess. Taking note of small details helps readers with comprehension skills.

EXERCISE 1.3

1. The literal meaning of a word	Denotation
2. A note-taking strategy to read a text closely	Annotation
3. Guessing what will happen next based on prior reading	Prediction
4. The feeling a word evokes	Connotation
5. Noticing something in the text	Observation
6. Responding to the text with feeling and emotion	Reaction
7. Reaching a conclusion based on text evidence	Inference
8. Drawing parallels between a text and the world or another text or to life experiences	Connection
9. Asking for more information	Question
10. Learning a word through the sentence's meaning	Context

2
Components of Fiction

EXERCISE 2.1

1. B. A young adult novel would be a work of fiction. The other examples are all nonfiction.

2. D. Characters, setting, and conflicts are all components of fiction.

3. A. Matthew Cuthbert does not share information. The reader can infer that he is shy.

4. A. The exposition is the part in the plot where readers learn about characters and setting.

5. B. An antagonist opposes the protagonist and would most likely be the villain.

6. D. Characterization is revealed through a character's actions, thoughts, appearance, and speech.

7. C. Through indirect characterization, readers learn that Matthew Cuthbert is a private person. He is shy, withdrawn, and reticent.

8. C. The novel is written from a third-person point of view. We know this from the use of the words *he* and *she*.

9. B. The setting of *Anne of Green Gables* is a rural community. Everyone seems to know each other. There are fields and farms and brooks mentioned. Matthew is traveling by horse and buggy.

10. B. If a student were debating about whether or not he should cheat, the struggle would be inside himself.

EXERCISE 2.2

1. D. Plot, characters, and setting are all components of fiction.

2. C. Rainsford comes across as arrogant, dismissing the fears and concerns of the crew.

3. D. Poisonous is an adjective. The rest of the answers are nouns because they are objects.

4. A. The captain is normally brave. His hesitancy now is alarming to the crew.

5. A. Rainsford is dismissive of the crew's concerns.

6. B. This passage is exposition because it is establishing characters and setting.

7. A. *Gravely* means seriously.

8. C. The story is written from a third-person point of view.

9. D. All of the above. Rainsford does not believe in superstitions and, therefore, does not take the crew's concerns seriously. He and the crew have differing opinions.

10. C. Rainsford falls overboard and now must face nature's elements.

EXERCISE 2.3

1. D. All of the details show that Rainsford is observant of his surroundings.

2. B. Rainsford sees a chateau in the distance.

3. D. Rainsford is observant and skillful. He is able to recognize the type of gun and size of the animal hunted.

4. A. Rainsford notices an empty cartridge on the ground, which indicates that people are present.

5. B. The descriptive words *jagged, rocky*, and *swirling* indicate danger.

6. D. Rainsford's thinking, actions, and behavior all indicate he is resourceful.

7. A. General Zaroff must be an experienced hunter. He has many mounted animals.

8. C. General Zaroff is arrogant. He claims he has discovered a new animal.

9. B. General Zafoff is most likely the antagonist because he enjoys hunting men.

10. A. This passage establishes a conflict between the two men. General Zaroff enjoys hunting men because they can reason. Rainsford is an experienced hunter. One can predict that General Zaroff would be happy to hunt Rainsford.

Analyzing Fiction

EXERCISE 3.1

1. D. All of the above.

2. A. The island's name is ironic. Rainsford doesn't believe the superstition, yet he falls off the boat and is left behind.

3. D. The sailor's instincts tell him to be wary. This is foreshadowing.

4. C. Captain Nielsen is normally brave, but even he feels anxious around Ship-Trap Island.

5. A. This scene foreshadows more unfortunate events to come.

6. D. A reader would want to know more about the abrupt sound. This line is suspenseful.

7. C. The captain is normally brave, but even he has the jitters. This is an example of situational irony. Don't be fooled by the quotation marks. The speaker is not saying the opposite of what he means. It is not verbal irony.

8. C. The mood is foreboding. The reader can tell something bad is going to happen.

9. D. All of the words contribute to the sense of foreboding.

10. D. Rainsford did not believe the crew. Now he is stranded in the water.

EXERCISE 3.2

1. D. A high screaming sound would be an example of foreshadowing.

2. B. The word *gloom* could foreshadow struggles to come.

3. D. The line is suspenseful. It contains words that convey an ominous mood and foreshadow danger.

4. D. All of the words have a foreboding connotation and foreshadow the danger to come.

5. B. Nature can present an obstacle in man's way. Rainsford struggled in the water, and now he continues to struggle in the jungle.

6. C. The jungle is a difficult place to survive. What men would choose to live here?

7. D. The line increases suspense, foreshadows events, and establishes mood.

8. A. It is easy to get trapped in the clutches of a jungle.

9. C. A chateau is a mansion.

10. B. The sight of the chateau would symbolize civilization; there are people who live here.

EXERCISE 3.3

1. Situational Irony: One would assume a police station is safe and free from crime.

2. Situational Irony: One would assume that a math teacher would not mess up an equation.

3. Verbal Irony: The customer says the opposite of what he means. The service was not great.

4. Dramatic Irony: The audience is privy to information that Romeo and Juliet do not know.

5. Situational Irony: One would not expect a spelling trophy to have a spelling error on it.

6. Dramatic Irony: The audience knows what Macbeth is thinking; the king does not.

7. Verbal Irony: Clearly, the woman does not really think she is having a good day.

8. Dramatic Irony: The audience knows about the surprise party; the character does not.

9. Situational Irony: One would imagine that a travel agent would love to travel.

10. Situational Irony: One would expect a lifesaving service would try to do more for a drowning woman.

4
Components of Poetry

EXERCISE 4.1

1. D. All of the statements are true about poetry.

2. C. Poetry and prose are written differently. Poetry is written in lines and stanzas.

3. A. A group of lines in a poem is a stanza.

4. B. Rhyme scheme is a pattern of rhymes that end at the end of each line.

5. C. Rhyme can occur in any location in a line.

6. B. Internal rhyme is rhyme that occurs in the middle of a line.

7. D. Rhythm occurs everywhere.

8. B. Limerick poems are known for their humor.

9. A. Elegy is a poem that honors someone who has passed on.

10. D. All of the statements are true about sonnets.

EXERCISE 4.2

1. Two lines of verse is a couplet.

2. A poem that features the elements of a story is a narrative poem.

3. A brief poem that originated in Japan is a haiku.

4. A poem that features a hero's journey is an epic poem.

5. Shakespeare wrote 164 poems known as sonnets.

6. A poem that is meant to honor the dead is an elegy.

7. A poem that is often humorous in nature is a limerick.

8. A group of lines in a poem is a stanza.

9. A line of verse that has five metrical feet and contains a pattern of stressed and unstressed syllables is known as iambic pentameter.

10. Four lines in a sonnet is known as a quatrain.

EXERCISE 4.3

1. There was an old man on the Border,
   Who lived in the utmost disorder;
   He danced with the cat,
   And made tea in his hat,
   Which vexed all the folks on the Border.
   —Edward Lear

   Limerick: a humorous poem

2. Let me not to the marriage of true minds
   Admit impediments; love is not love
   Which alters when it alteration finds,
   Or bends with the remover to remove.
   O no, it is an ever-fixed mark
   That looks on tempests and is never shaken;
   It is the star to every wandering bark,
   Whose worth's unknown, although his height be taken.
   Love's not Time's fool, though rosy lips and cheeks
   Within his bending sickle's compass come;
   Love alters not with his brief hours and weeks,
   But bears it out even to the edge of doom.
   If this be error and upon me proved,
   I never writ, nor no man ever loved.
   —William Shakespeare

   Sonnet: sixteen-line poem, three quatrains, a couplet

3. So, lovers dream a rich and long delight,

    But get a winter-seeming summer's night.

                  —John Donne

Couplet: two lines

4. Tell me, O muse, of that ingenious **hero** who travelled far and wide after he had sacked the famous town of Troy. Many cities did he visit, and many were the nations with whose manners and customs he was acquainted; moreover he suffered much by sea while trying to save his own life and bring his men safely home; but do what he might he could not save his men, for they perished through their own sheer folly in eating the cattle of the Sun-god Hyperion; so the god prevented them from ever reaching home. Tell me, too, about all these things, O daughter of Jove, from whatsoever source you may know them.

                  —Homer

Epic poem: features a hero's journey with gods

5. The outlook wasn't brilliant for the Mudville nine that day;

    The score stood four to two with but one inning more to play.

    And then when Cooney died at first, and Barrows did the same,

    A sickly silence fell upon the patrons of the game.

    A straggling few got up to go in deep despair. The rest

    Clung to that hope which springs eternal in the human breast;

    They thought if only Casey could but get a whack at that—

    We'd put up even money now with Casey at the bat.

    But Flynn preceded Casey, as did also Jimmy Blake,

    And the former was a lulu and the latter was a cake;

    So upon that stricken multitude grim melancholy sat,

    For there seemed but little chance of Casey's getting to the bat.

                —Ernest Lawrence Thayer

Narrative poem: tells a story, has characters and a plot

6. Thought I, the fallen flowers

    Are returning to their branch;

    But lo! they were butterflies.

        —Arakida Moritake

Haiku: short poem that captures a small moment

7. While I nodded, nearly **napping,** suddenly there came a **tapping,**

    As of someone gently **rapping, rapping** at my chamber door.

                —Edgar Allan Poe

Internal rhyme: rhyme that occurs in the middle of the line

8. O Captain! my Captain! our **fearful trip is done,** The ship has weather'd every rack, the prize we sought is won, The port is near, the bells I hear, the people all exulting, While follow eyes the steady keel, the vessel grim and daring; But O heart! heart! heart! O the bleeding drops of red, Where on the deck my **Captain lies,** Fallen cold and **dead.** <div align="right">—Walt Whitman</div>	Elegy: a poem that mourns the loss of a person
9. Friends, Romans, countrymen, lend me your ears. <div align="right">—William Shakespeare</div>	Iambic pentameter
10. My candle burns at both ends; It will not last the night; But ah, my foes, and oh, my friends— It gives a lovely light! <div align="right">—Edna St. Vincent Millay</div>	Quatrain

Analyzing Poetry

EXERCISE 5.1

1. Repeating a word or phrase over and over to emphasize a point in a text	Repetition
2. Creates a sensory effect, making readers feel as if they are actually hearing the sound for themselves	Onomatopoeia
3. Over-the-top exaggeration	Hyperbole
4. A comparison using *like* or *as*	Simile
5. The repetition of sounds that only appear in the beginning of words	Alliteration
6. Giving humanlike qualities to inanimate objects or nonhuman things	Personification
7. A play on words	Pun

8. A version of a metaphor that carries on over multiple lines	Extended metaphor
9. An expression that is not meant to be taken literally; it is figurative	Idiom
10. A poetic device that makes a comparison between two things for effect	Metaphor

EXERCISE 5.2

1. D. The repetition of the "d" sound in "dark and deep" is alliteration.

2. A. The horse is given humanlike qualities through personification.

3. D. "Miles before I sleep" is repeated twice.

4. C. The speaker reminds himself that there is much more life to live.

5. D. The "s" sound repeats. This is alliteration.

6. C. Hyperbole is exaggeration. The woods cannot fill up with snow to this extent.

7. A. Comparing love to a red, red rose is a simile.

8. B. It is an exaggeration or hyperbole to say the sea will dry completely.

9. D. The poet uses repetition, simile, and alliteration in the poem.

10. C. The poet says his love will last until "the rocks melt wi' the sun." This is hyperbole.

EXERCISE 5.3

1. Karma: What goes around comes around

2. Be patient

3. An impossible pursuit

4. It was easy

5. The children had a great time

6. Something rare

7. To figure out; to understand

8. Change the topic, distract
9. To take the quickest, cheapest, easiest way
10. Released from blame or punishment

Components of Nonfiction

EXERCISE 6.1

1. B. Nonfiction is fact based.
2. C. Poetry is not a genre of nonfiction. It is fiction.
3. D. All of the statements are true.
4. D. The table of contents tells a reader where a subject is covered in a book.
5. C. A glossary will provide definitions for terms used in the book.
6. D. All of the features will inform the reader about the content.
7. D. The purpose is to teach readers how to take care of bees.
8. A. The diagram shows readers how to care for the bees correctly.
9. A. It is a misconception that bees are always angry.
10. C. Bees are good-natured insects.

EXERCISE 6.2

1. D. The passage is fiction: It includes a plot, characters, and a setting.
2. A. The illustration shows beekeepers how to tend to their bees with care.
3. D. The author wants to inform readers how to build an effective Protector.
4. D. Protectors should be well-built to protect bees from the elements.
5. C. This is a manual to teach magic tricks.

6. C. The subtitles let readers know the examples of the most popular tricks.

7. C. The subtitles will lead readers to a discussion of how astrological signs affect magicians.

8. A. The illustration makes the directions more clear for the reader.

9. A. The purpose of this text feature is to outline steps to take to perform the trick.

10. C. The text feature lists the interpretations for each sum that appears on the dice.

Analyzing Nonfiction

EXERCISE 7.1

Subject: What is the main idea of the piece? What is this piece about?	The piece is about the value of education.
Occasion: Is there an occasion for this piece? Is the speaker reacting to an event? Is this a current controversy? Is it a holiday?	A student recently asked the teacher, "Will this be graded?" This question prompted the teacher to reflect about grades.
Audience: Who is the target audience? Men? Women? Adults? Teens? Parents? Teachers? Politicians? The general public?	This piece is directed toward students, hoping to change their attitude toward education. Other audience members may include parents, educators, and administrators—those in a position to make changes in the field.
Purpose: What is the speaker's argument? What does the speaker claim? What is the speaker's position about the issue?	The speaker argues that, too often, American students worry more about grades than about learning.
Speaker: Who is the speaker? What do you know about them?	The speaker is a teacher. The teacher has much classroom experience, which has shaped the argument.

Tone: How is the speaker feeling about the subject? Angry? Frustrated? Encouraged? Sympathetic? Sarcastic? Humorous? Serious?	The speaker is concerned, critical, and disappointed. The speaker uses words like "I wish," expressing a need for change. The speaker calls education a "luxury" that students don't appreciate.
Three Examples of Tone: Find three sentences or words that show the speaker's tone.	1. 2. 3.

EXERCISE 7.2

1. C. The ad claims that by drinking Coca-Cola athletes can maintain their condition.

2. B. The ad directly targets athletes.

3. B. Although the ad references baseball, the subject is Coca-Cola.

4. A. The speaker is Coca-Cola, the company that is sending the message. The company wants to sell the soft drink.

5. C. The tone of the ad is admiring. Words such as *prime, famous,* and *idol* all support and praise J. J. Callahan, who believes in Coca-Cola.

6. D. This advertisement relies on all three appeals to persuade. Using a celebrity to endorse a product appeals to ethos. The product must be good if a celebrity will use it. By calling J. J. Callahan a "Chicago boy," Coca-Cola appeals to the audience's emotions, mostly pride. The ad mentions that even the king threw a ball to J. J. Callahan, a fact that is meant to impress the audience.

7. A. Celebrity endorsements build up credibility and help establish faith and trust in a product or service.

8. A. This advertisement appeals to patriotism. J. J. Callahan is an "idol" to the people of Chicago. He is considered a "Chicago boy." He drinks Coca-Cola. Baseball is also a great American sport.

9. B. King George V threw a ball to J. J. Callahan. This is fact, which means it is a logical appeal.

10. A. By featuring a famous athlete on the advertisement, Coca-Cola wants its audience to believe the soft drink is good.

EXERCISE 7.3

1. This statement appeals to both ethos and logos. "Over one hundred dentists" appeals to logos. If dentists approve the toothpaste, then the audience should trust it.

2. This statement appeals to ethos. A person who grew up in a neighborhood is trying to appeal to history, experience, and credibility.

3. This statement is a fact, which is an appeal to logos.

4. This statement is an appeal to ethos. Because you know someone well, the person is hoping that you also share a mutual trust.

5. This is ethos because a mother is in tune with her children's needs.

6. This statement is trying to persuade through fear. It is an appeal to pathos.

7. A reference to studies, research, and data would be an appeal to logos. One could also argue that a person who is knowledgeable would also appeal to ethos.

8. This statement is both factual and sad. It appeals to both logos and pathos.

9. This statement appeals to ethos. People tend to trust the advice of those in the medical field.

10. This is an appeal to pathos. No one wants to be embarrassed.

EXERCISE 7.4

1. This is an appeal to vanity. You are so good at math, please help me.

2. This is an appeal to popularity. Everyone is going to the dance, and you should too.

3. This is an appeal to patriotism. If you love your country, wear our colors.

4. This is an appeal to novelty. The movie is new, so it must be better.

5. This is an appeal to tradition. It's what they always do here.

6. This is an appeal to vanity. You look good, so buy the car.

7. This is an appeal to tradition. If everyone in the family goes to Brown, you have to follow suit.

8. This is an appeal to popularity. You should vote for Sarah just because your friends are.

9. This is an appeal to vanity. Flattery is used to get a ride to the game.

10. This is an appeal to fear. Intimidation is used to get an A.

EXERCISE 7.5

1. B. The author argues that filters can negatively affect the way people view themselves.

2. D. All of the groups could be intended audiences.

3. C. The subject of the passage is filters.

4. B. The tone of the passage is critical. The author believes filters can cause harm.

5. A. Supporting evidence is an example of logos.

6. C. The author shares an embarrassing moment and appeals to emotions.

7. D. All the examples of ethos show that the author can understand and relate to those people who use filters. This common experience builds trust between the author and the audience. The author is not judging those who use filters. She understands.

8. C. The writer noticed the use of filters on TikTok. This occasion made her reflect.

9. A. The author reflects on her own experience as a teenager who thought a photo shoot could make her feel more attractive.

10. A. The tone shifts from intrigued to concerned. The author is fascinated by the new technology, but then wonders about the possible consequences.

The Writing Process

EXERCISE 8.1

1. A. An author's purpose is the reason the author is writing.

2. D. An author's purpose will determine the format, style, shape, and direction of the piece.

3. D. All of the above.

4. B. The writing process is flexible: Writers can go back and forth while writing.

5. D. There are many purposes for writing. Some main ones are to inform, persuade, and entertain.

6. C. A book review is written to persuade.

7. B. A poem is written to entertain.

8. D. Fixing punctuation would happen during the editing stage.

9. C. During revision, a writer can go back and add artistic touches, such as repetition.

10. C. Adding more descriptive language to a draft is part of the revision stage.

11. D. All of the strategies would be part of revision.

EXERCISE 8.2

1. B. Getting constructive feedback happens when you share your work.

2. D. Prewriting activities include mapping, a way to brainstorm ideas.

3. C. The purpose of the letter of recommendation is to inform the school about the student's performance and good qualities.

4. B. The crossed out lines are part of the revision stage.

5. C. The purpose is to inform the reader about global warming.

6. C. The purpose of this passage is to entertain the reader with a story about an argument between siblings.

7. B. The purpose of this review is to persuade the reader to watch *The Crown* on Netflix.

8. A. The author should include specific examples: What items are on the menu? Who was especially helpful?

9. D. When students receive an assignment, it's helpful to keep reviewing the rubric during each stage to make sure they are on track to meet the assignment requirements.

Writing to Entertain

EXERCISE 9.1

1. D. Personal narratives often imply a message or lesson. In this essay, the author wants the reader to realize that revenge often hurts both parties.

2. C. The author shows internal thinking in a reaction lead. The speaker is irritated and annoyed that the car is still not there.

3. C. The writer shows how upset her sister is when she realizes that the speaker has taken the car. The reader can see the pressed face against the window. The reader can hear the desperation in the sister's voice as she screams, "Stop!"

4. A. The isolated sentence creates suspense. What will happen next?

5. D. All of the sentences add to the conflict between the sisters.

6. A. The repetition emphasizes the speaker's frustration.

7. B. Samantha is inconsiderate.

8. A. The speaker is acting sneaky. She is slithering into the seat, hoping her sister doesn't see her.

9. C. *Scurrying* means moving quickly. Now that the car is returned, the speaker is rushing to class.

10. B. Samantha makes a mess in the car. She is inconsiderate by not cleaning the car before returning it.

EXERCISE 9.2

1. C. The author shows that working in a restaurant can be a good experience.

2. A. The writer shares his reaction from making his first paycheck. He is proud of himself.

3. D. The writer takes time to show how messy his uniform can get during a shift.

4. B. The repetition contributes to the mood: The restaurant is bustling.

5. A. Working at the restaurant pushed the writer to try new food.

6. C. The writer is famished after his shift and can't wait to eat.

7. D. All of the above. The writer has many lessons from working.

8. B. "Flaky white grains of sea salt" is descriptive language.

9. B. The dialogue contributes to the mood. The restaurant is busy.

10. A. *Clatter* is an example of onomatopoeia. It is a rattle sound.

10
Writing to Inform

EXERCISE 10.1

1. Opinion

2. Fact

3. Fact

4. Opinion

5. Opinion

6. Fact

7. Fact

8. Opinion

9. Fact

10. Opinion

EXERCISE 10.2

1. C. This passage comes from a newspaper article. Note the first paragraph answers the who, what, when, where, why, and how.

2. C. The purpose is to inform the community that students will return to school.

3. B. This is an example of a direct quotation. It is used word for word.

4. C. This is an example of a fact. Notice the date and the title and the percentage.

5. D. The lead includes all the most important details of the story.

6. A. This is an indirect quotation. The writer gives attribution but paraphrases Dr. Brown's words.

7. A. Dr. Brown is an administrator at the school. He is a valuable source of information for this story.

8. D. This story is important to the community because it is relevant, timely, and affects the community directly.

9. D. All of the above. Students, parents, and teachers are all credible sources for this story.

10. A. There are many differing opinions regarding learning during the pandemic. This is one opinion.

EXERCISE 10.3

1. Example

2. Narration

3. Process Analysis

4. Definition

5. Cause and Effect

6. Classification

7. Compare/Contrast

8. Description

9. Narration

10. Cause and Effect

EXERCISE 10.4

1. D. The purpose of this excerpt is to inform readers about the history of the Happy Meal.

2. C. This is a report about the history of the Happy Meal.

3. A. An outline for this report would begin with origins, the evolution of the Happy Meal over time, and some of the controversy it has faced.

4. D. The report includes multiple examples of toys that have been included in the Happy Meal.

5. A. The date of the original Happy Meal is a fact.

6. C. The author shares a brief anecdote about her children. This is narration.

7. D. The author includes these characters as specific examples of toys that have been included.

8. B. "Bright red" and "golden arches" are descriptive words.

9. D. "On the other hand" indicates a comparison.

10. C. The author is using classification to put fast food into three categories or groups.

11
Writing to Analyze

EXERCISE 11.1

1. C. The mood is enthralling and fascinating.

2. D. All of the examples are images, appealing to the senses.

3. C. These historical references, known as allusions, are men associated with wealth.

4. B. The men inspire the narrator to be successful.

5. A. The mood of the scene is tense.

6. A. Line 1 does not include imagery.

7. B. The clock symbolizes the passage of time.

8. B. The clock suggests you can't relive the past. Time moves on.

9. A. The mood is hopelessness; the inhabitants cannot rise or get ahead.

10. D. The setting symbolizes decay. The imagery reflects death and rotting.

EXERCISE 11.2

1. A. This literary analysis focuses on Joseph's character. Despite the rumors, he is not the person people imagine him to be.

2. D. The author asks the reader a question, shares a startling fact, and also builds sympathy for the main character, Joseph.

3. B. This sentence serves as a topic sentence, preparing the reader for the content of the paragraph.

4. C. The quotation marks indicate that direct words from the text are being used.

5. D. All of the examples are details that support the idea that Joseph eventually warms up to Jack.

6. A. *Despite* is a transition word. It indicates that Joseph is not what others believe him to be.

7. C. *Continues* is a verb.

8. C. Joseph is a complex character. He has been a victim of unfortunate circumstances, but he rises above.

9. D. All of the examples tell the reader more about Joseph and his past.

10. A. The purpose of the essay is to argue that Joseph is not one dimensional. He is a complex character who has made some mistakes, but these mistakes do not define him.

EXERCISE 11.3

1. D. All of the statements are true about a literary response. It is less formal and requires less structure and fewer guidelines than an essay.

2. A. When you write about literature, use the present tense.

3. C. Rubrics provide clear expectations to students.

4. A. Transitions help organize your ideas.

5. D. The transition *for example* should be used within the body of a paragraph to clarify your previous ideas.

6. C. Use italics or underline titles of books and other full-length works.

7. A. *Context* is the background information of a situation.

8. C. Writers use textual evidence to support their ideas.

9. D. A lead paragraph serves all of the following purposes: to hook the reader, provide background information, and establish a purpose for writing.

10. D. This sentence is an example of a clear topic sentence, telling the reader what the paragraph will be about.

EXERCISE 11.4

1. Rainsford does not believe the sailor's superstitions about Ship-Trap Island.

2. Rainsford argues that jaguars do not feel fear.

3. In the beginning of the story, the men are talking about hunting.

4. The men think hunting is the best sport in the world.

5. Whitney believes jaguars feel fear of pain and dying.

6. Rainsford hears a noise that startles him.

7. Rainsford loses his footing on the yacht and falls into the water below.

8. Rainsford swims to the nearest island.

9. Rainsford thinks the noise sounds like gunshots.

10. Rainsford does not recognize the sound of the animal on the island.

EXERCISE 11.5

1. C. The traditional gender roles in *The Odyssey*.

2. A. The writer begins the essay with the recent inauguration of Kamala Harris.

3. C. This example illustrates that women have made progress over time.

4. B. Men are expected to fight in wars and battle beasts while women are expected to tend to the home.

5. A. Finally, men are the ones in power and control while women are powerless.

6. D. All of the words are transitions.

7. A. In *The Odyssey*, Odysseus has been away from home for twenty years.

8. C. Circe also is shown to be a good hostess and homemaker as she invites Odysseus and his men into her home. This is an example of a woman who takes care of the home.

9. D. Textual evidence would be cited in the text.

10. C. The numbers reflect the book number and the line numbers.

EXERCISE 11.6

1. A. Hardships

2. D. Lines 8 and 9 show a shift in tone from despair to hopeful.

3. A. The first half of the poem reflects the mother's feeling of helplessness, but she is hopeful for her son.

4. C. The mother encourages her son to keep going despite hardships.

5. C. The mother was resilient during difficult times.

6. A. The mother's life was not comfortable.

7. B. The mother did not have the support she needed to change her situation.

8. A. The torn board is an image.

9. C. The dark symbolizes hopelessness.

10. A. With perseverance, one can overcome.

Writing to Persuade/Argue

EXERCISE 12.1

1. D. The piece is a review of a popular show.

2. B. The writer wants to persuade the reader to watch the show.

3. C. The writer begins the piece with a brief story about her time abroad and her memories about Princess Diana.

4. A. The writer was fascinated to learn that Princess Diana's life was challenging.

5. B. Princess Diana spends days under the covers in her bedroom refusing to come out.

6. C. The repetition of "we were" is an example of anaphora.

7. B. The dress details show why a little girl would be impressed.

8. A. This is an example of a rhetorical question.

9. B. The anaphora emphasizes why the girls were impressed.

10. B. Readers will challenge their misconceptions about royalty.

EXERCISE 12.2

1. D. This is an essay arguing that teens can be harmed by social media.

2. D. All of the groups mentioned would benefit from reading the essay.

3. C. In addition, being connected on social media has caused an increase in suicide because of cyberbullying. This is a reason to prove that social media can harm teens.

4. D. The writer explains why the evidence is significant.

5. B. It provides evidence for the claim.

6. B. This statement is a concession, admitting that video games do have benefits too.

7. D. It is a rebuttal to the benefits that screen time brings.

8. A. It is an example of the benefits screen time provides teens.

9. C. The writer used mainly statistics from articles.

10. D. The reader is given solutions: Teenagers can monitor their screen time.

13
Conventions to Know

EXERCISE 13.1

1. C. When citing a book, include the author's last name and page number only.

2. D. Use brackets to alter the words or tense of a quotation.

3. D. This quotation shows effective incorporation of a quotation into the writer's sentence, and it is cited correctly.

4. A. The ellipsis belongs in the middle, not at the beginning or end, of a sentence.

5. D. All of the above. Brackets can be used for all of these alterations to a quotation.

6. C. Remember to ICE all quotations: incorporate, cite, explain.

7. A. Plagiarism is the conscious borrowing of someone else's words or ideas.

8. D. These are some ways students are dishonest.

9. D. Include all of these when citing.

10. C. When you paraphrase, you can put the original ideas into your own words, but you must still provide attribution to the original source.

EXERCISE 13.2

1. A. This is a word-for-word quotation by Laurie Calvert.

2. D. This is the author's own words from her own experience.

3. A. Calvert explains that all skills need practice or you lose the skill.

4. D. All of the reasons provided make the internal citation effective.

5. D. The sentences in bold include the writer's explanation of the material taken from the source.

6. A. In this example, the writer is introducing the quoted material.

7. A. The student should add the source of this information.

8. B. This is an example of a footnote. The reader can find the coordinating information at the bottom of the page. The source can be found in the endnotes.

9. D. This is a source in a Works Cited page.

10. A. This evidence supports the argument that summer reading is valuable.

NOTES